ALSO BY HILARY SPURLING

The Unknown Matisse: A Life of Henri Matisse, vol. #1, 1869–1908

Matisse the Master: A Life of Henri Matisse, vol. #2, 1909–1954

The Girl from the Fiction Department: A Portrait of Sonia Orwell

La Grande Thérèse: The Greatest Scandal of the Century

Paul Scott: A Life

Ivy: The Life of I. Compton-Burnett, 1874–1969

PEARL BUCK

IN CHINA

Journey to *The Good Earth*

Hilary Spurling

Simon & Schuster

NEW YORK   LONDON   TORONTO   SYDNEY

Simon & Schuster
1230 Avenue of the Americas
New York, NY 10020

First Simon & Schuster hardcover edition June 2010.

SIMON & SCHUSTER and colophon are registered trademarks
of Simon & Schuster, Inc.

For information about special discounts for bulk purchases, please contact
Simon & Schuster Special Sales at 1-866-506-1949
or business@simonandschuster.com.

The Simon & Schuster Speakers Bureau can bring authors to your
live event. For more information or to book an event, contact the
Simon & Schuster Speakers Bureau at 1-866-248-3049
or visit our website at www.simonspeakers.com.

Text designed by Paul Dippolito

Manufactured in the United States of America

5   7   9   10   8   6

Library of Congress Cataloging-in-Publication Data
Spurling, Hilary.
Pearl Buck in China : journey to the good earth / Hilary Spurling. — 1st Simon & Schuster
hardcover ed.
p.   cm.
1. Buck, Pearl S. (Pearl Sydenstricker), 1892–1973 — Homes and haunts — China. 2. Buck,
Pearl S. (Pearl Sydenstricker), 1892–1973 — Knowledge — China. 3. Authors, American — 20th
century — Biography. 4. Americans — China — Biography. 5. China — In literature. I. Title.
PS3503.U198Z845 2010
813'.52 — dc22
[B]   2010007712

ISBN 978-1-4165-4042-7
ISBN 978-1-4391-8044-0 (ebook)

To the memory of Diane Middlebrook
who saw the point of this book from the beginning

CONTENTS

Pearl Buck's China

MANCHURIA

Sea of Japan

Beijing ★

KOREA

HEBEI

Yantai
(Chefoo)

Grand Canal

Yellow R.

*Yellow
Sea*

JAPAN

SHANDONG

Nagasaki

Xuzhou
(Hsuchowfu)

Suqian (Hsuchien)

Nanxuzhou or
Suzhou •
(Nanhsuchou)

Huai-an (Tsingkiangpu)

JIANGSU (KIANGSU)

Zhenjiang (Chinkiang)

Hwei R.

ANHUI   Nanjing

Shanghai

HUBEI
Wuhan

Yangtse R.

Hangzhou

*East
China
Sea*

Guling
(Kuling) ▲ *Mt. Lushan*

ZHEJIANG

•Yueyang

JIANGXI

HUNAN   *FUJIAN*

*Pacific
Ocean*

Han R.

GUANGDONG

Guangzhou (Canton)

•Hong Kong

0   100   200   300 miles

0   200   400 kilometers

Burying the Bones

T HE FIRST BOOK I remember from my early childhood was called *The Chinese Children Next Door*. It was about a family of six little girls with red cheeks and black pigtails who had given up hope of ever having a baby brother when one day their wish came true: the family's seventh child was a boy, the answer to his parents' prayers, a plaything to be waited on and adored by his older sisters. Many years later I came across this story again as a chapter in Pearl Buck's reminiscences. It turned out that she had taken a true episode from her own early years, and recast it in the form of a children's fable. The story's absurdity made Mahatma Gandhi laugh out loud when it was read to him on his sickbed by Jawaharlal Nehru. Its fairytale charm is if anything heightened by the realities of poverty, misogyny, and female infanticide that lurk in the backgound. Reading it for the first time as an adult, I recognized echoes of stories my mother told me about her own childhood when she, too, had been the last of six unwanted girls. After she was born her mother—my grandmother—turned her face to the wall. Two years later came the birth of the son who was all either of my grandparents had ever wanted in the first place. I knew *The Chinese Children Next Door* by heart when I was little, presumably because its consoling warmth and optimism made my mother's past seem more bearable.

I had no idea at the time who wrote the book that meant so much to me. Now I know that it is based on the life of Pearl's much older adopted sister, a Chinese girl abandoned by her own family and brought up as their own by Pearl's parents. The first two of this sister's six daughters were almost the same age as Pearl, who grew up seeing them count for nothing, and watching their mother publicly disgraced for bearing her husband six girls in succession. There is no hint of this sediment of suffering in Pearl's story. As a small child running free in a Chinese town where wild dogs foraged for babies routinely exposed to die on waste land, she often came across half-eaten remnants on the hillside outside her parents' gate. She tried hard to bury them just as she buried her memories of being sworn at as a foreign devil in the street, of fleeing for her life from marauding soldiers, of the young brides sold into slavery who hanged themselves at intervals in her neighbors' houses. Memories like these surface in her novels from time to time like a dismembered hand or leg. This ambivalence—the territory that lies between what is said, and what can be understood—is the nub of my book.

Fiction never lies; it reveals the writer totally.

—V. S. NAIPAUL

CHAPTER I

Family of Ghosts

P EARL SYDENSTRICKER WAS born into a family of ghosts. She was the fifth of seven children and, when she looked back afterward at her beginnings, she remembered a crowd of brothers and sisters at home, tagging after their mother, listening to her sing, and begging her to tell stories. "We looked out over the paddy fields and the thatched roofs of the farmers in the valley, and in the distance a slender pagoda seemed to hang against the bamboo on a hillside," Pearl wrote, describing a storytelling session on the veranda of the family house above the Yangtse River. "But we saw none of these." What they saw was America, a strange, dreamlike, alien homeland where they had never set foot. The siblings who surrounded Pearl in these early memories were dreamlike as well. Her older sisters, Maude and Edith, and her brother Arthur had all died young in the course of six years from dysentery, cholera, and malaria, respectively. Edgar, the oldest, ten years of age when Pearl was born, stayed long enough to teach her to walk, but a year or two later he was gone too (sent back to be educated in the United States, he would be a young man of twenty before his sister saw him again). He left behind a new baby brother to take his place, and when she needed company of her own age, Pearl peopled the house with her dead siblings. "These three who came before I was born, and went away too soon, somehow seemed alive to me," she said.

Every Chinese family had its own quarrelsome, mischievous ghosts who could be appealed to, appeased, or comforted with paper people, houses, and toys. As a small child lying awake in bed at night, Pearl grew up listening to the cries of women on the street outside calling back the spirits of their dead or dying babies. In some ways she herself was more Chinese than American. "I spoke Chinese first, and more easily," she said. "If America was for dreaming about, the world in which I lived was Asia. . . . I did not consider myself a white person in those days." Her friends called her Zhenzhu (Chinese for Pearl) and treated her as one of themselves. She slipped in and out of their houses, listening to their mothers and aunts talk so frankly and in such detail about their problems that Pearl sometimes felt it was her missionary parents, not herself, who needed protecting from the realities of death, sex, and violence.

She was an enthusiastic participant in local funerals on the hill outside the walled compound of her parents' house: large, noisy, convivial affairs where everyone had a good time. Pearl joined in as soon as the party got going with people killing cocks, burning paper money, and gossiping about foreigners making malaria pills out of babies' eyes. "'Everything you say is lies,' I remarked pleasantly. . . . There was always a moment of stunned silence. Did they or did they not understand what I had said? they asked each other. They understood, but could not believe they had." The unexpected apparition of a small American girl squatting in the grass and talking intelligibly, unlike other Westerners, seemed magical, if not demonic. Once an old woman shrieked aloud, convinced she was about to die now that she could understand the language of foreign devils. Pearl made the most of the effect she produced, and of the endless questions—about her clothes, her coloring, her parents, the way they lived and the food they ate—that followed as soon as the mourners got over their shock. She said she first realized there was something wrong with her at New Year 1897, when she was four and a half years old, with blue eyes and thick yellow hair that had grown too long to fit inside a new red cap trimmed with gold Buddhas. "Why must we hide it?" she asked her Chinese nurse, who explained that black was the only normal color for hair and eyes. ("It doesn't look human, this hair.")

Pearl escaped through the back gate to run free on the grasslands thickly dotted with tall pointed graves behind the house. She and her companions, real or imaginary, climbed up and slid down the grave mounds or flew paper kites from the top. "Here in the green shadows we played jungles one day and housekeeping the next." She was baffled by a newly arrived American, one of her parents' visitors, who complained that the Sydenstrickers lived in a graveyard. ("That huge empire is one mighty cemetery," Mark Twain wrote of China, "ridged and wrinkled from its center to its circumference with graves.") Ancestors and their coffins were part of the landscape of Pearl's childhood. The big heavy wooden coffins that stood ready for their occupants in her friends' houses, or lay awaiting burial for weeks or months in the fields and along the canal banks, were a source of pride and satisfaction to farmers whose families had for centuries poured their sweat, their waste, and their dead bodies back into the same patch of soil.

Sometimes Pearl found bones lying in the grass, fragments of limbs, mutilated hands, once a head and shoulder with parts of an arm still attached. They were so tiny she knew they belonged to dead babies, nearly always girls suffocated or strangled at birth and left out for dogs to devour. It never occurred to her to say anything to anybody. Instead she controlled her revulsion and buried what she found according to rites of her own invention, poking the grim shreds and scraps into cracks in existing graves or scratching new ones out of the ground. Where other little girls constructed mud pies, Pearl made miniature grave mounds, patting down the sides and decorating them with flowers or pebbles. She carried a string bag for collecting human remains, and a sharpened stick or a club made from split bamboo with a stone fixed into it to drive the dogs away. She could never tell her mother why she hated packs of scavenging dogs, any more than she could explain her compulsion, acquired early from Chinese friends, to run away and hide whenever she saw a soldier coming down the road.

Soldiers from the hill fort with earthen ramparts above the town were generally indistinguishable from bandits, who lived by rape and plunder. The local warlords who ruled China largely unchecked by a weak central government were always eager to extend or consolidate territory. Severed heads were still stuck up on the gates of walled towns like Zhenjiang, where the Sydenstrickers lived. Life in the countryside was not essentially different from the history plays Pearl saw performed in temple courtyards by bands of traveling actors, or the stories she heard from professional storytellers and anyone else she could persuade to tell them. The Sydenstrickers' cook, who had the mobile features and expressive body language of a Chinese Fred Astaire, entertained the gateman, the amah, and Pearl herself with episodes from a small private library of books only he knew how to read. This was her first introduction to the old Chinese novels—*The White Snake, The Dream of the Red Chamber, All Men Are Brothers*—that she would draw on long afterward for the narrative grip, strong plot lines, and stylized characterizations of her own fiction.

Wang Amah, Pearl's nurse, had an inexhaustible fund of tales of demons and spirits that lived in clouds, rocks, and trees, sea dragons, storm dragons, and the captive local dragon pinned underneath the pagoda on the far hill, who lay in wait for a chance to squirm free, swamp the river, and drown the whole valley. They inhabited an ancient fairyland of spells, charms, incantations, sensational flights, and fights with "wonderful daggers that a man could make small enough to hide in his ear or in the corner of his eye but which, when he fetched them out again, were long and keen and swift to kill." But even as a small child Pearl liked her fairy stories more closely rooted in reality, and she pestered Wang Amah to tell her about when she was little and how she grew up into a flawless young beauty with pale porcelain skin, plucked forehead, black braided hair that hung to her knees, and three-inch-long bound feet, so lovely that she had to be married off early for fear of predatory soldiers. By the time Pearl knew her thirty or forty years later, Wang Amah was wrinkled and practically toothless (the heartless little Sydenstrickers laughed when she knocked out all but two of her remaining teeth in a fall on the cellar steps), with scanty hair, heavy flaps of skin over her eyes, and a protruding lower lip. She was strict but kind and dependable, a source of warmth and reassurance, the only person in Pearl's household who ever gave her a hug or took the child onto her lap and into her bed for comfort.

She had been the daughter of a small tradesman in Yangzhou with a prosperous business destroyed in the seismic upheavals all over China that left at least twenty million people dead after the Taiping Rebellion. Wang Amah lost her family—parents, parents-in-law, husband—and with them her means of subsistence. She scraped out a living in the sex trade until hired by Pearl's mother to look after her children (an appointment badly received by the rest of the mission community). The traumas of her youth resurfaced in her new life as a sequence of thrilling set pieces, starting with her miraculous escape, when she was lowered on a rope down a dry well to save her from Taiping marauders, and going on to the firing of the great pagoda in her hometown, which was burned to the ground with all its priests inside it. Interrogated by Pearl about the smell of roasting men and whether the Chinese variety smelled different from white flesh, Wang Amah replied confidently that white meat was coarser, more tasteless and watery, "because you wash yourselves so much."

Even the dire process of having her feet bound became heroic in retrospect. Wang Amah explained that her father made her sleep alone in the kitchen outhouse from the age of three so as not to disturb the rest of the family by her crying at night. Rarely able to resist Pearl's coaxing, she took off the cloth shoes, white stockings, and bandages that had to be worn, even in bed, by women with the infinitely desirable "golden-lily" feet that enforced subjugation as effectively as a ball and chain. Pearl inspected the lump of mashed bone and livid discolored flesh made from forcing together the heel and toes under the instep, leaving only the big toe intact. She had witnessed the mothers of her contemporaries crippling their own daughters' feet and even suspected she might have ruined her chances of getting a husband by failing to go through the procedure herself. She watched her nurse put the bindings back on without comment. It was one of her first lessons in the power of the imagination to cover up or contain and make bearable things too ugly to confront directly. It was the same lesson she learned from the body parts she found on the hillside. The potent spell Pearl cast later, as a phenomenally successful writer of romantic best sellers, came in large part from this sense of a harsh hidden reality, protruding occasionally but more often invisible, present only beneath the surface of her writing as an unexamined residue of pain and fear.

The second major storyteller of Pearl's early years was her mother, whose repertoire transported her children to "a place called Home where apples lay on clean grass under the trees, and berries grew on bushes ready to eat, and yards were un-walled and water clean enough to drink without boiling and filtering." In the enchanted idyll of her mother's West Virginia childhood, America lay open and free, untouched by the taint of disease, corruption, injustice, or want. ("I grew up misinformed," Pearl wrote dryly, "and ripe for some disillusionment later.") The family were Dutch immigrants who had ended up a decade before the Civil War in a small settlement sixty miles west of the Shenandoah Valley, a corridor that allowed Confederate forces to launch raids on Washington from one end and move supplies into Richmond through the other, fought over with relentless ferocity for four years until victorious Federal troops finally laid waste the valley, destroying buildings, slaughtering livestock, and burning crops. Five years old when the war began, Pearl's mother grew up in a borderland repeatedly occupied by the scavenging, sometimes starving armies of both sides. Like Wang Amah, she reorganized her memories in later life into broad-brush narrative paintings depicting sudden dramatic reversals and hair's-breadth escapes, with streams of galloping gray and blue cavalry superimposed on the pagoda and the groves of bamboo her listeners could see beyond the veranda.

She applied the same bold graphic technique to her early experiences in China. Caroline Sydenstricker had set sail for the Orient as an idealistic young bride with only the haziest notion about what a missionary career might entail. For her it turned out in practice to mean housekeeping and child rearing in cramped, inconvenient lodgings in the poorer quarters of the more or less hostile cities where her husband parked his growing family, while he himself pushed forward into unknown territory in search of fresh converts. He drove himself on by totting up the staggering totals of heathen sinners to be saved and the pitifully thin line of men like himself standing between them and damnation, an insoluble equation that appalled and maddened him to the end of his life. When the Sydenstrickers first landed in Shanghai to join the Southern Presbyterian Mission in the autumn of

1880, they brought its numbers in the field up to twelve. Apart from a handful of foreign compounds in or near the main trading ports, the interior of China seemed to be theirs for the taking. Seven years later Absalom Sydenstricker persuaded the Mission Board to let him launch a personal assault on the vast, densely populated area of North Kiangsu, setting up his campaign headquarters in the walled city of Tsingkiangpu, nearly three hundred miles north of Shanghai on the Grand Canal, where no missionary had ever settled before. "He had to himself an area as large as the state of Texas, full of souls who had never heard the Gospel," his daughter wrote later. "He was intoxicated with the magnificence of his opportunity." The local people received him with passive and often active resistance. A younger colleague eventually dispatched to join him boasted that for three years he made not a single convert, coming home from country trips with spit on his clothes and bruises all over his body from sticks and stones hurled as he passed. Almost overwhelmed by the numerical odds stacked against him, Absalom spent more and more time on the road.

His wife had long ago learned to manage without him. One of the thrilling stories she told her children later was about the night she faced down a mob of farmers with knives and cudgels, who blamed an unprecedented drought on malevolent local gods provoked beyond bearing by the presence of foreign intruders. This was the sweltering hot August of 1889, when rice seedlings withered in the parched fields around Tsingkiangpu. Alerted by men beneath her window plotting in whispers to kill her, Carie found herself alone with Wang Amah and the children (by this stage there were three: eight-year-old Edgar, four-year-old Edith, and the baby Arthur, age seven months), surrounded by an angry populace, a hundred miles from the nearest white outpost, with no one to turn to and no time to send a runner for her absent husband. Her response was to stage a tea party, sweeping the floor, baking cakes, and laying out her best cups and plates. When her uninvited guests arrived at dead of night they found the door flung wide on a lamplit American dream of home-sweet-home, with the three small children waked from sleep and playing peacefully at their mother's knee. This preposterous story passed into family legend, along with its triumphant outcome: the hard heart of the ringleader was so touched by the spectacle laid on for him that he repented of his murderous mission, accepted a cup of tea instead, and left with his men shortly afterward, only to find rain falling as if by magic later that very same night.

This and similar incidents became part of a folkloric family epic, whose episodes were conflated, transposed, and repeated so often that Pearl, and in due course her younger sister, Grace, knew them and their punch lines by heart. The same stories figure in accounts published later by both sisters, where their mother's courage, resourcefulness, and determination stand out, burnished to a high gloss against a dull undertow of futility and waste, unfulfilled ambition, stifled hope and desire. There were other stories Carie knew but didn't tell. At Tsingkiangpu she set up one of a succession of informal clinics for women, where she taught young girls to read and offered sympathy and practical advice to their mothers. Even before they were old enough to understand what was said, her children could hear the urgent, uneven monotone of Chinese women explaining their problems to Carie. Pearl said it was a first-rate novelist's training.

As a public figure in the second half of her life, Pearl campaigned tirelessly for what were then unfashionable causes: women's rights, civil rights, black rights, the rights of disabled children and the abandoned children of mixed-race parents. As a writer she would return again and again to her mother's story, telling and retelling it from different angles in her various memoirs and in the biographies she wrote of each of her parents. Her analysis of Carie's predicament in *The Exile* and elsewhere is searching, frank, and perceptive. But it is in the daughter's fiction that the mother's voice echoes most insistently between the lines, at times muted, plaintive, and resigned, at others angry and vengeful. In her sixties Pearl published a lurid little novel called *Voices in the House* about a prime fantasist, a brilliantly precocious and imaginative child who might have grown up to be a novelist herself but descends instead into gruesome madness and murder. All the other characters in the novel are lifeless and bland compared to this energetic self-projection at its core. *Voices* is the book in which the author said her "two selves" finally merged, meaning not just her American side and her Chinese side, but also her outer and inner selves, reason and instinct, the two aspects of her own personality embodied in the cool, clever observer through whose eyes the story is told, and the implacable heroine who ends up possessed, "people would once have said by a devil, and yet there was no devil . . . except the reverse energy of dreams denied."

Pearl Buck knew perfectly well that most of her later novels had few literary pretensions, just as she understood why critical opinion dismissed popular fiction as trash. "But I cannot, I keep going back to it. It is what most people read." She wrote initially for herself and was genuinely astonished when her work spoke directly to the mass market, which she promptly adopted as her own, vigorously defending the magazine stories that kept her in close touch with her public. "One cannot dismiss lightly a magazine bought and read by three million people. . . . It is a serious thing for literature if three million read—not literature, but something that gives them greater satisfaction." *The Good Earth,* published in 1931 and still in print, sold tens of millions of copies worldwide in its author's lifetime and since.

Buck is virtually forgotten today. She has no place in feminist mythology, and her novels have been effectively eliminated from the American literary map. In the People's Republic of China her fiction remains unique because it accurately depicts the hard lives of an illiterate rural population ignored by the Chinese writers who were Buck's contemporaries and subsequently obliterated from the record by Communist Party doctrine. "In China she is admired but not read," ran a recent article in the *New York Times,* "and in America she is read but not admired." Both views could do with reappraisal. *The Good Earth* transformed the West's understanding of China, partly because of the picture it painted, and partly because it reached a readership most other books never could. Buck won a Pulitzer Prize for it and went on to become the first of only two American women ever to receive the Nobel Prize for literature. Everyone read her in her day, from statesmen to office cleaners. Eleanor Roosevelt was her friend. Henri Matisse said she explained him to himself as no one else ever had. Jawaharlal Nehru read her *Chinese Children Next Door* aloud to Mahatma Gandhi. My book aims to look again at the early years that shaped Buck as a writer and gave her the magic power—possessed by all truly phenomenal bestselling authors—to tap directly into currents of memory and dream secreted deep within the popular imagination.

SHE WAS BORN Pearl Comfort Sydenstricker on June 26, 1892, in her mother's family home in America, where her parents had returned to recover from a catastrophe that very nearly wrecked their marriage. A year after Carie's night with the farmers her youngest child, Arthur, who had never been strong, fell ill with a raging fever and died the day before his father could get back from the north. The family set out with the body in a sealed coffin on the long journey by canal and riverboat to bury him beside his sister Maude in Shanghai. There Carie and her surviving daughter immediately succumbed to a cholera epidemic. Edith died a fortnight after her brother, on September 5, 1890. Absalom, who had looked after the child while the doctor struggled to save Carie, retreated behind what had long since become an impenetrable barrier against emotions that threatened to swamp him. "We had a full cup of sorrow" was the most he would say then or later. The only flicker of personal feeling that surfaced in spite of himself in the many articles he published over a quarter of a century in the *Chinese Recorder* was an aside, in a piece written that autumn, on "the heart-rending bereavements that come to so many houses in spite of all medicine can do." Carie lay in stony silence, barely alive herself, unable to absorb or accept what had happened. "The deaths of these two children, coming so close together, almost deranged our mother," her daughter Grace wrote half a century later.

Husband and wife emerged from their ordeal each holding the other in some sense to blame. Every year Carie dreaded the tropical summer months, when disease flared in the towns, mosquitoes swarmed on ponds and streams, flies gathered in clouds over the great jars of human excrement used for fertilizer, and Absalom overruled her pleas to take the children to the comparative cool of the coast or the hills. "I shouldn't have listened to him," she said of an earlier defeat, "but I always did." Now that her worst fears had materialized, all she wanted was to go home. Warned by the doctor that Carie was on the verge of losing her mind, her husband reluctantly agreed to take her. "He went about Europe like a chained and quarrelsome lion," Pearl wrote of her father on their long slow journey, punctuated by sightseeing stops on the westward route to America. Absalom remained as always incredulous at his wife's inability to put the crying need of a whole nation of infidels before her own private setbacks. "I never saw so hard a heart, so unreasoning a mind as hers in those days," he said, looking back gloomily twenty years later. "Nothing I could say would move her."

It was an ignominious homecoming for both of them. Lively, pretty, and pleasure-loving, Carie had married the saintly younger brother of the minister in her hometown of Hillsboro, West Virginia, because he was preparing to go as a missionary to China, and she wanted to give herself to God. She said she had sworn a vow at her mother's deathbed, and she stuck to it in spite of stiff opposition from her father. Now she was returning damaged in body and mind, with only the oldest of her four children to show for a decade away. Pearl's birth eighteen months after they landed brought the consolation signaled by her middle name, Comfort, but it also marked yet another defeat for her mother, who was finally forced to accept that her marriage was a life sentence, "irrevocable as death," and that she must go back to serve it in a country she already feared and was beginning to hate. This new child tied her to both. "Had it taken the death of the other three to break her to God's will . . . ?" Pearl wrote somberly in *The Exile*. "She was broken, then, and she would do that will."

Absalom had extended his twelve months' furlough when his wife became pregnant, and now he could not wait to get back. In the ten years he had spent in China he had made, by his own reckoning, ten converts. Millions more awaited his call. "We are by no means overtaking these millions with the Gospel," he wrote grimly after another twenty years. "They are increasing on us." He was haunted by the specter of populations growing uncontrollably so that, as fast as young men migrated to the towns, "their place was taken by grinning boys." He listed with relish the components of a nightmarish vision: "a great and increasing host against us . . . Heathenism with all its vices still living and active . . . The darkness, widespread and deep, sin in all its hideous forms, intense worldliness as well as hydra-headed idolatry."

But the immediate problem confronting Absalom on his return to Tsingkiangpu in January 1893 was not so much heathen obstinacy as the intransigence of his fellow missionaries. The younger man who had arrived as an assistant twelve months before the Sydenstrickers left was not only living in their house but had stored their possessions in an outbuilding, where Absalom found his books mildewed and his bookcases eaten by termites. In the two years of his absence his system had been overhauled and Rev. James Graham, the colleague now starting to look more like a usurper, had pointed out its shortcomings to the mission meeting, which voted diplomatically to let Sydenstricker go. Interpreting this outcome as a triumphant endorsement of his vocation as a "Gospel herald," Absalom repossessed the house, settled his family back into it, and promptly set off with two new recruits by mule cart to stake out a fresh claim of his own in virgin territory seventy-five miles to the west. His new base of Hsuchien was a collection of straw-roofed mud houses on the edge of the immense, crowded, and poverty-stricken flood plain of the Yellow River, where he aimed to establish a network of small outstations within reach of his own post at the center, while incidentally putting as much space as possible between himself and the mission authorities, always far too ready to query his decisions in favor of crackpot schemes of their own.

His departure set a pattern for Pearl's childhood. Her father remained physically and emotionally distant, shut up in his study if not actually away prospecting for souls, never seeming particularly at home even when he was living in the same house. "His children were merely accidents which had befallen him," she wrote, describing the sense of relief his absence always brought to the family he left behind. "My father set off on a long trip northward, heady with excitement and hope," wrote her sister of one of these periodic partings that left everyone feeling as if a weight had lifted. Throughout the time Pearl spent in Tsingkiangpu, Carie was the center of a world confined to the house and its walled compound, where she had planted a garden. Respectable Chinese women were never seen on the streets; mission wives could expect to be cursed and spat at if they tried to go out alone. Two other American couples trying to establish a mission station a few years later in Hsuchowfu, eighty miles northwest of Hsuchien, reported that for six months the two wives were prisoners in their own houses, neither of them daring to walk even the few hundred yards to call on the other. Pearl's only view of anything beyond her high garden wall was the procession of feet she was short enough to see passing in the gap between the heavy wooden gate and the ground.

Her impression of this period afterward was of happiness and security. Sun shone on the garden and poured into the house. Carie could transform any lodgings, however unpromising, by applying the same cheap speedy formula (which would later be Pearl's): windows open to let in light and air, whitewashed walls, grass mats on the floor, the polished oval table she never traveled without, plain rattan chairs, and flowers everywhere. She planted a white rose grown from a cutting taken on the porch of her American home and hung up frilly curtains to shut out sights she didn't want her children to see. Edgar, who had been reading Dickens, Thackeray, and Scott since the age of seven, was currently working on a novel of his own and producing a weekly newspaper, which he printed on a toy press for subscribers among the tiny scattered mission community. In the mornings he had lessons with his mother, who had been a schoolteacher before her marriage and provided a basic education that included learning how to draw, sing, and play the violin. For Carie this was a time of renewal and hope. By the end of the year she was pregnant again.

Pearl learned to talk from Wang Amah, who fed, bathed, and dressed her, crooned tunes to her, and taught her riddles and rhymes. In the summer of the child's second birthday her mother was eclipsed altogether by the nurse. For three months Carie lay seriously ill,

racked by dysentery, unable to eat or keep food down if she did, struggling to nourish the baby she was carrying, and too weak to see even
her children for more than a few minutes at a time. Pearl remembered
twice-daily visits to "the other one's, the white one's room," when her
mother could only stare at her from the bed. Wang Amah made the
child put on a fresh white muslin frock, a petticoat and leather shoes
for these inspections; she combed her long hair free of tangles and
pinned a fat yellow curl in a sausage shape on top of her head. But
most of the time Pearl wore the Chinese jacket, trousers, and cloth
shoes in which she felt comfortable (unlike her father, who forced
himself to dress like the Chinese so as not to stand out more than
he must, but never got used to the loose cotton robes that flapped
around his long limbs, impeding his stride and making it impossible
to move at more than a slow amble).

Pearl escaped thankfully from the tight clothes and strict rules of
her parents into the indulgent world of the kitchen, where the whole
household—nurse, cook, houseboy, and anyone else who dropped
by—played with her and told her stories. They brought her kites,
whistles, and sugar candies from the market. Wang Amah kept hens'
eggs inside her jacket, where Pearl could reach in and find them when
they hatched into chicks. She ate the simple, highly flavored food of
the poor, dishes she loved ever afterward: soup, brown rice, bits of
salt fish or meat, pickled mustard greens, bowls of white cabbage and
bean curd, crisp chewy crusts from the bottom of the rice pot. For
Pearl China always remained the place where she felt at home. When
she looked back from the far end of her rootless and fractured existence, the landscape of her childhood shone in her memory as America did for her mother. She loved even the hot rainy season that Carie
dreaded, and the rice harvest in September when low autumn light
made everything hazy and soft. Her descriptions have a hypnotic,
almost incantatory rhythm: "The masses of feathery, waving bamboo,
the low green hills, the winding, golden waters of the canal, the small
brown villages of thatched houses . . . the drowsy rhythm of the flails
beating out the grain upon the threshing floors . . . deep blue skies
above the shorn gold fields and the flocks of white geese picking up

the scattered grains of rice. . . . The very air is sweet and somnolent with that broken, rhythmic beating of the flails."

In the fiercest heat of the summer of 1894 Pearl's father came home to announce that they were moving again. "My memory of his middle years when I was a child and a young girl was the ceaseless journeying to and fro," she wrote when he died. Tension always rose at this time of year for Carie, who had already lost three children at the end of long hot summers. Eight months pregnant, still shaky from prolonged illness, she was reluctant to pack herself and her family into carts to head for an unknown town so violently opposed to foreigners that it had taken Absalom nearly two years to find anyone prepared to rent him a place fit to live in. War had recently broken out with Japan, exacerbating the suspicions of the Chinese, who now lumped all foreigners together with the Japanese enemy, regardless of race or color. Absalom was tall and rawboned with reddish hair, a beard, and piercing blue eyes. In the traditional plays and stories, which were the main source of information available to country people, red hair and colored eyes were the distinguishing marks of a villain. Pearl's father produced much the same shock and dismay in the villagers of North Kiangsu as Wang the farmer feels in *The Good Earth* when he sees his first missionary: "a man very tall, lean as a tree that has been blown by bitter winds. This man had eyes as blue as ice and a hairy face. . . . His hands were also hairy and red-skinned. He had . . . a great nose projecting beyond his cheeks like a prow beyond the sides of a ship." In places where no one had seen a white man before, people treated a missionary preaching in the teahouse as a one-man traveling freak show, or else set the dogs on him.

Absalom was in his element. Difficulty and danger proved that he was getting to grips at last with the practicalities of wholesale conversion. The only way it could be done was by regular "itinerations," when he crisscrossed the region, methodically visiting and revisiting every town, village, and clutch of mud huts (his wife said his brain was a map of China). Genuine converts were still hard to come by, but he was planting chapels—often no more than a borrowed room in a local home—and recruiting lay helpers to run them. His grotesque and alarming appearance had always drawn crowds, but now they were starting to listen. As his grasp of the vernacular increased and grew saltier, he gained confidence, learning the tricks of a professional showman to rouse Chinese audiences often, as he freely admitted, sedated with opium: "almost as devoid of mental and spiritual life as the idols they worship." Absalom had no patience with more conciliatory colleagues who liked to point out the many similarities between Christ and Buddha, an approach he compared scornfully to dosing a drug addict with chloroform. "When we deal with a case of opium poisoning we do not administer soothing doses and put him to sleep, but on the contrary force down an emetic and trot him round the court, in spite of his resistance and his protests." Part showman, part salesman, Absalom liked to start his pitch with a bang: "Give them the Jehovah God and the divine savior of the Bible. Instead of dwelling on their good qualities show them their sins and abominations in fiery colors." His model was Jesus Christ, who brought not peace but a sword. "Such was the effect of His preaching, *and it produced results*."

His unshakeable conviction made Carie give in as usual, but even Absalom felt dubious about the premises he had finally secured from a landlord in need of the rent to feed an opium habit. The family's new home was one of a pair of unfurnished village inns, hardly more than stables with dirt floors, mud walls, rough thatched roofs sealed with paper inside, and gaping holes for windows and doors. Crowds of sullen unwelcoming men collected to inspect the newcomers from the far side of a low earthen wall. Doors could be fitted but they gave limited privacy, and there was no space for a garden. The family slept on improvised plank beds. The new baby, born in Hsuchien on September 16, was no more robust than Arthur had been. Carie called him Clyde Hermanus after his Dutch grandfather.

Absalom's departure after the birth left her more isolated than ever before and farther from any American or European support line. She was starting to worry about Edgar growing up for all practical purposes without a father, cut off from contact with boys of his own age and kind, beginning to turn moody and mutinous at thirteen with the onset of adolescence. Jealousy made even Pearl, so far the sturdiest and most responsive of babies, hard to manage now that Wang Amah's attention had shifted to the new little brother. Cold weather set in, rain fell, and water welled up through the earth, turning the floor to liquid mud. Carie's portable organ, a gift from her oldest brother in America, had to be hoisted on boards out of the wet. Absalom himself admitted in his memoirs that the situation was dire: "The people were afraid of us and official influence unfavorable. . . . We . . . suffered much from sickness during the winter." In one of his father's absences Clyde contracted pneumonia.

Pearl skimmed over this period in her nonfiction accounts, or left it out altogether. But the details—whether taken in at the time or picked up from what others said afterward—lodged deep in her memory, surfacing half a century later in a novel called *The Townsman,* set on the rolling prairie of the American West at the time of the Gold Rush. Like Carie, Mary Goodliffe in *The Townsman* gives birth without doctor or midwife to her sixth child (not counting the first, who plays no part in the story and seems indeed to have been largely forgotten by the author). She, too, had been persuaded to abandon a relatively settled existence in order to follow her husband, a perennially dissatisfied visionary driven westward all his life in search of an illusory future prosperity that blinds him to the hardships imposed on his wife and family in the present. "They were living like beasts in a den. She had no furniture. Her bed was a mattress on posts driven into the ground and crossed with slats. The children slept on pallets spread on dried grass." *The Townsman* is a solid, workmanlike family saga with inadequate emotional underpinning and a fairy tale ending, except for this bleak portrait of a woman pushed to the limits of endurance, camping out in winter in a mud dugout on the prairie with an absent husband, a restive teenage son, a refractory toddler, and a sickly newborn baby.

Clyde survived the first part of an exceptionally hard winter thanks to intensive care from his mother and Wang Amah. When Absalom got back from itinerating he found his wife waiting with the house dismantled, its contents sorted and packed, the organ tied up in matting, even the rose dug up and ready to go. This was the first head-on collision Pearl witnessed between her parents, and, like everything to do with Absalom, its scale was transcendental. "For neither of them was it a struggle between a man and a woman. It was a woman defying God. She fought against God, against [Absalom's] call, against the success of his work, against the promise of the future." Pearl's father told her long afterward that his wife in this mood was unstoppable, "like a wild wind." Ambushed and outmaneuvered, he had no choice but to accept her ultimatum when she threatened to return alone with the children to America if he didn't. Carie's eloquent and carefully rehearsed declaration of independence shaped her daughters' future. It is repeated almost word for word in Pearl's biographies of her parents, *The Exile* and *Fighting Angel,* and it returns even more circumstantially in her sister's *The Exile's Daughter,* where their mother speaks in a voice that must have been only too familiar to both daughters, uttering words neither of them ever forgot:

> In the white hot temper which was hers when she was provoked too much, she said in a dreadful still voice: "You can preach from Peking to Canton, you can go from the North Pole to the South, but I and these little children will never go with you again. . . . I have no more children to give away to God now."

Absalom never fully forgave his wife for once again sabotaging a critical campaign just as it began to get going. After dropping off his family by mule cart in Tsingkiangpu, he raced back to Hsuchien to retrieve the situation, failing in his haste and distress to grasp the depth of disturbance caused by the war. Japan's modernized army and navy, trained and equipped to Western standards, had inflicted a series of crushing defeats by land and sea in the north on outmoded and ill-prepared imperial forces, still armed in some sections with bows and arrows. Atrocities took place on both sides. Rumor and counterrumor swept the country. News of what was happening filtered down to the rural population via cheap garish prints of the demonized foreign enemy sold in markets and fairs. Disorganized groups of soldiers, bandits, and criminals headed north all winter toward the fighting in

Manchuria. Mounting tension erupted in violence. Absalom driving his mule cart picked up a colleague at Hsuchien and hurried on to Hsuchowfu, where they were besieged in an inn by a mob who stoned the two Americans and chased them up the main street, attempting to rope them like steers using girdles as improvised lassos.

Hampered by their heavy padded Chinese coats, long skirts, and the clumsy cloth shoes that came off as they ran, the two men sought refuge in the office of the local magistrate, who had signally failed to come to their aid. Even in peacetime there was widespread resentment against the aggressive meddling of missionaries, their automatic assumption of superiority, unlimited sense of entitlement, and ruthless exploitation of the unequal treaties that put them above Chinese law. Ejected under guard from the city, Absalom retreated via Hsuchien only to be badly beaten on the road by brigands or soldiers, who claimed he was Japanese and made off in his cart with all his possessions. By his own account, the thick wadding of his coat saved his life. He walked the last thirty miles back to Tsingkiangpu barefoot in his underwear, bleeding from three sword wounds on his back. When he burst in on his family at breakfast they were about to be evacuated again with the other wives and children by Yangtse riverboat to safety in Shanghai. Absalom stayed behind to make one last abortive attempt to regain Hsuchien, accompanied this time by his old adversary, Jimmy Graham. Heavy snowfall blocked their way, the Grand Canal froze over, and the pair had to retreat, carrying their baggage on foot through ice and snow to the Yangtse River, where they finished the journey by junk, eventually rejoining their wives in Shanghai in time for the Chinese New Year, January 26, 1895.

ABSALOM'S INORDINATELY AMBITIOUS plans for extension had ended in total rout. There was no longer any place for him in Tsingkiangpu, where the team that functioned well under Graham had no wish to jeopardize its smooth running by taking on Sydenstricker. "My father seemed oblivious to the fact that there were those in the mission group who opposed his individualistic way of working," his daughter Grace put it crisply long afterward. In the end an opening was found for him as stand-in for a colleague on furlough in Zhenjiang, the city he had left a decade earlier to open up Tsingkiangpu and its hinterland. A newly declared treaty port, commanding China's prime trade routes from the junction where the Grand Canal meets the Yangtse River, the rich, cosmopolitan, rapidly expanding city of Zhenjiang was the last place Absalom wanted to be. "No large cities have any considerable number of converts in them," he had written when he moved out. He had spent his first seven years in China delivering impromptu sermons on street corners, distributing tracts, and setting up street chapels, and it left him no illusions about an urban population inured to being preached at and skeptical about the promised rewards. Absalom preferred to push forward into unspoiled countryside, where villagers believed his stories and listened open-mouthed, once they got over their initial stupefaction, to his colorful accounts of abominable sin and the pains of hellfire.

Zhenjiang, prototype for "the great sprawling opulent city" in *The Good Earth*, with food spilling out of its markets and merchandise crammed into its warehouses, proved Absalom's point. After laboring for thirteen years the Southern Presbyterian Mission force of two men and their wives had made little impact. By January 1896, when the Sydenstrickers arrived, one couple had returned on furlough to the United States, and the other had been posted elsewhere, leaving behind ten Chinese converts, two street chapels, and a small boys' school. Proposing to waste no more time on the city's ungrateful inhabitants, Absalom carried on itinerating instead. The physical weakness and moral depression of the past year dropped away as he set about recreating the country networks successively smashed or seized from him at Hsuchien and Tsingkiangpu.

Zhenjiang would become from now on the family base. After much anxious correspondence with her siblings, Carie had decided that the only way for Edgar to grow up truly American was through further education beyond anything she could provide, and he was dispatched a few weeks after his fifteenth birthday to sail home alone to a country he had seen only once. At the age of four and a bit, Pearl now became the oldest child at home. Clyde had grown into a handsome, comical, intelligent little boy, precocious like all Carie's children, and old enough to join in his sister's games. Their mother, who had always loved the way the hills swept up from the river in Zhenjiang, was happy again, and in his own strange absent way their father was too ("they did not even know him well enough to miss him"). The children took walks along the magnificent, newly built stone embankment, or Bund, on the riverfront, picnicked on the grassy slopes above the town, and were regularly invited to tea aboard the Jardine-Matheson hulk by the river master, a retired Scottish ship's captain, and his hospitable wife. They celebrated Thanksgiving and the Fourth of July with firecrackers and a homemade flag, attended birthday parties for Queen Victoria at the British Club, and put up a tree hung with gingerbread men at Christmas, when they were allowed one toy each from the annual box of supplies shipped out by mail order from Montgomery Ward. They watched steamers discharging and taking on the cargoes stored in the Bund's high shadowy godowns that smelled "of hemp and peanut oil and the acrid sweetness of crude red-brown sugar." Once a young English customs officer slid with them down the long sloping chute that transferred loads to the backs of donkeys or men on the ground.

But the Sydenstrickers never properly belonged to the foreign community that occupied the British concession, a spacious orderly enclave with green lawns and shady trees protected by strong walls and iron gates, reinforced when necessary by British or American gunboats moored in the river. After a few months, when the occupants of their borrowed mission house arrived back from the United States, Pearl's family moved downhill to noisier and more cramped quarters behind the port, with no sanitation and refuse piled in the streets. Absalom rented what seem to have been the same lodgings he and Carie had first occupied as a young couple ten years before: three small rooms above a liquor store in an alley opening onto the brothels and bars of Horse Street, the widest thoroughfare in Zhenjiang after the Bund itself, smelly, crowded, and dangerous, frequented by drug dealers, prostitutes, and drunken sailors who congregated under the Sydenstrickers' windows at night.

The apartment's main advantage was cheapness. Mission salaries, generally lower than those paid to doctors, lawyers, or teachers, did no more than cover basic necessities, even in Asian countries, where domestic help cost next to nothing. But the Sydenstrickers were poorer still because of the great passion of Absalom's life, second only to conversion itself, which was his translation of the New Testament into the Chinese vernacular. He had been a member of the official committee set up in Shanghai in 1890 to produce a revised Mandarin version of the Bible, but he resigned or was pushed off at the committee's first working meeting the following summer. A natural linguist himself, he never concealed his opinion of other translators' work as misguided, inept, or inaccurate. The year before Pearl was born he decided to produce an unauthorized rival edition and publish it in installments himself, an enterprise that drained his wife's household budget for the next three decades. "It robbed her of the tiny margin between bitter poverty and small comfort," Pearl wrote, describing her mother's progressively more desperate attempts to economize. It was why they left a mud house in Hsuchien to end up in Zhenjiang's red-light district.

For Pearl the new surroundings were magical. Still too young to read fluently, she was already a voracious observer, intensely curious about the new world outside her window and the people in it. She asked questions so insatiably that her mother had to tell her not to ask any more for fifteen minutes (during which Pearl just as assiduously watched the clock). She was mesmerized by the sights Carie tried to keep from her: beggars ("They snatched at us with hands like the skinny claws of fowls"), lepers with chewed-up faces and stumps for arms or legs, street brawls, and the street vendors whose sweetmeats she was forbidden to touch. Just watching a man divide flat round cakes of barley-sugar brittle into pieces with a tiny chisel, or dip up strands of hot thick melted sugar to twist into sticks of candy, was a delight. In the evenings she listened with interest to the songs and shouts of American sailors disembarked from the merchant ships in the port and the high cries of Chinese girls floating over the crash of broken bottles. Whiskey and opium fumes drifted up through cracks in the floorboards. Once an intruder got into Pearl's bedroom, or she dreamed he did, in spite of Wang Amah's laying out her bedding roll to sleep on the trapdoor in the passageway that provided the family's only access to the street. Another time revelers woke the whole household by smashing up the shop downstairs. This was altogether too much for Carie, and after a marital showdown with packed bags and another terse ultimatum, Absalom was obliged to move his family to more sheltered accommodation inside the Baptist compound farther along Horse Street.

With her brother and Wang Amah Pearl explored streets lined with portable one-man cook shops and puppet shows, barbers, tailors, and letter writers at work in the gutter. They listened to professional storytellers and watched entertainers like the Pig Butcher in her novel, *Sons* ("if he took a pair of chopsticks he could pluck the flies out of the air as they flew, one by one he plucked them . . . and they roared with laughter to see such skill"). Even the markets were a form of street theater: "the silk shops flying brilliant banners of black and red and orange silk," the vegetable market with glittering stalls of red radish, green cabbage, and white lotus root, mounds of live yellow crabs and silver fish in the fish market, rows of shiny brown ducks turning on spits over hot coals in front of the duck shops. The children stopped to look at men measuring out grain from baskets big enough for an adult to step into and suffocate: "white rice and brown, and dark yellow wheat and pale gold wheat, and yellow soybeans and red beans and green broadbeans and canary-colored millet and grey sesame." They sucked illicit unhygienic candy from paper cornets and bought paper lanterns shaped like birds, butterflies, or a rabbit on wheels. Pearl even had a horse lantern made in two parts, the head held in front and the tail strapped on behind, so she could walk the streets in the dark as a horse.

In spring they climbed up the hill behind their house to fly homemade kites and watch teams of up to twelve men launching a gigantic paper pagoda, a dragon or a centipede thirty feet long. Sometimes there were soldiers tilting with spears and swords on the parade ground or firing off the antiquated cannon embedded in the mud walls of the fort. When she wasn't out walking in the afternoons with Wang Amah or doing morning lessons with her mother, Pearl spent her time at the window, looking down at the street or out over the vast expanse of the Yangtse River:

> I learned to know its every mood during the hours I spent at the window. On a crisp spring morning it looked as innocent as beauty itself, the sun caught in all its pointed yellow wavelets and shining upon brown and white sails and painted junks and bobbing sampans. . . . But there were other days when the river boiled like a muddy cauldron. Storms could beat upon it as fiercely as though it were a sea, and in the rough waters I have seen a ferry ease over upon its side and slide hundreds of people off as though they were insects, and turn still further until it floated bottom up. Those black bobbing heads were visible only for a moment and then the river sucked them down.

Pearl's mother drew the curtains even in daytime to shut out sights like this. Carie hated the Yangtse because it symbolized the overwhelming, implacable, impersonal forces that governed human life in China and made her own attempts at resistance seem futile. Like other mission wives, she did what she could to treat the sores, boils, cankers, ulcerated and gangrenous limbs, the infections and contagious diseases contracted by people who drank the polluted waters of the river, and worked waist-deep in the flooded rice fields. She saw to it that the family's three rooms on Horse Street were scrubbed with carbolic acid, all utensils dipped in boiling water at table, all fresh food either thoroughly cooked or disinfected with potassium permanganate before being touched. The children lived under perpetual surveillance to stop them putting anything, even their fingers, into their mouths. Carie's vigilance never let up, but it was Absalom who, for all his apparent indifference, solved the problem of summers spent in temperatures of 100 degrees or more on the fetid malarial flatlands of the Yangtse Valley.

In 1897 he was one of the first five missionaries to buy a building plot from the Kuling Mountain Company, set up the year before by an enterprising young English missionary-cum-businessman to market the top of a mountain that rose sheer from the stifling hot plain three hundred miles upstream of Zhenjiang. Nearly five thousand feet above sea level, thickly wooded, and laid out like an Oriental equivalent of Hampstead Garden Suburb in London, with cool air, fresh streams, and luxuriant greenery, Kuling on Mount Lu (or Lushan) was the first purpose-built mountain resort in China. It was also, as Pearl said, a lifesaving station. Absalom put up a stone shack on plot number 310, where for the first time in their lives his children could run barefoot on the hillside, drink water straight from the stream, and eat the wild strawberries they picked in the woods without boiling them first. From now on summer holidays became the high point of their year.

Pearl was six years old when this period of relative normality came to an end. Clyde contracted diphtheria in January 1899, struggling convulsively for breath with rasping throat and livid gray face, and dying (as Arthur had done before him) too suddenly for his father to be fetched back from the field. Pearl, who caught the fever from her brother, said she understood what had happened when she heard a Chinese woman's voice calling to the spirit of a dead child, and realized that the cries came from inside the house instead of outside on the street. Absalom came home to bury his son. Carie, who was five months pregnant, roused herself sufficiently to see Pearl past the worst danger, then relapsed into oblivion and torpor, exhausted in body and spirit, too weak even to nurse her remaining child back to health. Mother and daughter were looked after by a friend, who moved into the house once Absalom had gone back to work. By February Carie was well enough to help Pearl compose a letter to the *Christian Observer* in Louisville, Kentucky, describing the siblings whose invisible presence filled the child's life and her mother's: "I have two little brothers in heaven. Maudie went first, then Artie, then Edith, and on the tenth of last month, my little brave brother, Clyde, left us to go to our real home in heaven. Clyde said he was a Christian Soldier, and that heaven was his bestest home." The sentiments and phraseology, if not the actual wording of this melancholy epistle, must have come from Pearl's mother, who was struggling herself at this point to retain her faith in God. Pearl remembered a passionate outburst as the coffin was carried out of the house in the rain, and someone urged Carie not to worry about the child's body because his soul was in heaven. "But his body is precious," she cried. "I gave it birth. I tended it and loved it. . . . They are taking his body away, and it is all I have."

When Grace Caroline Sydenstricker was born on May 12, Carie developed puerperal fever. Her milk dried up, and the house filled with the hungry baby's cries. Pearl prayed in her father's church and also, on Wang Amah's advice, to Kuanyin in the local temple, a small dusty inconspicuous goddess who looked after women in childbirth. Bewildered by loss and by her own inability to comfort her mother, Pearl had for months added desperate private prayers for another baby, and now she helped their nurse tend the new sister and coax her to accept tinned milk. "I was so happy I did not know how close my mother was to death," she wrote long afterwards. Carie recovered slowly. When she began to tell stories again there was a new edge of bitterness to her childhood memories of the mountains of West Virginia. "Bred in this sparkling and cool sunshine, in these pure and silvered mists of America, it was no wonder that sometimes she fainted in the thick sultriness of an August noon in a southern Chinese city, filled too full of human breath and of the odor of sweating human flesh. . . . The stench from the garbage-filled streets rose into the three little rooms. . . . The flies swarmed from the piles of half-rotting filth smoking under the burning sun. The hot air hung like a foul mist."

Having tried and failed to provide consolation, Pearl now became her mother's confidant. At some point after the child's seventh birthday in June, Carie told her for the first time how Maude died. As an adult Pearl would retell this story three times over thirty years in biographical and autobiographical narratives, expanding and elaborating on a scenario conceived in the operatic terms of a Gothic novel to match the horror and pathos of the event. It happened in a typhoon on a boat carrying the Sydenstrickers with their first two children back from an unaccustomed holiday at a seaside resort in Japan.

Maude at eighteen months was tiny, frail, and malnourished, unable to digest the artificial milk that was all her mother had to give her that summer. Carie said she had been forced to wean the child early because she was already starting a third pregnancy (if so, she must have miscarried), and that they were returning too soon in great heat on account of Absalom's work. The baby died on September 15, 1884, in a stranger's arms because she refused to go to her father and her mother was too seasick to hold her. In the graphic account Carie gave Pearl she spent a whole night rushing from the heaving deck down to the cabin and back again, nauseous, soaked by saltwater, frantic with dread, rounding hysterically on her husband when he tried to calm her: "If it had not been for this other one coming too soon, I could have nursed her through the summer and saved her." The story ended with Carie huddled on a pile of rope in the ship's stern, cradling the body in her arms. "The sea was in great black waves, a leaden, livid light gleaming where a faint dawn shone upon them. . . . A wave of spray fell over them. How she hated this sea, the great heaving, insensate thing! . . . Over the roaring grey sea hung the grey sky. Where was God in all of this? No use praying. . . . She wrapped her arms about the child defiantly and crouched staring out to sea." Forced back below decks by sickness and vertigo, she found her husband staring through the thick glass porthole: "The dark water covered it as though they were running under the sea."

Images like these imprinted on a receptive and still unformed imagination bred a protectiveness that colored Pearl's view of her mother ever afterward. Carie's bouts of seasickness took the form of migraine, vomiting, and back pain. All three had afflicted her ever since her honeymoon voyage, when she found herself alone at close quarters for the first time with a husband she hardly knew in a ship's cabin crossing the Pacific, which "remained for Carie to the end of her life an ocean of horror." She conceived her first child on this voyage, and years later she spelled out the horror in question in terms a child could understand. After Maude's death she had collapsed mentally and physically, developing the early symptoms of tuberculosis and being ordered by her doctor back to the United States for a cure. Her religious faith wavered, and she contemplated leaving her husband, an unattainable fantasy that she abandoned, settling instead for the riskier but more realistic option of treating herself by fresh air and bed rest at the resort of Chefoo (Yantai) on China's northern seacoast. The couple set out (if Carie was indeed pregnant, she must have lost the child on or soon after this journey) on a slow dirty Yangtse junk infested by rats that ran up and down the low beams over their bunk. Still distraught with grief, Carie woke one night to find a huge rat squirming in her long loose hair. "She had to plunge her hand in and seize it and throw it to the floor, and the sleek writhing body in her hand turned her sick, and she would have cut off her hair if she could for loathing of it." Carie's account of the crisis in her marriage is immediately followed in Pearl's narrative by this sickening symbolic rat.

Pearl understood well enough even then. She and Grace both remembered conversations at night in their parents' bedroom next to theirs, a low murmur of voices, their mother's rising occasionally to vehement remonstrance, interrupted by weeping or the urgent angry creaking of her rocking chair. The same conversations recur in Pearl's novels, most notably in the semi-autobiographical *The Time Is Noon* and *The Townsman* (where Mary repulses her husband for fear of yet another unwanted conception, and has nightmares of snakes emerging from the sod walls to invade her bed). For the Sydenstrickers there would be no more babies after Grace.

Seven months after the birth they moved up above the town to a newly vacated property belonging to the Presbyterian Mission, with broad verandas looking out over green grave lands to a pagoda on the far side of the hill. This was the place Pearl remembered fondly ever after as her childhood home, with a climbing rose spilling over the covered porch that ran around two sides of the house, and a garden already planted with old trees and now filled by her mother with flowers. In blacker moods she saw it as "a small, decrepit brick cottage, whose sagging floors were full of centipedes and scorpions." She remembered her parents inspecting the bedrooms every evening, her father holding a lantern while her mother batted with an old slipper at the six- to eight-inch-long centipedes that fascinated the child: "Their segments were covered with hard black shell, each having a double pair of bright yellow legs, and on the tail a stinger which could give a dangerous wound. In spite of them I loved the tropical nights, the great luna moths, jade green and spotted with black and silver, clinging to the big gardenia bushes in the garden, and the bamboos dim in the mists from the river." Pearl explored the hillside beyond the back gate, made friends with the farmers' daughters who lived in the valley below, and kept her own rabbit with a cage of pet pheasants in the dark shady storage space under the veranda. She attended classes for Chinese girls at the mission school and played with the American boy next door, a redheaded missionary's son named James Bear, who taught her to smoke (he later denied the charge). In the afternoons it was Pearl's job to rock her sister to sleep in their mother's rocking chair.

This was the most dangerous period of Absalom's professional career. "In the year 1900 the famous 'Boxer' uprising broke over the land like a tremendous tornado," he wrote with an uncharacteristic flourish in his memoirs, "and all work was more or less suspended while it raged." The Boxers were a militant sect recruited initially from young northern farmers who blamed foreigners—which meant missionaries in rural China—for their country's misfortunes: social and political inanition, the inability to repel Western or Asiatic predators, and a cycle of flood and famine that devastated Shandong and Honan as the Yellow River burst its embankments and the Grand Canal silted up in the late 1890s. The movement spread rapidly with tacit and eventually open backing from the imperial throne, itself helpless to contain or control the opportunistic incursions of Japan, Russia, and the great European powers. Xenophobia simmered and flared in the countryside. Absalom never went out without a stick big enough to beat back the dogs loosed on him wherever he went in these years. People started cursing him in the street again. Once an innkeeper almost killed him with a cleaver. He was forced to close down chapels rented from landlords no longer prepared to do business with Christians. He spent much time cooped up at home, visiting local converts only in secret with a lantern after dark. All through the spring and early summer of her eighth birthday Pearl slept with her clothes folded ready for flight on a chair beside the bed. Her mother kept a bag beside the door packed with spare shoes and a set of underwear for each of them, together with a basket of tinned milk for the baby.

After fierce arguments about whether to go or stay, Pearl's parents compromised by hiring a junk to wait on the river at the far end of a concealed escape route, down through the bamboo at the back of the house, so that Carie could get away fast if she had to with the children and Wang Amah. For the first time the Sydenstrickers were shunned. Chinese visitors stopped calling on Pearl's parents, and her friends no longer came to play or shared her desk at school. On one of his clandestine visits to the city to administer communion to the aged mother of a parishioner, Absalom was caught by soldiers who raided the house, roped him to a post, and forced him to watch them torture to death his Christian convert, Lin Meng, before carrying off Lin's ten-year-old son. Lin's mother died the same night. When he was eventually released the next day, Absalom came home exultant and bloody. "Then he looked at us all strangely, his ice-colored eyes shining, his voice solemn and triumphant: 'Lin Meng has entered into the presence of our Lord, a martyr, to stand among that glorified host!'" Buoyed by the prospect of martyrdom himself, Absalom refused even to consider evacuation long after most of the white population had left Zhenjiang.

White refugees began trickling down from the north, small groups of ragged, hungry, frightened adults whose children had died from starvation or fever on the way. Carie told brave stories of Civil War battles in the United States and buried her few valuable possessions in the yard as her own mother had done forty years before. An imperial edict dated June 20, a week before Pearl's eighth birthday, declared war and death to all foreigners. Chinese troops opened fire the same day on the foreign quarter in Beijing, laying siege to Western diplomats in their own legations. On July 9 forty-five Christians were killed in the governor's compound at Shanxi. More atrocities followed. The American consul in Zhenjiang ordered the few remaining white people to evacuate by gunboat at a prearranged signal, which came at noon on a day so hot that the whole family of Sydenstrickers was resting in a darkened room ("even Father with his collar off," said Grace). Looking back half a century later Pearl described their departure as if it were a scene on a Chinese willow pattern plate: "The air that summer's day was hot and still and from the verandas the landscape was beautiful, the valleys green as jade with their earthen farmhouses shaded beneath the willow trees. White geese walked the paths between the fields and children played on the threshing floors. . . . Beyond the dark city the shining river flowed toward the sea. . . . The actual leave-taking was entirely unreal."

Absalom escorted his family to Shanghai, taking only what they could carry, and returned alone to Zhenjiang, the only white man in the region, dressed once again in formal Western clothes, looking weirdly conspicuous in the Chinese crowds on account of his crumpled white suit and pith helmet as much as his great height. When his two chapels were burned to the ground he preached on the streets to people who responded by stoning him. The single Chinese disciple who stayed with him told Pearl years later that he had expected her father over and over again to be killed. Absalom lived through the summer, by his own account in an ecstatic trance: "I seemed without the body. For I was conscious of the presence of God with me like a strong light shining, day and night. All human beings were far away from me." He came as close as he could to claiming a martyr's crown, regarding this near miss ever afterward as one of the high peaks of his life.

Pearl retained almost no memory of her own time in Shanghai, where the foreign community buzzed with rumors about Western troops preparing to move on Beijing and every steamer brought yet more refugees from the farthest parts of the empire. "The white people in Shanghai seemed to be clinging to the edge of China, waiting to be shoved off." Pearl saw great gray foreign warships in the harbor, and listened to her mother's stories of sanctuary in America. She remembered reaching up to pull the pigtail of a portly Chinaman ambling ahead of her and being terrified, not by his anger but by Carie's abject attempt to placate him: "I had never seen her afraid before in all my life." In the semi-tropical heat of that ominous summer Pearl played with her little sister in a tub of cold water in their boarding-house on Bubbling Well Road, where for the first time she saw water come out of a tap. Afterward she thought they were away for almost a year, but in fact it was a few months before their father arrived to fetch them home that autumn, looking so strange Grace didn't recognize him. The Boxers had been defeated, their leaders executed, the countryside pacified, and humiliating public capitulation forced on the dowager empress, who surrendered to virtually all the demands of the victorious Western powers.

In October Absalom convened the annual meeting of the newly formed North Kiangsu Presbyterian Mission, which assembled in Shanghai, and tabled a formal resolution urging him to go home at once on furlough to the United States. On July 8, 1901, he finally sailed with his family for San Francisco, taking the train on to West Virginia, the home his children had heard so much about and now saw with alien eyes as they traveled "down through the states, through wooded hills that looked strange and furred after the shorn Chinese hills, over rivers that looked like creeks after the flooding Yangtse and the Yellow River, through towns that looked unreal, they were so orderly and clean after the heaped mud and the confusion of Chinese villages."

CHAPTER 2

Mental Bifocals

W HEN PEARL LANDED at nine years old in America, she came in effect from a war zone. Pitched battles had been fought against Christians in northern China, foreign railroads ripped up, churches looted and destroyed, their adherents murdered or driven out. According to figures established later, no more than two hundred foreigners were in fact killed, none of them (thanks to a prescient political pact negotiated by two local governors) in the Yangtse Valley. But at the time white people lived in an atmosphere of terror heightened by stories, real and imaginary, of whole communities imprisoned and slaughtered by Boxers. Three thousand Chinese Christians lost their lives, many tortured to death like Lin Meng by the often ingenious and always excruciating standard procedures of Chinese punishment. Pearl had heard adults telling individual horror stories in whispers in Shanghai all through the previous summer. Children had been included in the massacres, and she herself had got used to people shouting routine death threats on the street. In the eight months between the suppression of the Boxers and the Sydenstrickers' departure, she heard many more dreadful accounts of missionaries who survived persecution or failed to, and whose followers were caged, hanged, sliced to pieces, or left out to shrivel in the sun. Christian newspapers published rolls of the glorious dead. Her father, who had hoped to join their ranks himself, totted up the numbers with satisfaction: "thousands of Christians suffered martyrdoms, which gave us great encouragement, as showing that the work which had been accomplished was not merely on the surface, but a genuine fruit that would stand the severest test."

Pearl, already expert in strategies for dealing with fears she could not face, suppressed many of these memories. "Did I not see sights which children should not see, and hear talk not fit for children's ears?" she asked rhetorically half a century later. "If I did, I cannot remember." The mood in her American world was upbeat. Missionaries returning to their posts all over China found themselves indemnified, amply compensated, privileged and protected more effectively than ever before by new government treaties that provided opportunities even Absalom conceded were "immensely better than they had been." The defeated Chinese were acquiescent, even obsequious, and almost suspiciously eager to enlist in the ranks of a religion that had so decisively demonstrated superior supernatural strength. Pearl moved uneasily between the two worlds of her childhood now that she had seen for herself the sudden ferocity that could erupt from beneath a surface as sunny and calm as the Yangtse. She said that in all this unaccustomed civility only the dogs still snarled at her, "for those savage, starving village dogs alone still dared to show the hatred they had been taught to feel against the foreigners."

It was high time to exchange the ambivalent actuality of China for the dreamworld of the West. When Pearl finally saw her mother's home at Hillsboro, tucked under the Allegheny Mountains in Pocahontas County, West Virginia, she knew as in a dream exactly how it would be: a handsome, unpretentious, white-painted house with a pillared portico set in a wide level valley beneath gently sloping green hills, surrounded by a broad meadow and shaded by sugar maples, with flower beds under the windows and wild honeysuckle growing along the picket fence. She recognized everything from the layout of the rooms and the grapevine shading the porch to the family spilling out onto the front steps: her tall brother Edgar dressed as a student in a high collar, straw boater, and glasses; her aunts and cousins and the two gray-haired old gentlemen she knew to be her grandfather, Hermanus Stulting, and his oldest son, her mother's favorite brother, Uncle Cornelius. She made friends at once with Cornelius's youngest daughter, Cousin Grace Stulting, who was two years older. For the first time Pearl had an American contemporary to play dolls and swap confidences with in the bedroom they shared at night. The two girls fed the turkeys together, built tree houses, picked grapes trained along the side of the big wooden barn and ate the fallen apples lying on the grass in the orchard. ("I knew every tree," said Cousin Grace, "the Early Harvest and the Early Ripe, the hard apples and the Maiden's Blush.") Pearl's mother slipped back into the routines of her girlhood, sitting gossiping and sewing with her sister-in-law on the front porch, baking bread, bottling preserves, churning butter, washing clothes in the shade of an elm tree and ironing them in the cool stone buttery under the house.

Everything was exactly as Carie had said it would be, and yet Pearl could see that her mother never felt entirely at home in the house she had inhabited for so long in her imagination. For one thing, her memories of living there were more fantasy than fact. Throughout her childhood her family had lived in rented accommodation in Hillsboro, scraping together the funds to buy enough land for a house of their own only a few years before Carie married and left the country, at which point her family began to break up. Within four years the two Stulting brothers and four of the five sisters had married and moved away, all except Cornelius, who for as long as anyone could remember had been their mother's mainstay and a father in all but name to his younger brother and sisters. Their actual father, Hermanus, eighty-five years old when Pearl met him, was a small, fastidious, immaculately turned-out figure, aloof and choleric, a lover of music and painting, who had apparently played no more part in family life than her own father in China. Born and bred in Utrecht, nostalgic all his life for the thriving Dutch metropolis he had left as a married man with a wife and two children, he described himself in official documents variously as carpenter, silversmith, and clockmaker, but his attempts to start a business in the United States had failed, and he seems to have resigned the practical running of his domestic economy to his wife and son. "He was a city man, never anything else," Grace Stulting said pityingly long afterwards. "He would chop kindling and do it like a woman."

Pearl's mother inherited her hot temper from Hermanus and also her gift for telling tales. He warmed to his strange little semi-Chinese granddaughter, leading her away to the room full of clocks and watches where he lived separately from the rest of the family, and enthralling her—as Carie had done before him—with highly romanticized accounts of "the Old Country," which in his case meant Holland. He filled Pearl's receptive ears with stories of her great-grandfather, Mynheer Cornelis Johannis Stulting, a pious and prosperous merchant who had uprooted his five sons to set out at the head of a party of three hundred persecuted pilgrims seeking religious liberty in the promised land of America, where, after many disastrous setbacks along the way, the family finally settled in Virginia, clearing primeval forest, hauling tree stumps and facing down parties of Indians, "frightening and savage to see." Very little of this was strictly true. The history of the Stultings' arrival in New York in 1847 and their subsequent establishment in Hillsboro, carefully documented from local archives by Grace Stulting more than a century later, was decidedly more prosaic than the alternative version published by her cousin Pearl. But his children and grandchildren all agreed that Hermanus (who had first learned English in his thirties) was a first-rate storyteller: "all that he said was like a fairy-tale," said Grace.

The heroine of the stories Carie told was always her mother, Johanna Stulting, who, like her daughter, had also abandoned her own familiar world to follow her husband to an unknown continent, where she made a life for her family from scratch, with scant support from Hermanus. Survival meant physical labor almost beyond the strength of a woman contending with regular pregnancies, whose only helper was a young son (Cornelius was not yet into his teens when the family reached West Virginia, and his only brother, Calvin, still unborn). Daily life consisted of digging, planting, hoeing, chopping, keeping a cow and chickens, making bread, butter, and cheese, spinning and weaving wool, cotton, and flax, producing enough to feed and clothe seven children. The family boasted that they eventually emerged from the Civil War self-sufficient in everything except tea, coffee, and chocolate. Carie, who idolized her mother, was eighteen when she nursed her through the final stages of the tuberculosis that killed her, worn out and used up at the age of sixty. Nearly all of her children became teachers. Having had to make do without education during the war, Carie herself was sent away by Cornelius to catch up in two years at boarding school after their mother's death. She had seen enough of life at home to know that she needed more. If social and religious convention required her to sacrifice herself for others, she planned to do it in a completely different way from her mother. Foreign missions offered the nearest means of self-immolation, and at the same time the only available escape route from unending domestic drudgery together with the narrow horizons that closed down round it.

The Stultings were admirably suited to their time and place. They were stubborn, resilient, puritanical people shaped by the Calvinist teachings of their Presbyterian church, which still saw China and its inhabitants in much the same terms as Carie had done when she sailed away with her young husband for God's sake in search of a cloudy vision, "a harvest of dark, white-clad heathen being baptized, following them with adoring eyes . . . two brave young missionaries . . . two white and cloud like shapes, blessing the dark, bowed multitudes bending in devotion before them." The gap between reality and imagination, which would be Pearl's chosen territory as a writer, opened up for her wider than ever before in the Stulting household. Her new family were the first Americans she had ever known at close quarters, and they made her feel foreign in the country she had been taught to call home. None of them had any inkling of the suppressed anxieties she lived with, or how exposed she felt in a house and garden without the protection of high compound walls. The assembled household was baffled and faintly embarrassed by her hysterical tears when her grandfather gravely announced the assassination of President McKinley in September 1901. Only Carie understood the shock and terror—"must we have the revolution here, too?"—released in her daughter by news of regime change.

The Stultings had never owned black slaves and they could not afford to pay servants, but their allegiance lay with the southern states. They had bitterly resented finding themselves just inside the border of Federal West Virginia when war split the state in two (Carie said that as a small child she believed the grown-ups who told her that Yankees had horns like devils). Although in theory they opposed slavery, they belonged by instinct and choice to a white society that treated black people as subhuman. For all their idealism, the same prejudice accompanied Pearl's altruistic parents when they left for China. After more than twenty years in the field neither Carie nor Absalom could ever quite see the Chinese in the way their daughter did, as people like any others.

Layers of mistrust and mutual incomprehension blocked any traffic between Pearl's two worlds. Dearly as she had loved her cousin as a child, Grace Stulting in later life disapproved strongly of Pearl's upbringing in a household of Chinese servants who expertly subverted all Carie's efforts to discipline her children, and ensure that they grew up in the hardworking, egalitarian, self-reliant American way. The Stultings were dismayed to find that Pearl had no idea how to sew, cook, clean, or wash up. "That amah, she raised her," Grace said sniffily. At the end of the summer holidays the Sydenstrickers moved to Lexington, Virginia, where Edgar was due to start as a freshman at his father's old college of Washington and Lee, and Pearl entered school in third grade. This was one of the periods she preferred to forget, for she could no more blend in with her southern classmates than she had gotten on in Zhenjiang with the sheltered and segregated daughters of foreign businessmen and diplomats, growing up behind the barred gates of the British concession. The ladylike white girls she met at Zhenjiang's British Club seemed condescending and dull to Pearl, and for their part they could make nothing of a child burned brown by the sun, accustomed to wearing loose Chinese trousers at home, and speaking an idiomatic street slang incomprehensible even to her parents (for whom Chinese was always a second language, as English was for Hermanus). Pearl was fluent enough to trade uninhibited insults with local boys who swore at her on the streets of her hometown. "She didn't feel like she was an American," said Cousin Grace. "It handicapped her terribly. Never felt like she belonged here . . . felt like she was odd."

The practical, hardheaded Stultings took a dim view from the start of the austere, unwordly, incorrigibly intellectual Absalom Sydenstricker, whose unremitting righteousness made them uncomfortable. The marriage had been categorically forbidden by Carie's father. Pearl's comical account of her parents' strangely impersonal courtship, in *The Exile*, started with her father finding his path barred by Hermanus, hopping mad and armed with a stick ("'Sir, I know your intentions! . . . You shall not have my daughter!' The young missionary . . . gazed down on the little man and answered mildly, 'Yes, I think I shall, sir,' and proceeded on his way"). By 1901 Pearl's Sydenstricker grandparents were dead, the family scattered, and their home just outside Lewisburg, forty miles away in Greenbrier County, had been sold, but the child picked up stories then and later about the early life her father said as little as possible about. He was the youngest but one of nine children brought up on a large rough hillside farm in servitude to their father, Andrew Sydenstricker, a God-fearing giant of a man who read the Bible right through aloud to his family every year and drove his seven sons off the property one by one, cursing their ingratitude, as each became legally free to go at the age of twenty-one. All of them hated the land that remained their father's abiding passion. All became ministers save one, who was a church elder.

Their mother, Frances Sydenstricker, born Feronica Kauffman, was a grandmother Pearl liked the sound of: clever, competent, combative, sharp-tongued and short-tempered, a fine cook, a formidable manager, and a powerful personality in her own right. She was responsible for the family's intellectual ambitions, a member of the proud and prolific Coffman family, Swiss Mennonites descended from a celebrated eighteenth-century dissident and scholar (the name change from Kauffman to Coffman signified their new American identity). She and her two downtrodden daughters serviced the household with the help of a wood-burning iron stove and a washtub in the woodshed. She ran her big, rambling, ramshackle farmhouse and its floating population of children, relatives, and visitors lavishly and well until at the age of sixty in 1873, the year her son Absalom was old enough to leave home, she decided she had had enough and never did a day's work again. Local legend said that for the next two decades and more old Mrs. Sydenstricker held court in her rocking chair, entertaining the wives of the neighborhood, impervious to her children's bewilderment and the stupefaction of her outraged husband, dispensing gossip, providing a subversive role model, recruiting more and more subscribers to her tacit declaration of female liberation until, on one memorable day, twenty-two likeminded women gathered to give one another strength and support on her porch.

His mother permanently shaped Absalom's ideal of womanhood, in which the only two qualities that mattered were meekness and docility. "In that house bursting with its seven great sons, roaring with the thunder of the quarrel between man and woman, he heard it often shouted aloud that the Bible said man was head of the woman. It had to be shouted often to that indomitable old woman, eternally in her rocking chair. It made no difference to her, but it made a deep impression on her seven sons." Absalom was the smallest, skinniest, and most insignificant, ostensibly the plain, timid weakling in a handsome, burly, turbulent family. He grew up the butt of his brothers, afraid of his father, and terrorized by the ghost stories he heard from his Mennonite grandmother, who spoke only German, which Absalom said afterward was the language of his childhood (the Sydenstrickers came originally from Bavaria). Most of the attention and perhaps also the affection he got seem to have come from this grandmother, who died when he was seven. Two years later his older brothers started enlisting one after another in the Union Army to fight the Yankees, leaving only the three youngest—Hiram, Absalom, and Frank, age eleven, nine, and seven—to work the farm under their father for the duration of the war. Absalom endured the hardship and humiliation of these formative years by shutting down his feelings inside a protective shell, telling his daughter long afterward that the occasional day when he could sneak off to school was always his greatest pleasure.

"I saw him an overworked boy, starving for books, hungry for school, loathing the land and tied to it until he was twenty-one," wrote Pearl, who came in the end to understand better than anyone except her mother the inner furies that scourged Absalom, "his austerities, his shynesses, his fires so deep and so strangely banked, the powerful mystic motive of his life." He escaped by the same route his brothers had taken, putting himself first through college, then through theological seminary, living at subsistence level, working with a frenzied concentration that ensured outstanding academic success and cut him off more completely than ever from other human beings. He was twenty-eight before he was finally ready for action, which meant picking a wife (admittedly one who was neither meek nor docile) on his mother's instructions and sailing halfway around the world to stake out a spiritual territory of his own on a scale incomparably grander than anything that had ever occurred to his father. Returning home on furlough always brought back the old sense of impotent grievance that Pearl gave long afterward to the youngest son of Wang Lung, the farmer in *The Good Earth,* another patriarch whose sons grow up crushed by a dread that comes back to haunt the youngest long after his father lies dead and buried. "It was the same sick helplessness he had been used to feel in the days of his youth when the earthen house was his gaol. Once more his father, that old man in the land, reached out and laid his earthy hand upon his son."

At the age of nine or ten Pearl was too young to grasp the root of the problem, but she could see perfectly well that her cousins looked down on their Uncle Ab, with his long-winded sermons and his baggy suits made by a cheap Zhenjiang tailor. America robbed Absalom of the confidence and authority he possessed in China, and he spent much of his family's time in Hillsboro away preaching or fundraising ("when he came back no one was quite as much at ease as we were in his absence," Pearl said). The only way she herself managed to inspire even a flicker of interest in him was by demanding to join the church on the same Sunday as her cousin Grace. The two girls were duly received by the local minister, Absalom's oldest brother, the Rev. David Sydenstricker, an initiation Pearl dismissed afterward as a complete letdown, claiming she had only suggested it in the first place because it gave her the chance to show off a new frock. She was beginning to realize that the yellow curly hair and "wild-beast eyes" so repulsive to the Chinese had the opposite effect on Americans. Her younger sister, Grace, remembered Pearl as already strikingly pretty with a "slender face, broad forehead, pointed chin, straight, stubborn mouth, narrow nose and gray-green eyes beneath black brows which contrast with the near-fair hair." She certainly looked her best in the new white dress with a sash and a broad-brimmed Leghorn hat. But, whatever she may have felt later, joining the church looks like a gesture of solidarity at a stage when Pearl still badly wanted to please her father.

SHE WAS ALSO beginning dimly to sense the limitations of the cohesive, coercive, and highly judgmental Presbyterian society into which she was born. When the family returned to China in the autumn of 1902 Pearl qualified as a newly admitted church member at just ten years old to attend Zhenjiang Mission meetings, where she found her father once again under attack. Absalom disagreed with his fellow missionaries, on most issues as a matter of principle. His opposition roused unconditional loyalty from his wife in public and blind family patriotism in his children, all of them "impregnated," as Pearl said, "with the feeling that the hands of their own kind were for ever against their parents and therefore against them." Contact with her Puritan origins in West Virginia shed new light on a side of her father that others found hard to bear: "He was a spirit . . . made by that blind certainty, that pure intolerance, that zeal for mission, that contempt of man and earth, that high confidence in heaven, which our forefathers bequeathed to us."

Station meetings were stormy affairs held once a week in the Sydenstrickers' house in Zhenjiang, where mission personnel met to discuss strategy, review progress, and vote democratically on how to allocate the funds provided by the financial board of the Southern Presbyterian Church in the United States. There was constant wrangling over the cost of repairs, maintenance, building programs, the price and distribution of tracts, and whether or not to raise the salaries of native helpers, who received a meager monthly wage of eight to ten Mexican dollars (worth roughly half as much as U.S. dollars). The women recruited to help spread the Bible story got even less. Provision in the minutes for "Mrs. Sydenstricker's Bible woman" was five dollars a month, in spite of bitter remonstrations from Carie in private (mission wives were permitted to attend but forbidden to speak at these meetings).

There was unanimous disapproval of Absalom's interminable schemes for extending the Work, and constant protest that his increasing number of conversions reflected an obsession with quantity over quality. His colleagues deplored his reluctance to pool the funds entrusted to him by American benefactors, his obstinate insistence on educating his Chinese staff (the conventional view was that teaching the natives too much was asking for trouble), and his point-blank refusal to fall in with official policy of dividing the available territory among competing Christian denominations in much the same way as the European powers apportioned their landgrabs. What infuriated his fellows perhaps more than anything else was his unauthorized translation of the Bible into a vernacular that ordinary people could understand for themselves ("We are better judges than the Chinese of what they need," ran an authoritative article in the *Chinese Recorder,* urging preachers to stick to the simple trusty formula of exhortation, admonition and reproof). Absalom was proud of his ability to whip up quarrels with himself at the center. Asked if he had succeeded in reconciling the two feuding missionaries in charge of his very first junior posting, he said with a disarming glint of self-mockery, "I succeeded to this extent—they united in turning on me!" At the end of her life Pearl told a close friend that as a girl she never felt free from the strain of his altercations. "My memory of that circle of half a dozen soberly dressed people is grim," she wrote of the regular Monday afternoon sessions in her parents' parlor:

On Sunday everyone had been religiously whetted by three church services—not only religiously whetted but physically exhausted and emotionally strained. . . . I have sat, hundreds of Mondays, a small bewildered child, looking from one stubborn face to the other of my elders, listening to one stubborn voice and then another. . . . Listening to them, my heart swelled with helpless tears. It seemed to me they were always against [Absalom] and Carie, those men with their leathery skins and hard mouths and bitter determined eyes. [Absalom] sat there never looking at them, but always out of the window, across the valley to the hills, that brow of his white and serene, his voice quiet and final. . . . "I feel it my duty to push further into the interior. I regret if it is against your will, but I must do my duty."

As an adult Pearl came to feel that her father had been ahead of his time in his work on the Chinese vernacular, as in his belief that the Church could not hope to survive in China except on a basis of further education, local autonomy, and increasing participation by the Chinese in its administration and government. Some of the harshest and also the funniest passages in her brief, unsparing, beautifully balanced biography of her father, *The Fighting Angel,* come from these years, when she became a firsthand witness of church politics, viewing them retrospectively in double focus as part idealistic child, part skeptical adult, often with startling results. The juxtaposition of childish bias with adult impartiality gives an exuberant spin to her account of the rivalry between her father and Zhenjiang's one-eyed Baptist minister, who for thirty years disputed Sydenstricker's territory and persisted in poaching his converts. The problem was total immersion, which appealed to the pragmatic Chinese more than the Presbyterians' modest baptismal sprinkle, on the grounds that "if a little water was a good thing for the soul, more was better." Persuading good Presbyterians to sneak off to the Baptists was a form of blatant religious theft that assumed diabolical proportions in the Sydenstricker home: "We sat silent through many a meal while [Absalom] with unwonted fluency said what he felt about other denominations, especially about the folly of immersion." The missionary with one eye became one of the arch bogeys of Pearl's childhood.

Absalom, whose distrust of women meant that he could not

quite bring himself to believe they had souls, never brought the full force of his excoriating zeal for salvation to bear on his daughters. Pearl's problem was how to attract his attention, not how to deflect it. He whipped his children for serious infringements such as telling a lie, but he hit them in anger only on rare, terrifying occasions, "when something he kept curbed deep in him broke for a moment its leash." Like her sister, Grace learned early to watch for warning signs when his hands shook and a muscle twitched in his jaw. At the age of eleven, as incipient teenage mutiny started to temper her first uncritical devotion, Pearl announced to her father's face that she hated him. In these years, when she was increasingly aware of tension between her parents, she transferred her allegiance exclusively to her mother. The sense of perspective she finally achieved in her adult recollections is both persuasive and poignant, as if somewhere between the lines of her hard-won objectivity there still lurks the ghost of a small distressed child trying not to burst into tears. "I have seen other lesser and more bureaucratic missionaries grow almost demented trying to control [Absalom]. They shouted bitter words at him, they threatened him with expulsion if he did not cease disobeying rules, over and over they called him a heretic, once even called him insane because he seemed to hear nothing they said. He was . . . so determined, so stubborn . . . that I know there have been those who, seeing that high, obstinate, angelic tranquillity, have felt like going out, groaning and beating their heads against a wall in sheer excess of helpless rage." Pearl admitted in private long afterward that the onset of puberty and adolescence in the period following the family's return to China in 1902 was when she came closest to being actively unhappy at home.

These were triumphal years for her father. Absalom agreed for once with the rest of the mission community in putting the post-Boxer era of unopposed white supremacy down to the direct intervention of divine providence in China's defeat by the West. Everything that had aggravated Christians about the Chinese—"Their language as well as their thought . . . contaminated by centuries of association with idolatry . . . Their ideas of truth and morals . . . distorted and wrong . . .

The residuum from the old religions . . . a system of demon worship . . . the source of untold misery as well as of spiritual and moral degradation"—was to be swept away. A surge of rhapsodical jubilation swept through missionary ranks now that God had at last given them a sign that they were His chosen people. "Assyria, Babylon, Greece, Rome . . . have passed away. Only China remains," wrote one of many exultant contributors to the *Chinese Recorder,* arguing that God had preserved this last great heathen empire intact for thousands of years precisely so that its inhabitants might be ripe for the plucking as the second millennium approached. "God has saved China for entire collapse. Morally, China is rotten to the core." A wave of revivalist meetings swept the north in the aftermath of the 1900 uprising, with huge congregations of hysterical Chinese confessing their sins, lacerating themselves, forgiving their enemies, and declaring with tears pouring down their faces that their resistance had been broken in a grotesque spiritual reversal of the Boxers' military campaign. "Even the smallest children began to cry out for mercy."

Absalom approved of revivalist tactics ("so hopeful and encouraging," he wrote with unusual warmth), conducting similar, if smaller meetings himself on spring and autumn tours of his expanding circuit, when he visited each one-room chapel in every walled city or market town, performing mass baptisms and preaching sermons that left him physically exhausted but emotionally transfigured. Pearl said that as a small girl she convinced herself she could see light streaming out from his body at these times. Even as a teenager, old enough to start learning Latin from her father, "I never stood up to recite to him—and not to stand was unthinkable—without feeling that more than man was listening." A supernatural imperative consumed him. He was nearing the goal he had schooled himself to attain all his life, and the urgency of his mission raged in him like fever.

Absalom gathered around him a small group of young Chinese followers, modeled by his own account on Jesus Christ's band of disciples, who met in his study in Zhenjiang for theological and practical training. This class, a perpetual irritation to Absalom's fellow missionaries, had started in Tsingkiangpu and was still running strong two decades later, when it was finally disbanded in 1906 on the foundation of the Nanjing Theological Seminary, another of Absalom's pet schemes for training Chinese evangelists, fiercely opposed by his peers. The most faithful of all his disciples was Ma Pangbo, who had begun as his prize pupil in Tsingkiangpu and remained at his side throughout every subsequent campaign. A Muslim from the north with Arab blood, disowned by his own family when he entered the Christian Church, the boy was still in his early teens when he joined forces with Pearl's father before she was born. Ma collaborated on Absalom's translations, accompanied him on his travels, preached in his chapels, planned strategy with him, and supervised his native staff, standing in as a kind of adoptive son in place of the actual Sydenstricker sons, who were absent or dead, becoming a trusted collaborator, consultant, second-in-command, eventually a spiritual brother. Both men were tall, dark, and lean, with strong bony features, hooded eyes, and hawk-beak noses. A Calvinist predestinarian and believer in the Second Coming, Absalom was a justified sinner who found his alter ego in Ma. Pearl said it was almost impossible to tell with your eyes closed which of the two was preaching or praying. "There is fire in him," Ma said when she asked what had drawn him as a boy to her father. "There is fire in me. The flame in his soul leaned over and caught at the flame in me, and I was compelled."

Ma had been Absalom's sole human companion in the summer of 1900, when the Boxer storm raged in Zhenjiang. "Many times I stood there," he told Pearl, "thinking I must, like Saul of Tarsus, be witness to the death of a martyr." Missionaries were frequently urged to model themselves on Saint Paul, but Absalom was among those who embodied in practice "the Pauline spirit of consecration," "the living aggressive force," "that spirit which irreligious people will call variously 'fanaticism,' 'intolerance,' 'narrow-mindedness,'" qualities every missionary strove in theory to emulate. For someone as steeped from infancy in the Bible as he was, accustomed to set aside hours every day for translation and exegesis, a large part of China's appeal lay in its superficial resemblance to Old Testament Israel. Absalom was not the only one to find conditions unchanged since the time of Abraham in China with its lepers and devil-worshippers, its superstitious rites, sympathetic magic and belief in demonic possession, its temples full of painted idols, and its stringent solutions to the problem of women. In spite of or possibly because of his refined erudition, he believed literally in every tenet of his fundamentalist faith, from bodily resurrection to miracle working. "The power to work miracles is promised, their need is apparent, real and great," he wrote, deploring what he hoped was only a temporary suspension. "No one seems to have the power in exercise, but the reason why the power is withheld we are unable to give."

There is a kind of insular absurdity about attempting to superimpose nineteenth-century biblical orthodoxy on an ancient, highly civilized culture underpinned in its customs and thought by Confucianism, Daoism, and Buddhism, a broad consensus organized, in Pearl Buck's words, "into three great types, naturally tolerant, non-evangelical, and mellowed by long human experience to a philosophy of humanism." Militant Christianity, backed up by armed force and gunboats, subverted deep-rooted systems of ethical belief, judicial practice, and administrative organization in favor of a simplistic morality that denounced any but the most basic education as elitist claptrap, regarded tolerance as a vice, and prized "aggressive evangelistic work" as a self-evident good. Of all the punitive measures imposed on China in 1900—freedom for Westerners to travel, trade, and settle where they wished, the payment of huge indemnities, and the lifting of virtually all restrictions on missionaries—the one that dismayed Pearl most in later life was the tacit insistence on an exclusive, prohibitive, alien religion. "The effrontery of all this still makes my soul shrink," she wrote half a century later.

The right to pride of place assumed by the Christian Church was possible only because, as many observers pointed out at the time and afterward, it chose to confine its attention to illiterate porters, gatemen, servants, and rural laborers. Absalom Sydenstricker himself freely admitted that "a stinging conviction of sin" was easier to induce in this sort of people. Without sin, guilt, and atonement, concepts with no place in Confucius's definition of virtuous conduct, the puritan mechanism of reward and punishment became frankly meaningless. People who failed to understand they had sinned could not be brought to repent. Simple mathematics starkly outlined the scale of the difficulty for the handful of Southern Presbyterian missionaries who had elected to hold themselves responsible for saving the souls of ten million people in North Kiangsu. The logical answer was to set up the redemptive equivalent of a production line, calculating two minutes per person as sufficient to spell out the message. Absalom himself managed to compress "all the essentials of Salvation" into a single sermon so short that, by his own account, "the unsaved soul, hearing perhaps but once, could understand and so take upon itself its own responsibility." Pearl, who must have heard her father's homily countless times as a girl, could recite the formula by heart: "God—His Son—believe—not perish—everlasting life. His whole creed was there."

Seen from Absalom's point of view in *The Fighting Angel,* his patent sermon was a reasonable, ingenious, and eminently practical device. But to his daughter, looking back "in anger and indignation" as an adult from a different perspective, this kind of quick-fix solution had little or no relevance to the Chinese peasants taught to repeat it by rote on the promise of rewards that never materialized from hellfire-breathing missionaries more interested in their own than their converts' problems. "I hear them repeat a memorized jargon to a group of eager, suffering, uncomprehending men and women," Pearl wrote after her father was dead, in a detailed, dispassionate analysis of mission practice that caused scandal throughout the United States and severed forever her connection with the Presbyterian Church.

In the first decade of the twentieth century all this lay far in the future. But already as a young girl, just beginning to distance herself from her father, Pearl felt uneasy about his preaching. "Somehow I had learned from Thoreau, who doubtless learned it from Confucius, that if a man comes to do his own good for you, then must you flee that man and save yourself." Pearl first encountered Confucius through Mr. Kung, who was engaged as her tutor in the autumn of 1902, a singular act of intellectual bravado on the part of her parents at a time when more conventional missionaries dismissed Chinese reverence for Confucius as rank idolatry. Perhaps the Sydenstrickers recognized that China had marked Pearl indelibly, and perhaps they felt she should learn literary *wen-li* as an antidote to the racy popular language she spoke with her friends and Wang Amah. Possibly her father wanted to help out a fellow scholar in need of a job, for Mr. Kung was a refugee, forced to flee after German soldiers had smashed up his ancestral home in the sacking and looting unofficially sanctioned by Western powers as part of the post-Boxer reprisals in Beijing. Whatever the reason, for the next three years Mr. Kung came for two hours every afternoon to teach Pearl calligraphy and to read aloud to her "in his beautiful polished Peking Mandarin" the ancient classical texts of Confucius, Mencius, and the canonical poets.

Teacher Kung was tall, slender, and stately, with courtly manners, long swaying robes, and an elegant black silk queue. Pearl had often watched elderly Chinese scholars disappearing into her father's study, but this was the first time any of them paid her the slightest attention. Her teacher seemed old to her, but in fact he was in his late forties, shrewd, kind, and, in his own judicious and considerate way, radically subversive. He gave her a solid grounding in Confucian ethics and their contemporary implications, pausing often to fill in the historical context of whatever book they were reading and to explain simply and clearly to his young pupil the relationship of China's past to its present and its future. He instilled in her a sharp sense of the hatred and humiliation smoldering behind the deferential faces of his proud and envious people, and of their perfect right to feel as they did. Mr. Kung was the only teacher Pearl ever had (apart from her mother) who commanded her unconditional respect. He laid the foundations of a liberal, inquiring, secular education, based on a breadth of vision and a tolerance beyond the reach of her father. He opened her eyes to much she had seen but not understood. His version of events was often at odds with that of the mission community, and under his guidance her view of the turmoil she had lived through began to shift and expand. "I became mentally bifocal, and so I learned early to understand there is no such condition in human affairs as absolute truth."

One thing Mr. Kung made unequivocally clear in their first lessons together was that the current state of truce in the country could not last. He quoted the Bible in ways that might have surprised its Western adepts: "His favorite text was the one about reaping the whirlwind if one sowed the wind, and he reminded me often, in his gently lofty manner, that one could not expect figs from thistles." He warned Pearl explicitly that revolutionary violence would erupt again, and that next time she and her family could not be sure of getting away with their lives. The shock overwhelmed her and she burst into tears, just as she had done in America when she heard from her grandfather that President McKinley had been assassinated. Afterward Pearl tried to find a way of passing on to her parents what her teacher had said, giving up in the end for fear they might overreact or misunderstand. Like many children who successfully negotiate the treacherous ground of a divided inheritance, she did it by cultivating two distinct personalities: "When I was in the Chinese world, I was Chinese, I spoke Chinese and behaved as a Chinese and ate as the Chinese did, and I shared their thoughts and feelings. When I was in the American world, I shut the door between." Keeping that door closed was the price of survival for Pearl as a child, but she spent the greater part of her adult life trying to open it, and keep it open.

IN THE GAMES of Chinese cops and robbers Pearl played with her friends on the hillside, she was generally cast because of her dubious looks as a trusty American ally, bearing gifts to aid the noble Chinese in their ceaseless battle against rapacious and ruthless Europeans. Now that she was starting to realize the ambiguous nature of American gifts, she looked back with new eyes on what was "so strangely called in Western history" the Boxer Rebellion, pointing out that it had been essentially a nationwide resistance movement aimed at strengthening the ruling Manchu Dynasty by cleansing the country of foreigners. At the head of the dynasty sat Dowager Empress Tz'u Hsi, whose fairy-tale history fascinated Pearl. A real-life Cinderella, she had started as a penniless orphan, working as a kitchen maid for her uncle until she was picked out to become an imperial concubine and embarked on a steady ascent, rising up through palace plots and intrigue to end up ruling China, installing successive young puppet emperors and remaining for nearly half a century the ultimate authority behind the Dragon Throne. Like every single one of her playmates, Pearl herself had believed for a time that she too was descended from this Venerable Ancestor. Tz'u Hsi's attempt to exterminate foreigners in the summer of 1900 had been one of the traumatic shocks of Pearl's childhood. But the defeated and pragmatic empress had rapidly returned from exile, regained her composure, and reversed her policies, staging a magnificent reentry into Beijing and eagerly embracing the modernizing process of Westernization she had so adamantly opposed for so long.

In 1904 Pearl watched the coming of the railroad from Shanghai, a British investment that involved the construction of China's first railway tunnel in the teeth of stubborn opposition from people who feared that any form of excavation would drive the dead from their graves, scatter the ancestral spirits, and rouse the dragons that lay waiting under the hills to destroy the world. Migrant laborers poured into Zhenjiang from city and countryside, beggars, outcasts, desperate and destitute refugees from famine areas, putting up makeshift hovels at the side of the line they dug out by hand, gouging into the rock with hammers and shifting the clay soil with shovels. "Gradually the workers disappeared into the depths of the earth, to come out white-faced and covered with moisture. Once there was a cave-in and panic stopped all work. . . . Soon the digging was going on at both ends. . . . The people darkened the banks of the cuts where they entered the hill, standing for hours, watching and talking." Pearl sat on Fort Hill above the Sydenstricker house with her mother and sister to witness the ceremonial arrival of the first train, belching smoke and breathing flame, erupting from the hill with a roar that changed forever the Zhenjiang her parents had known even before its transformation into a treaty port, in the days when it was still a sleepy country marketplace clustered along a single main street. "The West had pushed in. Like possessive arms of steel, the rails lay glistening in the sun."

Pearl idealized the empress as a child and identified with her as an adult, following her career, collecting a small library of books about her, and eventually writing one of her own, *Imperial Woman,* part biography, part fiction, and on some level a transposed and refocused self-portrait of Pearl herself. As the emperor's chief concubine, Tz'u Hsi had studied history, philosophy, and literature with a tutor (clearly based in Pearl's book on Teacher Kung), while at the same time pursuing her passion for the popular plays that brought real and imagined characters from the past back to life. The history and folklore Pearl studied were rich in the kind of heroines she needed at this stage, clever, powerful and beautiful women like the empress herself and the semimythological Mulan, a Chinese Joan of Arc, who put on her father's armor to fight for her country in the army of a fifth-century khan. Mulan was a particular favorite with audiences in these years, silencing restless or gossipy spectators by her dramatic first entrance, "a brilliant figure" heralded by flutes and drums, galloping in on an invisible horse, singing in high falsetto as she "dashed upon the stage . . . in the ancient garb of a warrior, and shouts burst from the people."

Pearl was a regular playgoer, always the only foreigner in the crowd squatting in temple courtyards or on hillside threshing floors, and she was also by now an enthusiastic reader of the novels she had first gotten to know through the family cook. "I decided well before I was ten to be a novelist," she said, relinquishing her ambition only briefly, when Teacher Kung scornfully dismissed her taste for pop fiction. "Such books poison the thoughts, especially of females," says the empress's tutor in *Imperial Woman.* "Such books ought not even to be mentioned by a virtuous lady." But Pearl could never resist these ancient stories for long. The countryside around Zhenjiang was impregnated with them. The heroine of *The White Snake* still lay in captivity beneath the pagoda on Golden Island, where she had once lived with her lover in a cave on Jingshan Mountain, inscribed with texts carved into the rock in or before the time of Confucius. The hero of *The Romance of Three Kingdoms,* another of Pearl's favorites, had married the princess of Wu in Ganlu Temple overlooking the Yangtse, just outside the old city wall.

Pearl had started reading fiction in English almost as soon as she could read at all. She claimed to have consumed every book on her parents' shelves by the age of seven, searching out anything that promised stories about real people—Plutarch's *Lives,* Foxe's *Book of Martyrs*—and surreptitiously combing her father's bound volumes of *Century Magazine* for fictional content. She devoured the works of Charles Dickens, a complete set of small blue cloth-bound volumes that she read over and over again, curled up in a corner of the veranda with a pocketful of peanuts or lodged in the branches of an old elm tree looking down on the road over the compound wall: "And there quite alone above the crowded Chinese scene I sat and read or sobbed and dreamed, not there at all but thousands of miles away, in a land I had never seen, among people I never knew." She read these particular volumes until they became interchangeable, so that she could reach one down at random from its high shelf, knowing it would serve her purpose without even bothering to check which title she held in her hand.

At one point Carie grew so alarmed by her daughter's inability to do without what had evidently become an escape mechanism that she tried hiding the books, but nothing could break Pearl's addiction to Dickens. "He was almost the sole access I had to my own people," she wrote. "I went to his parties for I had no other." In spite of disapproval from her parents, who shared Mr. Kung's view of fiction as inherently coarse, trashy, and time-wasting, she read Shakespeare, Scott, Thackeray, and George Eliot. She even tried *Tom Sawyer* and *Huckleberry Finn* by Mark Twain, but put them aside on the grounds that boys' adventures set on the Mississippi River had too little in common with anything she herself knew (an objection equally applicable to Dickensian London). None of them left any obvious trace on her own fiction, and none produced on her the same narcotic effect as Dickens. Her obsession with him lasted for a decade or more, during which she read everything he wrote at least once a year. Perhaps it was the art of popular fiction in general, as much as anything specific to Dickens, that held her attention. As a prospective writer herself, she responded avidly to the haunting power of an imagination that accesses horrors lurking deep beyond the reach of the conscious mind through symbolic imagery and drama, gluing the narrative together on the surface with a bland sentimentality that soothes and reassures readers. The split between dreamlike purity and contaminated reality, bred into Pearl at her mother's knee and rediscovered in Dickens, would become a crucial part of the implicit bargain she too would make later with her American public.

The habit of reading to distance herself from the life around her, hidden away alone in holes and corners where she could remain undisturbed, was an intrinsic part of the solitary, internalized Western world Pearl constructed for herself in these years, so different from the gregarious Chinese existence she was free to take up again once she had finished her daily lesson with Mr. Kung. In the late afternoons she ran down the hill to join her friends in the courtyards of any one of half a dozen neighboring farmhouses, where she was once again a welcome and familiar visitor. Pearl's Chinese manners were excellent and she was an attentive listener, eager to hear all the stories, "plaguing everyone with questions sometimes too intimate and personal," intrigued by the endless farming talk about crop failures, pest control, and appalling weather conditions. In times of drought she walked in procession with her friends' families to ask help from the paper gods of the fields, who lived in mud shrines looking out over the land. When the semitropical rains finally arrived she skipped through the bamboo barelegged in a waterproof hat the size of an umbrella made of layers of plaited bamboo.

Eccentricity on this scale raised comment in the foreign community, which was perplexed by Pearl's disorderly conduct at an age when most mothers were trying to wean their amah-raised children away from questionable habits and lax vocabulary picked up from servants in the kitchen. The mission wives would have been even more censorious if they had realized quite how frankly and freely Pearl discussed sex and religion with her contemporaries. The farmers' daughters questioned her closely as to whether Americans made babies in the same way as their own Chinese parents. Anxious for clarification herself, Pearl asked her mother, who said unhelpfully that all babies were made by God, "and in His image." Scarcely less baffling was the mystery hanging over Mary and Joseph and the conception of their problematic Son: "I heard talk about this from Chinese Christians who had no enthusiasm for Mary, and felt sorry for Joseph."

Pearl's closest confidants were the daughters of her Chinese sister, T'sai Yun, or Precious Cloud, whom she called Chieh-Chieh (Elder Sister), and who addressed Mr. and Mrs. Sydenstricker as Father and Mother. T'sai Yun seems to have been taken in as an unwanted child by Carie after the death of her own first daughter, probably around about the same time as Absalom selected Ma Pangbo as a young boy to train as his ally. Brought up in the Chinese manner and educated at a Chinese boarding school, T'sai Yun married before Pearl was born, producing six girls in rapid succession. "They grew up with me, and we told each other everything," said Pearl, who was close in age to the two oldest. "These six little Chinese girls were the nucleus of my childhood." Their father was the son of one of Absalom's native assistants, Pastor Chang, who caused increasing trouble in the church with his disruptive public demands for a grandson. Prayers were offered up by the congregation each time the couple announced the arrival of another daughter: "A first girl they accepted with welcome, a second one a year later with equanimity, a third with gravity, a fourth with consternation." Pearl remembered Pastor Chang as an aggressive old man with a skimpy white pigtail and a jutting goatee, preaching shrill sermons in which he threatened to revoke his allegiance to the Christian God, who had so abysmally failed to bring off a sex change for his fourth, fifth, and sixth granddaughters.

T'sai Yun's story was tragic in a country where girls were dismissed as worthless, routinely crippled as children and often identified by numbers rather than names, bringing irredeemable loss of face at birth on their mother, her family, and in this case the Christian Church. Long afterward Pearl turned her adoptive sister's experience into a captivating children's book, *The Chinese Children Next Door,* about six little girls with scarlet bows on their black pigtails, who idolized the plump placid baby brother their mother eventually achieved on her seventh try. This was the fable that delighted Nehru and Gandhi who must have been as familiar as the author herself with the actuality underlying her story and its fairy-tale ending. Infertility, infanticide, the institutionalized physical and mental abuse of women, the suicides of young wives blamed for transgressions often far less significant than repeated failure to produce a son, all these were commonplace in Pearl's childhood, constantly discussed and publicly dramatized in a society where nothing could be kept secret for long. Neither she not her sister ever forgot another of their neighbors, a childless wife from the Fu family, whom they watched one afternoon screaming curses for an hour or more at her husband as he stolidly followed the plow with his buffalo in the valley below their back gate: "She rocked back and forth in her howling, her voice broken and hoarse, the saliva dripping from her lips, her hair stringing down the sides of her face." Both Sydenstricker sisters had grown up watching processions of women coming to confide their troubles to Carie or lay them at the feet of the clay figure of Kuanyin in the temple, the goddess Pearl adopted as her tutelary deity, bringing wild flowers herself as an offering in spring: "I used as a small child to go to sleep more quietly at night because of her."

Disaster, and how to cope with it, were part of their practical education. At regular intervals, when the sky darkened and the wind rose to a sullen throaty roar, the whole Sydenstricker family retreated behind locked doors and windows to wait for a typhoon that hurled itself on the landscape, smashing trees, breaking down walls, tearing off the thatched roofs of mud huts, making their own brick-built mission bungalow quake on its foundations. Cholera raged in Zhenjiang every autumn, striking with terrible speed and finality. One year Wang Amah developed symptoms overnight and would have died if Carie had not risked her own life to fight the fever, shutting herself up with the patient for a week in a stone shed at the bottom of the garden, gripped by a bitter avenging rage for the lives she had already lost and the ones she still had to lose. She and Wang Amah had been friends and companions for so long and had gone through so much together that she said she had no intention of being left alone now. That same autumn Absalom left for the annual general meeting of the

North Kiangsu Mission in Hsuchowfu, accompanied by their next-door neighbor, an energetic younger man named James Bear, father of the red-headed boy who played with Pearl under the veranda. Absalom came home alone, sick and shaken, very nearly defeated himself by the cholera that had killed Bear as soon as he reached Hsuchowfu.

Carie escaped every year with the children to Kuling, packing up to leave as the rice seedlings were transplanted to the flooded fields in the steamy disease-ridden heat of late June, traveling upriver for days to Kiukang (Jiujiang), and then another day's journey inland across the parched plain. At the foot of Mount Lu the party transferred to flimsy bamboo chairs hanging from ropes on carrying poles, each borne by four mountain bearers, for the three-mile climb ending in one thousand twisting stone steps cut into the sheer side of the mountain:

> The road wound around the rocky folds of the cliffs, and beneath us were gorges and rushing mountain rivers and falls. Higher and higher the road crawled, twisting so abruptly that sometimes our chairs swung clear over the precipices as the front bearers went on beyond the rear ones, still behind the bend. One misstep and the chair would have been dashed a thousand feet into the rocks and swirling waters. . . . Somewhere near the top of the mountain we turned a certain corner and were met . . . by a strong cold current of mountain air. Until then the air had gradually cooled but now it changed suddenly and the bearers welcomed it with loud hallooing calls and a spurt of running, the chair swaying between them. As a child I could never keep from laughing. . . . The air of the plains had been hot and heavy, breathed in and out by millions of human lungs, but here on top of the mountain it was charged with fresh cold purity, and one breathed it in like lifesaving oxygen.

The Sydenstrickers' two-room stone house stood in a clearing on the sloping side of a valley with a stream running along the bottom between groves of acacia, bamboo, maple, and juniper, yellow-flowered dogwood, pink crape myrtle, and sweet-scented bushes of white osman. Pearl's first job each morning was to climb up through the woods past the rivulet at the side of the house to pick ferns, wild clematis, ornamental grasses, and lilies—"the tall white Madonna lilies, the red black-spotted tiger lilies or the white ones with red spots"— so that her mother could dress the house. There were picnics, walks, games, and even a handful of other mission children to play with as year by year more houses appeared along the brick paths, reached by shallow flights of stone steps and shaded by forest trees with everywhere the sound of water trickling or falling. The sense of being at home was intensified for Carie by the views from rocky platforms and sudden openings in the trees, where you could look down through layers of cloud on jagged peaks and crags or vertiginous drops to glimpses of river and lake far below. The mountain air, the pure water, and the paper-white mist reminded her of the famous "cloud seas" of Droop Mountain in the Alleghenies, where she grew up. After two or three magical months the family came back down again to make their way home by junk between the fields of high ripe yellow rice now lining the banks of the Yangtse.

At times like this Pearl forgot the forebodings of Teacher Kung, whose warning had been reinforced by the father of one of her friends: "Mr. Lu said there would be wars and more wars." But sometimes she felt she was the only member of her family to realize that the way they lived was precarious and finite. "Peace covered China like a sheet of thin ice beneath which a river boiled." The empress died in her seventy-fourth year in 1908, soon after Britain's Queen Victoria, another great empress whom Tz'u Hsi had thought of in her last years as a sister. Mr. Kung died too, carried off in a single day by cholera in the autumn of 1905. Pearl observed the funeral rites, wearing a white mourning band and bowing to the coffin with her father (both of them on strict orders from her mother not to join in the feast afterward for fear of contagion). It was a salute to her teacher, and also to the rich, dense, complex past he had opened up for her. Teacher Kung had lost all he possessed, and his life had been ruined in the havoc that marked China's entry into the twentieth century. If he understood and accepted that traditional scholars like himself had no part to play in their country's immediate future, perhaps it gave him some faint satisfaction to have passed on the humane and rational core of Confucius's teaching, even if only to one small, serious American girl. "Not until justice has been done," he said gravely to Pearl, explaining why his country was unlikely to be safe for Westerners for many years to come. She held on to his saying as her guiding rule for the rest of her life.

TOO OLD TO run freely in the valley any more, indeed no longer allowed out at all without Wang Amah as escort, Pearl at thirteen was beginning to part ways with her Chinese contemporaries, whose mothers were preparing them for marriage. Her own mother, belatedly worried by Pearl's intimacy with the local peasants and anxious to salvage what remained of her social credentials, encouraged her to make overtures to the few girls they knew in the expatriate white community, daughters of traders and business people temporarily posted abroad, all of them preoccupied with the life they had left and longing to get back to the West. None of these girls spoke more than kitchen Chinese or would have dreamed of having Chinese friends. Pearl made the most of a sweet-natured but thoroughly conventional English Agnes and three bright, smart, self-assured Longden sisters from the United States. The Longdens were the first American teenagers she had ever met, and they fascinated her, especially the oldest, Mary, who became for a while Pearl's dearest friend. But in the Longdens' terms she was young for her age, and could never keep up with their jokes or their expertise in the latest slang, clothes, and hairstyles based on fashion magazines from Shanghai. Her knowledge of their world came from nineteenth-century English novels and from the schooling she got from her mother in morning lessons with Grace. The Sydenstricker sisters worked through a correspondence course supplied by the Calvert School in Baltimore—history, geography, scripture, composition, and mathematics—with extra tuition in painting, music, and calisthenics (compulsory gym sessions on the veranda, led by Carie and detested by Pearl).

Carie compensated for the loss of Mr. Kung by enrolling her

daughter in the Methodist school for Chinese girls, part of a new mission settlement a little farther around the hill from the Sydenstrickers' house. The gray-haired American principal, Miss Robinson, seemed stiff and intimidating to Pearl, but she agreed to take the child three mornings a week as both pupil and part-time teacher. This was a highly unsatisfactory compromise. Chinese education was generally felt by Westerners to be a catastrophe ("mental infanticide on an enormous scale," wrote the venerable Dr. Martin), consisting of learning by rote classical texts wholly incompatible with modern scientific principles, and in any case reserved exclusively for boys. Mission schools admitted the first generation of girl students in China and equipped them to face the twentieth century by giving them the rudiments of a Western education. There was no other white girl in Pearl's school, and although she wore her American dresses to teach English to a class of eight pupils barely younger than herself, she kept her Chinese name, reverting to her own level in breaks between lessons, when she gossiped and giggled with contemporaries on the playground. Her best friends picked English names—Dottie Wei, Su-i Wang—and dreamed of becoming teachers or doctors themselves.

The experiment can't have lasted much more than a year because, in the winter of 1906–7, it became too dangerous for either Pearl or her sister to leave their compound. Floods followed by famine on an almost unprecedented scale laid waste the north of the country, and for months on end vast, sluggish, menacing, unstoppable streams of refugees flowed into and around Zhenjiang. The exodus started in Anhui and North Kiangsu, provinces already scoured and picked clean when icy winds from the Gobi Desert drove the inhabitants south. Entire populations on the move devoured everything in their path, stripping bark from the trees and grass from the hills. No birds, animals, or children survived in their wake. They brought sickness, infection, contagion, violence, and rumors of cannibalism, which spread panic and were met with reciprocal savagery. The Manchu government's response was ineffectual and slow. Ad hoc Western efforts to give aid were coordinated on a piecemeal basis. The Zhenjiang Mission force treated dying and destitute patients without adequate drugs or medical facilities. Pearl's father spent the winter distributing American supplies in the north for the Famine Relief Committee, hastily formed in Zhenjiang as it became clear that many millions of people would die of hunger and disease.

Her mother worked in the city, visiting pitifully inadequate shelters and soup kitchens, returning appalled, unable to eat or sleep, almost unhinged at times from exhaustion, impotence, and grief. She had to work after dark, dressed in Chinese clothes to escape being mobbed, but somehow people found out her name and traced her back to where she lived. Sinister, barely human bundles of bone and rag shuffled up the hill to beat at the Sydenstrickers' gate and lie in "dreadful shivering hordes," heaped against the compound wall. All night they wailed Carie's name: "The sound . . . drove her nearly mad . . . She no longer tried to shield her children; indeed, she could not." They too lay awake listening to groans and whimpers and soldiers dragging bodies away every morning. Pearl spent Christmas day with her mother cooking "great vats of rice and distributing it bowl by bowl through a crack in the gate until none was left." She recognized ever afterward the signs and stages of starvation in children and adults, gaunt pregnant women gnawed from within by their unborn babies, infants with sunken eyes and shriveled blue gums "like a toothless old woman's lips," swollen and distorted bellies, protruding bones with the skin glued to them turning an unmistakable dark purplish color, "the hue of a liver that has been dried for a day or two" which faded only when people started eating again.

At the time Pearl tried hard to blank out the images lodged at the back of her mind so tenaciously that, as her sister said, "not even her avid reading could make her entirely forget." Amnesia was her sole defense against nightmares impossible to tame or withstand. "She could not think of suffering and so again she went to the people of books. Now in an even more voracious way she began to read everything she could get hold of." Pearl went back to school that spring as life stirred again in the countryside. Women and children could be seen emerging like insects from hibernation, as Pearl described them long afterward in *The Good Earth,* swarming over the grave lands in search of the first green leaves of dandelion and shepherd's purse, "with bits of tin and sharp stones or worn knives, and with baskets made of twisted bamboo twigs or split reeds." Northerners who had survived the winter straggled back to their fields as the time for rice planting approached. A sense of release and recuperation is palpable in Grace's recollection of the five girls—herself and Pearl with Mary, Ruth, and Florence Longden—lounging companionably in late afternoon sun on the Sydenstrickers' porch to listen to "the normal sounds of summer . . . the cheerful talking of the farmers, the call of evening vendors, the sleepy cooing of wild doves, the croaking of frogs."

Pearl emerged from the crisis a disturbed and withdrawn adolescent, venting her own agitation in increasingly sharp conflict with her mother. Stormy, strong-willed and decisive, the two were so alike, according to Grace, that it was hard for either to back down from head-on collision. Carie was anxious and apprehensive, as she had been about Edgar when he too showed signs of rebellion at the same age. Pearl felt lonelier than ever before as the end of the school year approached and the gap between her and her friends began to reopen. Dottie Wei, Su-i Wang, and all the girls Pearl liked best left, one after another, weeping or stony-faced, to abandon their fantasies about independent careers and embark with men they had never seen on marriages arranged by their parents. Mary Longden was sent back to school in the United States, leaving Pearl cut off once again from contemporaries in the foreign community, who were themselves being groomed by their families as they approached marriageable age.

She was charmed and disconcerted that summer by a missionary couple newly arrived from America, Charles Hancock and his young wife, who lodged with her parents and took Chinese lessons from her father. She said it was the Hancocks, newly married and still clearly in love, who provided her first inkling that there could be more to marriage than working out a practical compromise between the wife's duty and her husband's needs. Carie had struggled to contain her own mutinous feelings, but her efforts had not deceived even Grace, by far the more submissive of her two daughters. Both girls understood the tension released in the emphatic creaking of the rocking chair in their mother's room and the eloquent speeches rehearsed under her breath. "Mother is angry," Grace wrote of one of these occasions. "Not angry at anyone, for Father is away—but just angry at Things." They both knew and feared the bright red stripes on their father's white forehead, when he emerged from the study after long solitary prayer sessions with his head resting on a chair back pressed against two bony fingers. "Only when he goes and shuts himself in the study is there any peace," wrote Grace.

Like his father, Absalom looked for justification to Saint Paul, announcing flatly and often "that as Christ was head of the church, so man was head of the woman." Quicker, bolder, and more intellectually agile than he was, Carie unequivocally repudiated the Pauline doctrine that tolerated females as a necessary evil, denied them souls or minds of their own, and prohibited them from participating in or even speaking at meetings of the mission to which they belonged. She brought up her daughters to think in ways that flummoxed her husband ("It did not occur to him to look for or desire intellectual companionship or spiritual understanding in a woman"). In these years the prime cause of friction between them was further education for Pearl. She turned fifteen in the summer of 1907, and her mother had no intention of repeating the mistakes that had been made with Edgar. Sent away too soon with too little backup or preparation, he had shocked both his parents by squandering his chance to polish a brilliant mind in favor of drink and girls. Marriage had made Carie a proto-feminist—"and I must say with cause," wrote Pearl—and nothing was going to stop her sending this next child to college. The problem was how to pay for it, since Absalom had a rooted objection to spending money on his wife or daughters. In spite of his own long absences from home and the fact that Carie earned nearly half their joint salary (eight hundred dollars for a married missionary, five hundred dollars for a single man), he banked the money and refused her a checkbook of her own. "He was penurious for God's sake," wrote Pearl, "that everything might go into that cause to which he had dedicated his life—and to which also he ruthlessly and unconsciously dedicated all those lives for which he was responsible."

These were the years when he published his Chinese New Testament in defiance of the Church, putting it out gospel by gospel and funding publication with the housekeeping money. His daughters had grown up picturing their father's translation as a bottomless well that swallowed the toys, books, and dresses they never had. As they got older Pearl was painfully conscious of the "incredible pinchings and scrapings and even begging" that marked the Sydenstrickers out from other missionaries at a time when, as Grace said, "Absalom's New Testament stood like a boulder between her parents." Both sisters dreaded the scenes Absalom made on journeys, when he refused to tip coolies or porters in spite of their furious complaints and Carie's pleading. Pearl detested her beautiful lace-trimmed underwear, handmade by charitable ladies as gifts for the needy, and she traveled reluctantly by coolie class now that her family could no longer afford the fares to go "upstairs with the other white people" on the Yangtse riverboats: "We put on Chinese clothes and traveled below decks with the Chinese." They slept at night crammed into small dirty berths doused with carbolic lotion by Carie and spent their days in the crowded salon, dimly lit by oil lamps, with a couch for opium smokers down one side and a big central table for gamblers:

> As for me, beginning then to see and feel, to perceive without knowing, I can never forget the smells of those ships . . . the thick foul sweetish fumes rising and creeping into every cranny. From the half-closed doors of the tiny cabins came the same smell, so that the close air seemed swimming with it. . . . In the middle of the table was a pile of silver dollars, which every one watched closely, covetously, with terrible longing. . . . Occasionally it was swept away by a single lean dark hand. Then a strange growl went over the crowd of gamesters and over the crowd of onlookers.

Absalom's indiscriminate preaching embarrassed Pearl in her new role as her father's most hypersensitive critic. She said she could never bring Chinese friends home in case he set about saving their souls.

She had long since stopped listening to his sermons herself, and now she watched him at work on the boats with a captive audience of drug addicts, who responded to his fervid exhortations with yawns of boredom. "They did not know what he meant by sins, or who this man was who wanted to save them, or why he did. They stared, half listening, dropping to sleep in grotesque attitudes upon the deck, where they slept, leaning against their bundles." Pearl would come eventually to understand and feel for her father, and to write calmly and humorously about his predicament, but at this stage her entire future hinged on her mother's will and the frugality that was its practical expression.

One of the results of Carie's stringent economizing was a term at the newly formed Kuling American School, an experience Pearl did not repeat and afterward preferred to forget. Her mother complained that the teaching was substandard and transferred her daughter to a school in Shanghai run by a couple of puritanical New England spinsters. Miss Jewell's School was next door to a mission boardinghouse kept by an older sister in a seedy part of town very different from the prosperous tree-shaded French concession inhabited then as now by business people. Pearl's account of this heavily barred, grim, gray brick establishment, and its frightening headmistress with her short heavy figure, cold eyes, and limp handshake, owes more to *Jane Eyre* than to anything in Dickens.

Absalom delivered his daughter as a boarder to Miss Jewell's School in the autumn of 1909. Pale, slender, and studious, socially immature but intellectually advanced for her age, Pearl made no headway with the other girls, who were as shocked by her knowledge of Confucius as she was by their contempt for the heathen Chinese. She got on better with the staff, who found her shy, aloof, and almost suspiciously clever. "She said she read Lewis Carroll's *Alice in Wonderland* at least once a year for its deeper insight," one of her teachers told Grace thirty years later. She impressed her classmates by reading aloud to the Friday Literary Club from work in progress ("a real novel with chapters"), and having a long poem published in the *Shanghai Mercury* (Pearl was an old hand at the *Mercury,* having won its monthly children's competitions so often that she treated the prizes as regular pocket money).

She also fell in love for the first time, with a handsome, charming, and sensitive college boy. The older brother of a school friend, son of an American father and a Chinese mother who had died, this intelligent and unhappy boy discussed his divided heritage at length with Pearl (fifty years later she used his story, by her own account, as the basis for her novel *Letter from Peking*).

Pearl was not used to living under surveillance, nor to being tightly hemmed in by rules, and least of all to the perfervid religiosity that pervaded the school. Martha Jewell and her younger sister Eugenia belonged to a sect of Holy Rollers, American fundamentalist fund-raisers, who called regularly to collect donations and conduct prayer meetings in the school parlor. Prayers that began normally enough rapidly degenerated into gibberish as teachers and pupils began "speaking in tongues," moaning and crying for the Holy Ghost, repenting nameless sins, and urging Pearl to join in while she tried with glazed eyes to absent her mind. "Religion I was used to, but not this dark form of it, this grovelling emotion, the physical confusion, a loathsome self-indulgence of some sort that I could not understand." When it became clear that Pearl was never going to conform like the others, the school turned against her. Miss Jewell declared her a heretic, and she was ostracized by fellow pupils, including her roommates, Ruth and Florence Longden, Mary's younger sisters. The preparatory training that was to have taught her to mix with girls of her own age and kind ended with Pearl being exiled alone ("lest I contaminate the others") to a small room in the attic.

Looking back later, Pearl recognized in Miss Jewell a passionate, iron-willed idealism that had corroded, leaving as its residue only the indestructible need for power and control. "She was expressing . . . a sort of sex instinct," Pearl wrote of her teacher in the first article she ever published in the *Chinese Recorder.* "She would have been horrified to have heard it called that." As part of Pearl's rehabilitation program, Miss Jewell took her to revivalist meetings and charitable reformatories. "Both terrified me," said Pearl. Once a week she was obliged to teach knitting and sewing at the Door of Hope, a refuge for women undergoing correction after careers in prostitution and slavery. As the only one of the white lady volunteers who spoke the language of the Chinese inmates, Pearl heard atrocious accounts of physical and mental abuse, violence, torture, starvation, and rape inflicted on girls thrown out or sold by their families into forced labor, working in brothels or as domestic slaves terrorized by the mistress of the household and passed from hand to hand by the master, his sons, and his menservants. She listened to their stories by day and dreamed about them by night. Still haunted by her experiences in the famine, Pearl was too young to be exposed so soon and so brutally to the exploitive squalor of Shanghai sex trafficking. Miss Jewell's School had been cheap (the fees barely covered expenses), but Pearl paid a heavy price. She was removed after two terms, as soon as Carie realized what was happening.

Pearl's formal schooling so far had been a series of steadily more disastrous experiments. Once again the sound of low voices arguing and occasional weeping emanated from her parents' bedroom at night. The campaign to secure university entrance for Pearl was one of the few that Carie won by settling for a compromise solution. Wellesley College ruled itself out as a Yankee institution, and in any case prohibitively expensive, so they settled instead on Randolph-Macon Woman's College in Lynchburg, Virginia, where the fees were just over half of Wellesley's, which pleased Absalom. The curriculum suited Carie: "My mother approved it because the education there was planned to be exactly what a man would get." In academic terms this was the best the South had to offer girls. Carie emerged triumphant from the last of a series of confrontations behind closed doors to announce that there would be a new dress for Pearl and that the rest of the family would accompany her on furlough, traveling home westward by the overland route.

Hostilities continued intermittently right up to the packing. Carie planned this journey as a do-it-yourself induction course, during which she and Pearl would study a trunk full of books about Europe at the same time as sampling its highlights in practice. Absalom washed his hands of the whole affair. "There was nothing of very special importance or interest in this our last visit home as a family," he wrote defiantly in his memoirs. His own packing consisted of the official, newly completed *Revised Mandarin New Testament,* which he subsequently demolished in a succinct and scathing review. They set out in early June, traveling north to Harbin in Manchuria, then for ten days through imperial Russia by the trans-Siberian railway, with a day's stop in Moscow, where Pearl was sickened by a poverty and degradation beyond anything she had seen before. They went on via Warsaw and Berlin to spend a month at a small Swiss pension in Neufchâtel so that Absalom might enjoy himself at last visiting Calvinist shrines, and Pearl could practice her French. They stayed one day in Paris (where Grace said her father was so disgusted by the naked statues that he refused to look), and a week at the China Inland Mission in London.

Pearl spent the last leg of the journey, onboard ship from Southampton to New York, contemplating the new world she was about to enter and the old world she had left behind. Sights she had seen in Zhenjiang and was still struggling to put into some sort of perspective would finally resurface decades later in her books. She mentally filed away the "grave and bitter look" on the faces of porters with no redress against unjust treatment by white men, and the grimaces of old men pulling rickshaws: "Their faces in repose were twisted as though in anger, only it was not anger. It was the years of straining at loads too heavy for them which had lifted their upper lip to bare their teeth in a seeming snarl." She had witnessed firsthand the hard labor, stench, and danger that made up daily life for the boat people living in picturesque sampans moored along the banks of the Yangtse, and she could not forget the coolies who lived on those boats, men she had watched as a child loading and unloading merchandise on the Bund: "They were always sweating . . . summer and winter, and their thighs and knees quivered under their heavy loads. Their eyes bulged . . . and their breath came out of them in singsong grunts and they kept step with each other and swung into rhythms to lighten their intolerable loads."

Pearl's premonition of an inevitable uprising was confirmed in a rare and surprising conversation with her father on the Atlantic crossing. He predicted a revolution within ten years in Russia ("It is clearly foretold in the Scriptures") that would spread to engulf the white races in Asia, including Americans. "The Chinese owe us nothing," was his stern response to Pearl's protest. "We must never forget that missionaries went to China without invitation and solely from our own sense of duty. . . . We have done the best we could but that, too, was our duty and so they still owe us nothing. And if our country has taken no concessions, we have kept silent when others did, and we too have profited from the unequal treaties. I don't think we shall escape when the day of reckoning comes."

They took the train straight to Lynchburg, where they were to stay with Edgar, now established in the town as a newspaper editor with a wife and a little daughter whom her grandparents had never seen. Pearl was just eighteen years old. "I entered America in September, 1910, with a sober heart and a mind too old for my years."

CHAPTER 3

The Spirit and the Flesh

A T RANDOLPH-MACON WOMAN'S College Pearl encountered a tribe unlike any she had met before. Her fellow students were confident, competent, energetic, and often highly intelligent southern girls brought up to run households and organize communities in a homogeneous, highly stratified, hierarchical society initially set up by long-established landowning families. This was a community very different from the rugged individualism of more recent settlers like Pearl's family in the mountains of West Virginia. Her mother's efforts to help out the women she met in Tsingkiangpu or Zhenjiang reproduced the straightforward neighborliness of Pocahontas County and Greenbrier. Nothing had prepared Pearl for the elaborately mannered and coded behavior of the society she came across for the first time at Randolph-Macon. Even its throwaway gestures typified a kind of worldliness that would have infuriated her father. "He never troubled himself to be thoughtful of anyone in small ways," Pearl wrote in *Fighting Angel*. "No one ever saw him pick up a woman's handkerchief . . . or rise to give her his seat."

Everything about Pearl betrayed an alien sensibility. She looked and felt wrong in this crowd of girls with bare throats, rounded bosoms, and curvy hips emphasized by tight-waisted, low-cut, flouncy frocks over boned corsets, and bouffant hairstyles bulked out with artificial curls and pads. Pearl's dresses were plain, high-necked, and long-sleeved, made from handwoven Chinese linen and silk to designs carefully copied by a Zhenjiang tailor from back numbers of outmoded American magazines. The cut of her jackets was dubious (Chinese women wore loose-fitting clothes designed to hide, not hug, the figure), and her skirts were the wrong length. Her leather shoes had been specially made for her in Zhenjiang, where cloth shoes were the norm, and her hair was plaited or pinned in a bun on the nape of her neck. "She knew she must seem almost severe in comparison with the coils and puffs and ruffles of the others," wrote her loyal younger sister. "Girls came in groups to stare at me" was Pearl's bitter memory fifty years later. The fact that she had been pointed out as a freak all her life in China made it no easier to bear the casual cruelty of her American contemporaries. Their attitude stiffened her resistance. The only full-scale portrait of a southern belle in Pearl Buck's books is the seductive, imperious, and irresistibly pretty Lucinda Delaney in *The Angry Wife,* who is also a mean-minded, cold-hearted, and egotistical racist shrew.

If Randolph-Macon girls were in some ways far more sophisticated than anything Pearl was used to, in others they were more childish. They readily accepted a time table regulated by bells, rising and going to bed when they were told, indulging in nothing worse than routine ragging or a little mild horseplay in the corridors after lights out. There was no smoking or drinking, and dancing took place in the gym only at Christmas and Easter. Girls rarely left the campus, although they were permitted to receive closely supervised visits from boys on a list vetted beforehand for social credentials. They amused themselves by getting up clubs, "college fights" (when they tore out each other's hair, leaving the ground littered with fake curls on pins), picnics, pageants, and parties enlivened by a good deal of intensely competitive same-sex petting and courting rituals. Excessive reading and scholarship for its own sake were not encouraged. Most students had little experience of anything beyond their immediate horizons, and their interest in the outside world was strictly limited.

Randolph-Macon was just ten years old when Pearl got there (the earliest women's colleges had been in existence in the United States for less than a century). Its founders had envisaged a haven of peace and learning in handsome and spacious surroundings, but the complex of Italianate brick buildings, surrounded in rainy weather by a sea of liquid red mud, still looked exposed and raw on its hillside above the town. Pearl found the work undemanding, and was not impressed by her teachers ("There was nothing I could do to help her," the English professor reported years later to Grace, "for she knew all I could teach already"). She majored in philosophy and psychology, escaping to spend hours in the library—"I read prodigiously, extravagantly and greedily"—and wasting no time on the sports facilities. Her main education came by her own account from the other girls.

The college already possessed a single Chinese student (who spoke no Mandarin, and whose dialect was unintelligible to someone from Zhenjiang), treated by her classmates with a distant civility that did not appeal to Pearl. Pearl's plan was to create a new self, and she did it with superlative success: "Externally I became an American . . . by the end of my freshman year, I was indistinguishable from any other girl of my age and class." Her first step was to get rid of the trousseau prepared with such effort and cost by her mother. She sewed her new wardrobe herself during her first vacation in her brother's house on his wife's sewing machine. One of the things that made her proud of Randolph-Macon ever after was the faculty's firm refusal to grant the students' annual petition for classes in home economy ("The theory was, and I think it entirely correct, that any educated woman can read a cookbook or follow a dress pattern"). Pearl's outfits went down well, and her best effort—a chic little hat with pheasant-feather trim—was coveted and borrowed by every other student on campus. She acquired the right slang and the correct "soft drawl of Virginia speech." She even outclassed the others as a practical joker, sabotaging the fancy-dress party of a rival faction by filling the fake fishnet decor with genuinely rotten fish.

In her junior year she was invited to join AMSAM, the oldest and most prestigious of the college's secret societies, an accolade restricted to no more than a dozen girls at any one time. Pearl was treasurer in her sophomore year, and class president the year after. She wrote deftly accomplished stories for the college magazine and belonged to the exclusive Delta Kappa sorority. In 1913 she was chosen as one of two college delegates to the YWCA conference at Bryn Mawr (by this time she felt sufficiently sure of herself to turn down

the loan of a pair of corsets—an article of clothing considered barbaric in China—together with a request that she wear them at the
northern gathering so as to uphold the honor of the South). She carried off prizes for both the best story and the best poem of her senior
year but failed to anticipate the unspoken resentment this caused.
Painfully sensitive herself to slight and rebuff, Pearl underestimated
all her life the effect of her own successes on other people. She would
have been voted president of the student government in her last year
if she hadn't answered frankly, when someone asked her who would
win the election, "I think I shall." It was her only false move, but it
cost her the job.

If Pearl could not always conceal the fact that she found her contemporaries narrow and parochial, they hurt her in return by their
lack of curiosity about the world she came from. This was her first
prolonged exposure to the standard American view of China as a land
of dirty, scavenging beggars and sinister, slit-eyed, yellow-skinned vil-
lains. Nobody asked, and she never told about her own background,
anxieties, and preoccupations. The only person who understood was
her brother Edgar, a kind, humorous, slow-spoken character whose
deceptively bluff manner concealed a keen analytical intelligence and
a sharp wit. He had grown into a big handsome man with the same
broad open forehead, generous mouth, and strong features as Pearl
herself. Brother and sister drew close in her years at college, when she
spent much time at his house, getting to know him and playing with
his children (a baby son was born during her time in Lynchburg). She
realized in the hours they spent sitting and talking alone together on
his porch in the evenings how alike they were, and how close Edgar
too had been to their mother.

His early experiences had shut down a side of him that his sister
opened up again. She understood probably better than anyone else
the cumulative impact on a young boy of the terrifying loss at intervals without warning of his three younger siblings, his mother's desolation, and her decision to send him away as soon as the next child
looked robust enough to survive. If Pearl sympathized with Edgar's
sense of abandonment, he recognized only too well her struggles to

establish a footing in a strange, sometimes incomprehensible new environment. With him there was no need to hide her shock and shame when she discovered from Carie that their father had written begging letters trying to extract money for Pearl's college fees from his charitable backers. Her immediate angry response was to find herself a part-time coaching job, but she never got over a betrayal that set her apart from her American contemporaries: "No one of them knew what it was to be always nothing in comparison to a cause, to a work, to a creed." Only Edgar shared the bitterness of that particular bereavement ("For [Absalom's] children were bereaved in what they never had, in what he could not give them, because he had given everything in him to God"). Like his sister, Edgar owed his moral balance and a residual belief in himself to their mother, who remained, in Grace's words, "the one against whom he had measured the real importance of his life." He relaxed in Pearl's company, and she came to depend on his comforting presence and his quick quiet jokes. "She saw things in Edgar which he could not see himself," wrote Grace: "a mind like Mother's in warmth and human understanding, like father's in careful, studious ability."

After a slow and uncertain start, Edgar was beginning to look beyond a career as a newspaperman to the possibilities opening up in the comparatively new field of medical and social statistics. He had been married too young to a wife his parents considered unsuitable, and now that the marriage was beginning to fall apart it was Pearl who helped extricate him from the consequences of his own rashness. For his sake she gave up the pleasures and privileges she had worked so hard to achieve in her last year of college, abandoning her chance to edit the student magazine, *Tattler,* leaving campus and moving into Edgar's house to provide support for his wife, while he left to take up a new job in Washington. Pearl regretted her decision later, claiming that her years at college had been overshadowed by the unhappiness and friction of her brother's marital breakup. Certainly she was deeply disturbed by her role as go-between. When Edgar decided that divorce was his only option, he persuaded Pearl to plead his case with their parents, who were so appalled that the scheme had to be dropped. For nearly twenty years he lived alone, apart from his wife, obtaining his divorce only after the deaths of both parents. Pearl explored his predicament (and her part in it) in two novels published long after he too was dead. The heroine's brother in *The Time Is Noon* follows roughly the same path as Edgar, marrying early for the wrong reasons with disastrous results. In *Portrait of a Marriage* the brilliant, ambitious, and highly sophisticated hero marries a simple uneducated farmer's daughter and takes the opposite course, making a decidedly implausible success of the marriage by allowing his career as an artist to fizzle out as he sinks steadily over half a century into professional obscurity and arrested development.

Pearl escaped from an oppressive situation in Lynchburg by spending summer vacations with the Stultings in Hillsboro. She also paid visits to her father's family, questioning his two elder sisters and drawing her own cool sharp conclusions about his six brothers: "most of them white-haired by that time, an amazing array of tall, passionate angry men, not one of them under six feet, every one of them with the same shining bright blue eyes and dry humor and intolerant mind. The quarrel between them was as hot as ever." Pearl got a first inkling of what lay behind her father's furious solitude of spirit during her own long lonely summers in Pocahontas County and Greenbrier. Now that her grandfather was dead, she felt as much of a misfit in this world as her parents had done before her. Her fondness for her cousins was tempered by their disapproval of the escape route her family had chosen, and by her own need for outlets beyond their local round of gossip, visits, and calls. "I did all that I could to seem like everyone else, while I knew I never could be, however hard I tried."

The same applied to her friends at college. The only close and durable relationship she made there was with a girl called Emma Edmunds, who singled Pearl out on their first day as someone even more out of place than herself. Tough, practical, and shrewd, Emma came from a large, unconventional, hard-up family that had gone down in the world. Hers was the only home where Pearl was welcomed and warmly invited to stay. Throughout their years in college Pearl confided freely in Emma, and for the next fifty years they continued their conversation by post ("It meant everything to me to know that I could and can depend on you utterly," Pearl wrote in an early letter; "I need you, Emma, and I need your friendship"). Pearl was popular and admired by the other girls but already protected by an aloofness that ruled out intimacy. She put it down to her background ("I was trained by Asian women to be self-effacing. . . . It shaped me in profound and basic ways"), recognizing detachment as part of the penalty she paid for her rapid remake as an American.

She would return again and again in her books to the drastic physical and emotional pressures on young people uprooted at a formative age, torn by conflicting cultures, attempting to adjudicate internally between the claims of America and Asia. "The shock . . . of the departure . . . and the end of all that she had known at a time when she was ceasing to be a child, was becoming a woman, the breaking off of deep emotional ties, not only with her friends, but with familiar landscapes, the necessity to conform to a . . . background, at once her own and yet alien, had set up restraints upon her spirit, certainly in her mind, which affected her body." In her senior year Pearl complained of putting on weight (always a sign of inner perturbation with her) and removed herself bodily from campus. In retrospect her overall impression was of four years' loneliness and isolation at Randolph-Macon, with details largely blotted out by the amnesia that runs like a refrain through her memoirs. "Of my college days I remember shamefully little," she wrote. "Of my senior year I can remember very little that is pleasant or that added to my growth. . . . Summing it up I am amazed at how little I learned in college."

Her graduation in June 1914 was attended by Edgar and their cousin Eugenia, the daughter of Carie's sister Nettie, herself a music student in Richmond. Pearl had no intention of leaving America at this stage. She had been asked by her professor in the psychology department to stay on as his research assistant, a job designed in theory to lead to a scholarship at a major university, followed by a career as an academic or a practicing psychologist, options that clearly suited her better than work in the mission field. America's limitless possibilities and its openness to the future spoke to something reckless and rootless in her. The imperial China of her childhood lay in the past, swept away soon after her parents' return in the autumn of 1911 by the uprising her father had so clearly predicted. The Sydenstrickers had come through the Revolution with characteristic aplomb, resisting diplomatic efforts to evacuate them with the rest of the foreign community, siding instead with the heterogeneous forces that finally toppled the corrupt and ineffectual Manchu Dynasty after more than two hundred years on the throne. Pearl's mother described lying in bed that winter listening to distant cannon fire as revolutionary troops stormed the emperor's former summer capital in Nanjing. Another night she reported rifle shots on the hillside at the back of their house and figures crouching in the bamboo grove beyond the compound wall; they were the wives and daughters of government officials, recognizable as Manchus by their elaborately styled hair, unbound feet, and court dress, put to flight by the gunmen of the new Republican regime. Powerless to intervene, Carie stayed indoors all through the next day with the twelve-year-old Grace, knowing and trying not to hear what was happening outside: "She never forgot the pity of those ladies, delicately nurtured and sheltered all their lives, hunted now like deer and lying among the bamboos dead, their satin gowns spotted with blood."

This was not the kind of news Pearl could pass on to her college classmates and, even if they had wanted her to, she knew it was beyond her to explain the root causes of a revolution that seemed initially more apparent than actual. Men were forbidden to kowtow or wear pigtails. The binding of girls' feet was discouraged. Absalom was stoned again in the street by revolutionaries whose fervor he cordially approved. "It was a young man's revolution and [he] was always drawn to young men. He gloried in every step they took—even in their ruthless new laws that cut off queues by force. [Absalom] liked ruthlessness. A thing was always either right or wrong, and if it was right, it was right to enforce it." He set up a language course for missionaries unable to leave Shanghai because of widespread unrest and pushed forward himself, patrolling his vast territory in a newly acquired junk, and ignoring as usual the increasingly determined attempts of younger colleagues to curb his plans for expansion. When the Sydenstricker bungalow was torn down to make way for a dormitory attached to the new mission school for boys, Absalom designed their next house himself, eliminating with satisfaction all the unnecessary conveniences and grace notes introduced by his wife, who wrote despairingly to Pearl about the destruction of her garden and the impossibility of creating a new one. Grace left home to attend the new American School in Shanghai, and Wang Amah died, leaving Carie more alone than ever. The unaccustomed pessimism and plaintiveness of her letters worried Pearl ("A little seed of anxiety sowed itself," Grace wrote, "and thrust down a torturing root"). When news came in the summer of 1914 that Carie was seriously ill, Pearl persuaded the Mission Board to find her a teaching job, a posting temporarily suspended by the outbreak of war in Europe in August. She started work in the psychology department at Randolph-Macon only to break off after a second bulletin from her father announced a sharp deterioration in her mother's condition. Pearl sailed for Shanghai that November.

SHE PLANNED A temporary visit, meaning to stay just long enough to nurse her mother back to health, but already on the boat she realized that in a fundamental sense she was going home: "I began again to think in Chinese." The journey back marked a shift in perspective in some ways more startling than the voyage out four years earlier. Pearl had experienced at firsthand in Virginia the mixture of incredulity, indignation, and shame felt by her Chinese contemporaries when they first encountered the American view of their country as irredeemably backward and ignorant. Now for the first time she saw China as an adult through Western eyes. The spiritual dislocation of this return in 1914 was one of the key factors that shaped her as a writer. She explored it in essays, short stories, and novels, perhaps most graphically in *A House Divided,* the third volume of *The Good Earth* trilogy, in which the student grandson of Wang the farmer takes the same train from Shanghai as Pearl. He finds that his years in America have transformed the ordinary familiar sights and sounds of the journey—the grimy overcrowded railway carriage, the passengers' belching and scratching, the floors sticky with spittle and urine, the blackened hands of attendants serving fly-spotted food—into the Chinese equivalent of a Dickensian underworld. An entire generation all over China in the long slow awakening that followed the 1911 Revolution would echo Wang Yuan's involuntary cry: "Why did I never see all this before? I have seen nothing until now!"

For the first time Pearl subjected her parents to the clear dispassionate gaze she had acquired in America. Absalom, who met her in Shanghai, failed to recognize his daughter when the boat docked and could give only the vaguest answers to her urgent questions about her mother. Pearl realized that the religion that had always cut him off from other human beings now cushioned him completely from even the most intractable reality. "In all the time that so many things had been happening to her, nothing had happened to him nor could anything ever happen to him, in the sense of change," wrote Grace, who was present at this meeting. "Nothing . . . would ever shake that unalterable inner security of his." Too weak to travel, Carie was waiting with her Chinese daughter and a band of friends at the station in Zhenjiang, so frail and shrunken that this time it was Pearl who barely recognized her mother.

The illness that had aged her so rapidly was sprue, a form of tropical anemia that attacks the mucous membranes in the mouth, throat, and digestive tract, making it difficult to swallow or digest food. Pearl fought it vigorously by all available means. There was no known medication, but she consulted new doctors, treated her patient with massages and baths, experimented successively with a banana diet, a milk diet, diets of rice, gruel, fresh fruit, soft-boiled eggs, liver, and spinach juice. Nothing worked (it would be many years before sprue was first successfully treated with massive doses of vitamin B). Not normally fatal, the deficiency was visibly destroying Carie, whose defenses had been depleted over a lifetime in China by tuberculosis and repeated bouts of cholera, malaria, and dysentery. Physical weakness was compounded by a profound underlying depression. She was often fretful and fractious, but even anger could not help her now. Grace, helpless and terrified, was amazed by her sister's strength, courage, and imaginative sympathy with their mother at times when "it seemed nothing Pearl could do would please her." The family regrouped around a new center. Pearl managed the sickbed, ran the household, reestablished her father's routines, supervised her mother's Bible classes, and played the wheezy little organ in church on Sundays. She had her own teacher-training class of up to twenty girls, and she took over the regular clinic her mother had established for women, listening attentively to the problems and confidences she had grown up hearing as a low troubled murmur in the background. "I was always touched and moved at their acceptance of me in her place," she wrote long afterwards.

She was welcomed by the whole community. "To other Americans in Zhenjiang, Pearl came as a fresh breeze from their homeland," wrote Grace, who was not the only one captivated by her sister's stylishness and sophistication. There were musical evenings when Pearl in black velvet with her fair hair pinned up in loose wavy curls sang American pop songs at the piano. But the experience that indirectly transformed her life was teaching the senior English class at the Presbyterian Mission's high school for boys. "It was a wonderful time in which to live in China," she wrote, looking back, "and I was at the right age for it." Education, and mission schools in particular, were at the heart of a revolution that had started and spread spontaneously from one province to the next, achieving its prime aim almost before people fully realized what was happening. Sun Yatsen, the Nationalist leader, had been away in the United States when the old regime fell, returning only in time to be sworn in as the first president of the new republic. "He was the crest of a wave of revolution and such a wave is always the rise of a deep ground swell of human events," Pearl wrote, "and Christian missionaries themselves continued to increase that ground swell, without knowing what they did." The church schools set up in China in the 1880s and 1890s had instituted an empirical, knowledge-based approach to education wholly different from the ancient imperial system based on poetry and calligraphy. Missionaries taught mathematics and science, introduced modern medicine, promoted interventionist policies such as famine relief, and actively campaigned for less oppressive treatment of women. "The impact of these ideas was terrific and radical," wrote Pearl, who grew up watching them take hold.

A Christian convert himself, trained as a Western doctor, Sun Yatsen was almost immediately ousted from the presidency, only to take on a more powerful role as prophet and theorist, "a Lenin for the Chinese revolution," in Pearl's phrase. He became a charismatic figurehead for progressive young intellectuals, many of them mission-educated and deeply impressed not simply by Western inventions but by the subversive principles of Jesus Christ, which they interpreted in aggressive and uncompromising ways never envisaged by their missionary teachers. "The wonder is that none of them . . . realized how revolutionary these principles were," Pearl wrote dryly. "They had been reared in the Western atmosphere where church members do not take literally the teachings of Jesus. . . . The Chinese, however, tended to be very practical, even about religion, and the result was often very upsetting indeed."

Pearl's students gave her a first taste of the kind of intellectual, political, and social ferment she had missed in her own years at college. Her class was small (founded in 1907 with eight boys, the entire school had sixty pupils when Pearl taught there), but it made up in urgency what it lacked in size. The students were in their late teens or early twenties, nearly the same age as their teacher, many already married, some with children of their own. They were hungry for knowledge, buoyed by expectation, almost giddy with their sense of release from the burden of inherited repression and inhibition. Most of them would be hemmed in again soon, like the hero of the first story Pearl published a decade later in the *Chinese Recorder,* a thin, pale, feverish seventeen-year-old forcibly removed from school by his father in order to mind the family shop and produce sons for the ancestors. Pearl's early fiction is full of quick, vivid, confident sketches of young men like this one, briefly confronted at school or college by the vision of a brave new world before being dragged back into line by their families and obliged to accept their submission "with the terrible sadness of defrauded boyhood."

Pearl brought her pupils probably as close to the West as they were ever likely to get, and they drank in all she could tell them. At a time when the country was already heading for chaos and anarchy, they stood for everything hopeful, generous, and forward-looking in a revolution commandeered from the start by the young. They marched under the Blue Sky and White Sun of Sun Yatsen's banner. For them the symbol of conservatism and retrogression was the queue, imposed by the hated and now defeated Manchus. The stern, crop-haired young revolutionaries stationed at the gates of Zhenjiang to intercept country farmers and chop off their queues by brute force included students of Pearl's. "They taught me far more than I taught them," she said. She listened at school to their idealistic aspirations and at home to the counterarguments of elderly traditionalists among her parents' Chinese friends. For her this was an intensely receptive period, when she absorbed impressions greedily and indiscriminately, soaking them up like a sponge as any prospective young writer must do. "It seems to me now, looking back, that I spent those first years of my return in almost complete silence," she wrote in her memoirs four decades later.

She heard the same progressive views repeated by the young husbands of her Chinese girlfriends, all of them mothers by this time and absorbed in family concerns of their own. Pearl's single status at the advanced age of twenty-two puzzled her friends, who held her parents severely to blame for doing nothing about it. Her father, by now "far more Chinese in his mentality and feelings than he was American," was inclined to agree with them, but Carie's libertarian American instincts were outraged. She was equally suspicious of what seemed to her a new laxity Pearl had picked up in the United States, apparent in everything from her social manner to her frivolous hairdo and flirtatious outfits. Pearl herself provoked the unconditional disapproval of the entire mission community by going out occasionally with the only available unattached Americans, lonely young males working on the Bund for tobacco companies or Standard Oil.

Her field of sexual experimentation had been even narrower than was normal for women of her age at the time. She had fallen briefly

in love as a schoolgirl with a half-American student (now safely married to a Chinese wife), and there had been some sort of affair on
shipboard coming back from America. Pearl confided her passionate response only to Emma Edmunds, who promptly tore up the letter at the writer's request. In old age Pearl vaguely recalled receiving
advances on the ship from a couple of older admirers, both of whom
she turned down, although not before she had enthusiastically learned
how to kiss from the younger of the two. Possibly this was the intense
physical awakening she seems to have experienced at some point in
that year or the next from a respectable middle-aged man who was
also a serial seducer, expert in techniques of arousal that stopped just
short of actual consummation. She described this encounter in con-
vincing detail in her most autobiographical novel, *The Time Is Noon,*
where the heroine finds herself driven almost wild by the "dry sterile
pain" of unsatisfied desire. ("'He'll never marry you, that's one comfort,' her mother said bitterly. . . . 'There's something downright queer
about him.'") Absalom's solution to the problem of his older daughter's future was an arranged marriage to the handsome, clever, highly
eligible son of one of his Chinese friends, a proposal that came to
nothing after a heated dispute between the parents of the prospective
bride, who remained wholly passive in the Chinese way. "I listened
and reflected and did not take sides," wrote Pearl.

By the time Carie began at last to show signs of reviving in the
warmth of her daughter's energy and will, Pearl had dropped any idea
of a return to the United States. Her immediate priority was to find
work in China and, even more important, to get away from the dogmatic opinions and censorious eyes of the Zhenjiang mission community. As soon as her mother seemed well enough to be left, she wrote
secretly to Cornelia Morgan, an independent American running a
mission school at Tsuyung in Yunnan province in the far southwest.
The letter that came back provisionally offering Pearl the job of assistant was intercepted by Carie, who lost her last shred of composure,
weeping like a child and insisting that without her daughter she no
longer wanted to live. Pearl protested that as a girl Carie herself had
run away in direct defiance of her own father, and was shaken to the

core by her mother's reply. "'I know it,' she said, 'and I did wrong. I wish I had obeyed him.' This was a terrifying revelation and I was struck speechless."

Carie relapsed, losing weight again with shocking speed, reversing all the progress made since Pearl's return. "Her flesh fell away until she was dreadful to see. Only her eyes looked bright and indomitable out of her little shrunken face." She no longer wanted to die, but her emaciated body was so weak that the slightest touch jarred her. In June 1915 Pearl took her to Kuling, cushioned as far as possible from the jolts of the journey on a padded stretcher carried by two Chinese servants. The original tiny mission settlement had grown into a prosperous, whites-only summer community, drawing visitors from all over China with large handsome villas standing in their own leafy grounds, shops, a church and a school, conferences and a concert program, a place for social and business contacts where young people could meet one another at tennis or bridge parties and go dancing in the evenings. Pearl had no time for any of it. She called in the English doctor and set herself once more to revive her mother, who could not leave her bed. "I studied my Chinese books while she slept, and every day I went for a long and solitary walk." Grace came from her school in Shanghai for the holidays, and Absalom joined them for the couple of weeks that was all he could spare from his work. Lying on a lounge chair on the porch, Carie made her daughters laugh by planning a riotous old age of leisure, pleasure, and placid self-indulgence. Gradually she began to tell stories again, entertaining their friends and inducing a subdued optimism in Pearl. By early autumn, when most other people had left and the town stood empty, Carie was strong enough to totter on her own legs into the garden. There was no one for company now but one American couple and the patients in the new TB sanatorium (Pearl had a brief encounter with one of them—"He was only a boy to my newly adult eyes"—which ended abruptly when she was warned off by his missionary parents).

Muffled reports of the Great War came from the single English weekly paper to reach Kuling from Shanghai. Mother and daughter talked about the future, when both agreed that China in general, and

Kuling in particular, would bid good riddance to the West. They also looked back to the past, drawing close again as they resumed the long, frank, free-ranging conversations interrupted by Pearl's stormy adolescence. "My love for my mother was a thing apart. It was rooted in my blood and bones," Pearl wrote of this period. In these months of grief and uncertainty Carie explained or implied enough for Pearl to begin to understand the underlying mechanism of her parents' disastrous mismatch. She came to see more clearly her father's part in the demoralization that had precipitated her mother's illness. "Born a generation earlier he would have burned witches. There was a deep unconscious sex antagonism in him," she wrote in *Fighting Angel,* describing Absalom's struggles to hold his own against his wife's quicker and sharper intelligence by invoking Saint Paul, as his own father had done before him. "Since those days when I saw all her nature dimmed I have hated Saint Paul with all my heart."

Carie said it was while she was nursing her own dying mother that she had sworn in her late teens to renounce the temptations of the flesh in the person of her current boyfriend, a big, blond, boisterous, good-looking, hard-drinking character named Neale Carter, a guitar-player with a rich singing voice and a hot lusty presence that threatened to unleash urges in herself she had been taught all her life to fear and repress. By her own account, she married Absalom Sydenstricker as an antidote to the lure of drink and desire. Her husband himself was still wrestling with the same problem alone in his study in his sixties, when he annotated steamy passages in a book about the Holy Ghost with penciled notes in the margin. "The word 'flesh' as used in . . . the Bible is interpreted as meaning 'the natural self,'" he wrote at the head of the first chapter, returning to the question again fifty pages further on: "What is meant by the word 'flesh'? It means the uncorrected human nature." The solution proposed by the same book was to burn out vileness, filth, and impurity.

Pearl had witnessed this process in practice throughout her childhood as a daily stifling of her mother's natural warmth, gaiety, and impetuosity in innumerable small defeats and reprimands. Carie's exuberance grated on her husband, and her spontaneity made him uneasy. He mistrusted everything that captivated other people about his wife: her infectious delight in pretty things, impromptu picnics and treats ("he did not enjoy whimsy and sudden plans and the discomfort of a plate and no table"), her full-throated singing when she flung back her head and belted out her favorite hymns, her rare zany jokes, and the absurd comic rhymes she could improvise until her children were helpless with laughter and her husband told her coldly to stop. All this Pearl had seen and resented as a girl. As an adult she was increasingly aware of the sensual and emotional deprivation that had made a desert of her parents' life together, bleakly exposed in the years when the departure of their two daughters for college and school left husband and wife confronting one another alone for the first time since the birth of their oldest child. Carie's talks with her daughter would be harshly reenacted in *The Time Is Noon* and touched on more briefly in the bright, shining, looking-glass world of Pearl's first novel, *East Wind, West Wind,* where another dying mother confides to her daughter the scary side of a long-lasting marriage. "I sat in horror at her words," says the young Chinese heroine, who might be Pearl herself speaking. "I saw suddenly into the inner halls of her heart. The bitterness and suffering there were bowels of fire within her. I had no words to comfort her."

As cold winter winds blew around the little house intended only for summer visits, Carie and her daughter moved partway down the mountain to be nearer the doctor, settling in a borrowed house, where Pearl faced the question of her own future: "I began what was to be the loneliest winter of my life. . . . I was struggling with the decision of what I was to do with myself." Her twenty-third birthday that summer made her the same age as her mother had been when she married. Pearl had always known she was a writer, but she also knew she was nowhere near ready even to think about what that might entail. Her immediate problem was practical. Job offers had not been hard to get so far, but one of the conditions imposed by the few professional careers open to women (basically, teaching and nursing) was compulsory celibacy. The Church, which gave single women in the mission field schools, hospitals, even outlying stations of their own to run—

an autonomy unthinkable for mission wives—demanded nunlike austerity in return. The price was too high for Pearl, who would enliven her Chinese stories with vigorous little snapshots, like gargoyles in the margins, of sexless, infantilized, and dried-up lady missionaries brooding over faded family photographs, pouncing hungrily on any stray widower, pursuing the hypothetical goal of wholesale conversion with dwindling enthusiasm and hope.

Pearl's own religious faith was contingent and variable. Like many ministers' children, she had learned early to blank out during sermons, switching her attention instead to more promising activities such as making up stories. She was prepared to teach Bible classes or play the organ for her father, but she adamantly refused to lead religious meetings or have anything to do with proselytizing. The station pecking order meant that older women, theoretically subject to their husbands ("repressed, strong, vigorous mission wives . . . their faces . . . stormy and hewn into lines of determination and grimness"), exercised power in their turn over novices like Pearl. Her mild escapades with the boys from Standard Oil had ended in a head-on collision with one of these weather-beaten old battle-axes, who threatened her with expulsion if she persisted in her offense. Pearl's critical detachment, and her inadmissible sympathy with the Chinese, would inevitably land her in further trouble, but for the moment she had no choice save to return to the mission school in Zhenjiang.

In February 1916 Pearl left her mother, whose old irrepressible energy was flowing back under the tonic effect of mountain air, careful diet, and twelve months' respite from her husband. This was the first time in her life that Carie had ever lived alone, and she celebrated her freedom in her sixtieth year by demolishing Absalom's cramped little house and building a bigger one to her own design, simple, airy, and efficiently planned, with three bedrooms, two bathrooms, a living room, and steps leading up to a broad shady porch looking over the ferny glades of the garden and out to the valley beyond. Carie's house embodied her American dream. Everything she disliked and feared about China was excluded from it. Even the plangent melancholy temple bell that had always given her the shivers when it sounded in the night on the hill below the house in Zhenjiang was replaced by the brisk reassuring little bell of the church a few hundred yards from her front door. The transformation, planned and carried out in secret from her husband as a surprise for her daughters, restored her sense of purpose. When she wasn't supervising masons and carpenters, she went tobogganning with the children from the American School. "She did the things she had not done since she was a girl," Pearl wrote, "and there was no one to be displeased with her merriment."

What Pearl herself felt that February when she climbed down one thousand steps cut in the rock and walked the rest of the way, turning and twisting for five miles down almost vertical slopes to the foot of the mountain, is hard to imagine. She was returning to keep house for her father and rejoin a mission community that seemed to her later—and was already beginning to seem to her then—blinkered, small-minded, and arrogant, above all in its invincible assumption of superiority to the people to whom it ministered. "The failure of missions and of Christianity . . . in China," Pearl wrote somberly in *My Several Worlds,* "was that no first-rate Chinese minds joined the Christian movement."

Her own allegiance lay with the ambitious young radical thinkers beginning to emerge as the only leaders capable of shaping a coherent vision of the future in an era of rapid political disintegration. At the end of March 1916 Sun Yatsen's successor (who had placed himself three months earlier on the imperial throne) abdicated and died. From now on the country was ruled in practice by intrepid, opportunistic, uneducated warlords, who split the territory and divided the spoils between them. Meanwhile a restive and increasingly militant student body in the big cities tackled the theoretical question of how to abolish the legacy of centuries of oppression by transforming the culture and consciousness of the Chinese people. Zhenjiang was swept up in a raging national debate that engaged the key figures of a whole generation, from Pearl herself to the young Mao Zedong.

Its forum was the magazine *New Youth,* founded the year before by a popular professor at the university in Beijing, Chen Duxiu, whom Pearl singled out as the most powerful mentor of her youth: "I think before all others of Chen Duxiu [Ch'en Tu-hsiu], brilliant, bold and radical." Chen (who would go on to become the founder and first secretary of the Chinese Communist Party in 1920) aimed to overthrow an entrenched, institutionalized, ossified Confucianism by launching a literary revolution with his magazine. An article in *New Youth* fired the first shot in the battle between *wen-li*, the ancient classical written language intelligible only to scholars, and *pai-hua* (baihua), the despised medium of ordinary speech. This was far more than a linguistic dispute. Its implications reached into every area of social and political reform. *Pai-hua* was an essential tool for understanding, or even thinking about, the three planks with which the movers and shapers running *New Youth* planned to build a new China: science, democracy, and modernization. "When in 1916 the magazine took up the cause of literary reform, the flame of new intellectual life spread everywhere through China," Pearl wrote in her memoirs.

At the heart of the furor as far as Pearl was concerned stood the Chinese novel. Fiction had been popular but despised by anyone who could read as intrinsically primitive and crude, fit only for illiterate storytellers and low-grade traveling actors, the kind of thing no one with the slightest literary credentials would have in the house. The first serious scholarly attempt to argue that the vitality, inventiveness, and range of vernacular literature had shifted it into the mainstream, ready and able to replace an impoverished and now obsolete classicism, was published in *New Youth* by Hu Shi. A Columbia PhD student newly returned from the United States, Hu was the champion of *pai-hua*, arguing his case with a "brilliance and persuasiveness" that electrified young people like Pearl: "We recognized a fresh force in modern China." The stories she had loved as a child and continued to read in secret in spite of Teacher Kung's prohibition became all the rage almost overnight. European novels published for the first time in translation—by Dickens, Scott, Hugo, Dumas, Tolstoy, Cervantes—sold in increasing numbers. Young people were not only reading fiction but beginning to write it as well. Little magazines published a flood of confessional stories, expressing straightforward emotion in a vigorous vernacular at the furthest extreme from the arcane and allusive literary rituals of the past. Pearl read everything she could find and discussed it avidly with her Chinese friends, whose sudden sense of intellectual empowerment—"vivid, articulate, world-questioning"—was part of a combustible atmosphere that made anything seem possible. "This was an enormous release to educated men and women. To be able to say what one felt without having to think whether it was written in a rigid and antiquated style was to free an energy suppressed for centuries. . . . It was a wonderful hour, young enough to be still pure."

Hu Shi, the most fearless of all the young iconoclasts Pearl admired, attacked another immemorial taboo by taking over a whole issue of *New Youth* to publish his translation of Ibsen's *A Doll's House*, with an introduction explaining that the heroine, Nora, freed herself from a society corrupted by the four evils—selfishness, slavery, hypocrisy, and cowardice—at the end of the play when she slammed the door on her husband and family. Nora promptly became a role model for radical young women all over China. Published in June 1918, the Ibsen issue came too late for Pearl, who was married by then to a friend of Hu's, and busily engaged in constructing a doll's house of her own.

CHAPTER 4

Inside the Doll's House

P EARL'S HUSBAND WAS John Lossing Buck, who had met Hu Shi
  as a fellow student at Cornell University when they were both
in their early twenties. The two took the same agriculture courses
together, until Hu switched to an arts program at Columbia and
Buck sailed for China as an agricultural missionary at the end of 1915.
Retreating to Kuling in the heat of his first summer, he met "that darling Mrs. Sydenstricker's daughter, Pearl," at a Sunday picnic given
by another Cornell graduate and embarked on a whirlwind courtship.
She was "the nicest girl in all Kuling." he wrote home to his parents.
"She is just one peach of a girl." In the first week of September he
escorted her down the mountain, accompanying her by boat as far
as Nanjing, where he took the train to regain his mission station at
Nanxuzhou in the northern province of Anhui. They corresponded
that winter, and he made the long journey to Zhenjiang to see her
again, treating himself to a first-class ticket on the train ("She was
worth it"). The couple had been alone together no more than four or
five times when, in January 1917, they announced their engagement.

Lossing was twenty-six years old, the oldest of four boys reared by
frugal, hardworking, God-fearing parents on a small farm in upstate
New York. He looked "like a nice big overgrown farmboy," said one of
his colleagues at Nanxuzhou, who was surprised and taken aback by
Lossing's impressive catch when Pearl came on a visit of inspection.
"She was so pretty . . . oval face, slender, wore her hair done attrac-
tively, pretty eyes, lovely smile." Asked many years later what he and
his wife had in common, Lossing cited Sunday school teaching and
Bible classes. It was not enough for Pearl's parents, who were united

for once in disapproval. Carie warned her daughter against rushing into marriage, pointing out that Lossing had never read a book in his life and that an agricultural degree was hardly what the Sydenstrickers considered education. But he was everything Pearl wanted at this stage: tall, purposeful, and strong, physically confident, passionate about his job, and reassuringly unfanatical in other directions: "he was not at all religious so far as I could see." Also, he thought she was perfect. "I am happier every day," Pearl wrote to Emma Edmunds at the end of April. "Lossing is all any woman would wish him to be and makes me completely happy. He is so *thoroughly good* and so fine and true." They were married a month later at a simple ceremony in the Sydenstrickers' garden. The bride wore white crepe de chine trimmed with chiffon, and shocked her younger sister by the lavish lace trimmings she considered essential on her honeymoon underwear. The young couple spent the next two months getting to know one another for the first time in Pearl's parents' house at Kuling before moving north to Anhui in mid- or late August.

Nanxuzhou was a nondescript settlement, mud-walled with mud houses and unpaved mud streets, barely a mile across, on the vast, flat, featureless, deforested flood plain of the Hwei River. Its drabness filled visitors from outside with dismay. Pearl's mother was horrified by its dry and dusty monotony when she came for Christmas with Grace. Pearl herself said it took time to adjust to the "downright ugliness" of a landscape that stretched like a desert without change as far as the eye could see. "Earth and houses were all of one color, and even the people were of the same dun hue, for the fine sandy soil was dusted into their hair and skin by the incessant winds." But the countryside transformed itself when Pearl saw it for the first time in spring, becoming radiant, alive with promise, and full of entrancing mirages, like her marriage:

> The bare willow trees around the villages put forth soft green leaves and the wheat turned green in the fields and the blossoms of the fruit-trees were rose-colored and white. . . . When the earth was still cold but the air was warm and dry

and bright, wherever I looked I could see mirages of lakes and trees and hills between me and the horizon. A fairy atmosphere surrounded me, and I felt half in a dream.

The young couple were enchanted by one another in those early months. They had been allocated a small, bare, boxlike mission house belonging to somebody else (George and Mary Hood, the previous occupants, were absent on furlough), but Pearl astonished the station by turning her husband's cramped bachelor quarters—two small rooms with bathroom and kitchenette over his agricultural workshop—into a family home. She extended the living room, resurfaced the floors, put up bookshelves, and painted the walls a rich warm ochre which she mixed herself, toning down a bilious mustard color with a handful of red earth from the yard. She hung yellow silk curtains, painted pictures to furnish the walls, and made her first garden in the courtyard with ferns in pots that came inside in winter, and fresh flowers in every room so that "the garden seemed part of the house." She grew sweet peas, nasturtiums, golden Shantung roses for summer, and chrysanthemums in the autumn. Lossing planted beds of asparagus and strawberries and a vegetable patch with rows of peas, beans, tomatoes, radishes, and pumpkins. Pearl kept a caged canary in the window and four hens in the yard. She taught herself to cook, writing to her mother-in-law for simple all-American recipes to try, experimenting with tinned cow's milk and improvised local ingredients, sometimes so disastrously that the young couple and their guests fell about laughing. Lossing installed two mud-and-brick Chinese beehives and planned to keep goats so they could have their own milk. Pearl made date jam and plum jelly. "My new housekeeper is working to perfection," her husband wrote exultantly to his younger brother after four months of marriage. "I wouldn't change for all the rest of the housekeepers in the world put together."

Pearl learned to use a typewriter to write her husband's business letters for him and type up his notes. He spoke only halting beginner's Chinese, so she became his go-between with the local farmers. Lossing had been recruited as the first step in an ambitious plan for "the economic salvation of the region" drawn up by the head of the Nanxuzhou mission station, the Rev. Thomas Carter, a Columbia graduate who had founded the station five years earlier, and staffed it with idealistic young people like himself: the Hoods, Dr. John Wiltsie and his wife, and an energetic schoolteacher, Marian Gardner, who promptly became Pearl's best friend. Lossing's role was central in Tom Carter's schemes for expansion—"We ought to have an agricultural man here . . . a fellow with a good practical turn of mind"—worked out in consultation with the dean of China's first agricultural college at Nanjing University. Dean Baillie had been guest of honor at the first formal lunch party given by the young Bucks on honeymoon in the Sydenstricker house at Kuling. Mission funds had been allocated to build them a house of their own, with a farm and workstation attached. Six months before his wedding Lossing officially registered Nanxuzhou Agricultural Experiment Station on the mailing list of the Department of Agriculture in Washington.

Like their friend Hu Shi in a different sphere, the Bucks were part of a nationwide drive to build a new China, and Pearl threw herself into the work. Together they visited the villages and hamlets that would be part of the station's outreach program, Lossing on a bicycle and Pearl for propriety's sake in a curtained sedan chair borne by four coolies. The Revolution had brought the railway to Nanxuzhou in 1915, and with it the first Westerners ever encountered by farmers scratching a subsistence living on these bare flatlands ravaged by harsh winds, cold winters, bandits, and a regular cycle of drought, flood, and famine. People no longer threw stones or cursed foreigners openly on the road, but they could not contain their amazement at the sight of this freak on wheels. "Poor devil, he's eating dirt," one of them said sympathetically when Lossing bit into a chocolate bar.

Pearl was the first white woman the country people had seen. They were aghast, like *The Good Earth*'s Wang Lung at the sight of an American woman in a winter coat with a fur collar: "He had no idea of whether it was male or female but it was tall and dressed in a straight black robe of some rough harsh material and there was the skin of a dead animal wrapped about its neck." Crowds gathered at the gates of any town Pearl approached, accompanied her to the inn, and returned no matter how many times the innkeeper drove them away. "They would bend down to the ground where for six inches or so there was no door and stare at me upside down. If the windows were papered, they licked their fingers wet and melted holes in the soft rice paper and applied an eye to watch me." Once they pressed around her on market day in a small town—"literally hundreds of people packed against my chair"—tearing at the sides and trying to get the top off because Lossing had ridden ahead on his bike. Later the same day Pearl was mobbed in a stable, the only room the inn had to offer, by men trying to break the door in while her husband was away fetching their bags. She shoved a chair against the door, climbed on the seat, and drew up her feet. When Lossing got back they pinned sheets over the windows and barricaded themselves in, spending an uncomfortable night on a wooden sleeping platform above a manure heap. They finally got home to find that their cook and houseboy had very nearly killed each other in a knife fight over a dishcloth, which left Pearl's kitchen bloodspattered. Lossing as always remained calm. "Mother, he grows better every day," Pearl wrote, describing this eventful trip to her mother-in-law. "We are happier all the time. He is so good to me in every little way and makes life so happy for me."

They had been married almost exactly a year. "They were having fun together in those early days," said Marian Gardner, who remembered Pearl as a great giggler and a natural diplomat, always able to make others laugh with a comforting knack of defusing potential catastrophes by turning them into tall stories. "We'd all go off into gales. We got along by laughter . . . she was a wonderfully humorous person . . . bubbling over with humor in those early days." For bewildered young Americans, almost all straight from college, highly trained in their particular spheres but ignorant and inexperienced in this context, Pearl was not just a translator. She interpreted conventions and customs, advised on how best to approach the local people, explained their reactions, and reported their gossip. "She got a great deal from her amah," said Marian. "She would sit and talk to her for hours . . . she was one of the best listeners I ever knew. . . . She could draw out torrents of conversation by a few questions and come back convulsed with mirth at the tales she had been hearing, or indignant at the injustice done someone, or grieving at the results of poverty and neglect." Pearl investigated the nearest villages on foot, walking from one farm to the next, talking to the women and playing with their children, listening to their stories as her mother had done before her, only with the advantage of being bilingual, indigenous, and familiar from infancy with their world. "You see, she understood what they said as we didn't," said Marian. "She knew the things that were going on. . . . Pearl had an uncanny ability to explain the Chinese to us. It came out in *The Good Earth,* which was laid right there."

Pearl herself felt like a stranger to start with in Anhui. After the active, restless, cosmopolitan interchange of a rich treaty port, the isolation and remoteness of Nanxuzhou belonged to another world, "a world as distant from the one I was living in as though it had been centuries ago." The place seemed immune to change. News that China was falling apart and Europe being torn to pieces mattered little to anyone in these parts: "The vivid intellectual and political turmoil of the country did not reach us here. We lived as serenely as though the nation were not in revolution." Poor, self-contained, and inward-looking, Anhui preserved intact a way of life barely touched by outsiders for thousands of years. There was no industry and virtually no trade except sale or exchange in the nearest market. Local transport meant shifting as much at a time as could be carried on a man's back. Farmers practiced an agriculture efficiently adapted by time and experience to their own soil, climate, and conditions. They grew just enough grain and cotton to feed and clothe themselves on tiny family farms, varying their staple diet of wheat bread or porridge with garlic and beans, and burning dried grass for fuel. They worked the land themselves or with help from a buffalo, using wooden tools made at home. The little clay gods of the earth lived in clay houses at the edge of the fields, and the people lived clustered together in villages of bigger thatched clay houses that cracked apart in heavy summer rains and dissolved in winter floods. Humans and animals slept together in a single unventilated room with the door closed and a charcoal stove burning in winter.

The villagers thought and talked in ways very different from the sharp incisive speech of Zhenjiang, where "people spoke in syllables which splintered from their lips and from the ends of their tongues." In the unhurried seasonal pattern of life in the country around Nanxuzhou, "the language is slow and deep and it wells from the throat." Nearly twenty years later in *A House Divided* Pearl described the delayed impact of village life on an impatient young intellectual, recently returned from college in America, who comes reluctantly to see a kind of grandeur in this harsh unprepossessing countryside under a sharp winter sun: "The land stretched out before him, far and smooth and plain, and he could see, upon its smoothness, the flecks of blue which were men and women working . . . and for the first time he saw the . . . hard bright beauty of this northern land, glittering in the cloudless sky, its very light seeming blue, it poured down from so blue a sky."

Both Bucks gave this land their full attention. Together they explored and examined it, interrogated its inhabitants, and stored away their findings for future reference. Lossing would spend the greater part of his life systematically gathering, sorting, tabulating, and processing this kind of material. His two monumental statistical surveys of Chinese farm economy and land use were the first, and remained the only accurate record of China's agrarian infrastructure in the early twentieth century. The picture he painted was bleak. Seventy-nine percent of the labor force (or 205 million men) were farmers. The average size of a family farm was 2.62 acres (40 acres was considered the minimum for raising a family in West Virginia). Food, virtually all grown at home, consisted of 77.8 percent grain of one sort or another in North China (too cold and dry for a rice crop), 10.3 percent beans, and 9 percent roots. Farmers ate no sugar, hardly any meat, and "practically no vegetables." An average family consisted of 4.3 adult male units, and each unit consumed the equivalent of $22.91 worth of food a year, or $1.90 per month. Fuel was a cash crop saleable in the market, which meant that some northern farmers could not afford to waste their own dried grass stalks on heating water for tea. 80.8 percent were in any case too poor to buy tea leaves, although 80.5 percent bought tobacco. They took no weekends off, and holidays were unknown except at New Year. Only 7.4 percent of households set aside money ($1.92 a year) for recreation. None of them had access to capital, and the 23 percent who gambled were crippled by gambling debt. "This hand-to-mouth existence works very well in normal years," Lossing summed up laconically, "but in years of low crop yields it is often a hard race with starvation before the first cutting of barley in spring."

Listening, watching, and interpreting for her husband, Pearl saw for herself the same story written in the lined dun-colored faces, bent backs, and sinewy calves of men who had never eaten their fill from the day they were born. She could read a farmer's whole life in his body without even looking at his face. "There was something eloquent in this man's two bare feet, knotted and gnarled in the toes, and the soles like the dried hide of a water buffalo." Things seen and heard on field trips with Lossing would be absorbed and distilled a decade later in the magical opening sequence of *The Good Earth*, which slides the reader imperceptibly into a mud house, where Wang Lung the farmer on his wedding morning lights a fire of dried grass and recklessly squanders twelve tea leaves in a bowl of hot water for his aged father. Wang takes as his wife a discarded slave girl from the local big house, who bears him a son and celebrates the birth by scheming and saving to scrape together materials for a batch of sweet pastries decorated with wild red haws and chopped green plums from the field. Wang feels unaccustomed respect for his wife when he realizes that these moon cakes are not for home consumption, but to present to the big house, where she had endured a lifetime of humiliation, abuse, and rejection. Sold into slavery by her parents as a child of three or four years old, too young for her mother even to have begun binding her feet, Olan had grown up as a kitchen drudge, mute, coarse-featured, big-footed, beaten daily with a leather strap, bullied by the women and ignored by the men of the household as too plain to be worth raping. Her fragile red-and-green moon cakes, made with white sugar and lard—luxuries even more wildly extravagant in a poor farmer's economy than a pinch of tea—answer a secret need. Handing them over to her oppressors as a free gift expressed a dumb silent pride she had neither means nor cause to articulate before.

Pearl got to know ordinary farming people—"so charming, so virile, so genuinely civilized in spite of illiteracy and certain primitive conditions of life"—for the first time as an adult in Nanxuzhou. "They were the ones . . . who made the least money and did the most work. They were the most real, the closest to the earth, to birth and death, to laughter and weeping. To visit the farm families became my search for reality." The search in these early years was a joint enterprise, initiated by Lossing and energetically seconded by Pearl ("He has a great future before him here," she wrote to her mother-in-law; "I try to help him all I can"). His life's work began by his own account as an attempt to speak to and for the illiterate, inarticulate, ignored, and excluded farmers who made up four-fifths of China's population. He investigated soil, seed, and irrigation problems, set up comparative trials of American and Asian varieties of wheat, beans, and sesame plants, tried out American strains of corn, cotton, and sweet potatoes, and planned crop rotation experiments, all on a three-acre plot that he hoped shortly to double. But his practical research was rapidly overtaken by the need to go deeper, to establish, document, and analyze the underlying "situations which limit or affect, in one way or another, the lives of millions of China's people." He aimed specifically to promote the kind of self-knowledge without which there could be no improvement by supplying Chinese college students with meticulously accurate data, "and not only data, but methods of collecting such information, so that these students might in the future discover for themselves the facts of their own country."

Lossing drew up questionnaires, gave lectures, and published progress reports in the *Chinese Recorder*. As chairman of the newly formed agricultural committee of the Honan-Shandung Education Association, he campaigned vigorously for more and better education. He started a club in Nanxuzhou for the exchange of ideas, and organized classes for young farmers coming in from the country as well as a more intensive winter program for the town's landowners to study scientific advances in farming. Pearl claimed that Lossing's questionnaires were her idea in the first place, and she certainly helped formulate the questions beforehand and evaluate the answers afterward. But this was two-way traffic. Pearl knew the background, sometimes also the wives and mothers, of Lossing's first students, who belonged to a handful of leading families, "the elders, merchants and teachers of Nanxuzhou," representing between them what Tom Carter called "all the style and dignity that our little town can boast." She heard Lossing talk about promising individuals like young Mr. Hwang, a rich idle playboy who made good by running fertilizer experiments on his farm, and the even more enthusiastic Mr. Wang, who took part in "the testing of new grains and grasses for this region." Wang was Lossing's star pupil in the pilot study program that started in November 1918 with twelve students and finished two months later with a waiting list of a hundred. "Mr. Wang the farmer (the one I speak of so often) said the other night, 'This is the first agricultural class Nanxuzhou has ever had in its four thousand or more years of history,'" Lossing wrote proudly to his parents. Wang the farmer figured in Lossing's bulletins in the *Chinese Recorder* long before he lent his name, and perhaps something more, to the hero of *The Good Earth.*

It was Wang who warned Lossing that Ni Shi Chung, the minor warlord officially installed as military governor of Anhui, was the worst in China. Warfare was endemic in these years, when powerful, ruthless, and ambitious generals and politicians jockeyed for power. Soon after the Bucks set up home in Nanxuzhou, the town's thirty thousand citizens were overrun by seven thousand soldiers ("idle, reckless . . . lawless . . . noted ruffians and of the very lowest class," Pearl wrote to her parents-in-law). They belonged to the disgraced and defeated army of Chang Hsun, a loyal Manchu general who had tried and failed to restore the emperor to the throne in July 1917. His disaffected troops quartered themselves in the houses, looted the shops, and terrorized the people, like the horde of men who come swarming out of the north toward the end of *The Good Earth,* "filling the street, filling the town . . . as though air and sunlight had been suddenly cut off because of the numbers of grey men tramping heavily and in unison through the town. . . . Before Wang Lung could move in his horror the horde was pouring past him into his own gates. . . . Into his courts they poured like evil filthy water, filling every corner and crack."

Pearl knew firsthand how it felt to live under occupation and to retreat behind locked doors in the run-up to one of the regular gun battles when Nanxuzhou's four great gates were barred and martial law was imposed on the town. Lossing sent his parents a graphic description of one of these battles in the autumn of 1918, when hundreds of bandits had been massing for weeks at the railway station outside the town wall, while people inside pondered reports of pillaging and burning farther down the line. The fight itself lasted a day, with bullets whizzing over the Bucks' compound and an answering cannonade every four or five minutes from inside the town. Pearl, who had lived with bandits all her life, dismissed these assaults later, claiming that anyone who took precautions had nothing to fear ("At least once or twice a year bullets would fly over our town. . . . These old-fashioned wars were often amusing rather than dangerous, provided one stayed out of the range of gunshot"). Neither Lossing nor Grace Sydenstricker shared Pearl's optimism. "This does not tell what a bandit attack is like," Grace wrote of her sister's account. "It does not describe the smothering stillness which falls on a Chinese town when word is brought by runners from the outlying country that the tu-fei [bandits] are coming. Nor does it make you see that hurried secret rush to hide every valuable thing from the shelves of shopkeepers. . . . It does not give the feeling of fear for daughters and babies, and the quick concealment of these in lofts, beneath heaps of fuel. . . . Most of all, it does not bring the clutching of the pit of the stomach which is fear of human violence. These all come and stay through interminable nights." During this interlude the town shuts down with barricaded houses and silent empty streets waiting for the screams, shouts, and crashes that accompany the battle itself, followed by battering at the gates. "The shattering blow comes. . . . The hinges hold against the next blow and the next. A voice shouts '*K'ai!*—open!' Another says in a lower tone, 'Foreigners in there.'"

Bandits lived by ransom, and foreigners paid more. Old hands like Pearl knew that at some point the bandits always moved on, leaving their dead behind if they had been significantly beaten, taking their plunder and a substantial bribe with them if not. Predatory stragglers still lay in wait on the roads, and even Pearl was afraid of the half-starved, wolfish dogs that infested the villages. The Bucks solved the problem by acquiring a motorbike, which Lossing drove at speed with Pearl hanging on behind. "I defy any bandit to catch up with us," she wrote home airily at the end of the year.

BUT THERE WAS a limit to when and where a wife could accompany her husband in a society that imposed almost entirely separate lives on men and women. Chinese women were confined to homes traditionally organized for multiple occupation by different branches and generations of the same family. Housekeeping for two persons in the American style could be, by comparison, a dismally isolated business. Pearl did her own cooking after both cook and houseboy had to be sacked for trying to murder each other, but with no running water, no heating or lighting except open fires and oil lamps, no sanitation save commodes that had to be emptied daily, servants were essential. Lossing grew steadily more absorbed by his work. "He seems so busy all the time," Pearl wrote to his mother as her world closed in on her and his opened out. "Agriculture was his life," said Marian Gardiner, who was fond of Lossing but dismayed by his blank indifference to history, literature or art ("to have Pearl marry Lossing made me wonder").

Pearl countered her loneliness by diving back into the Chinese world, where she felt most at home. Her sister's chief memory of the Bucks' hospitable little house was of the visitors who poured through it, "an endless stream of Chinese people who came in to talk over everything." As a married woman Pearl had regained the freedom of movement lost when she reached puberty and was no longer allowed out alone. She resumed her solitary roaming, taking long walks in the cool of the evening on the town ramparts, shifting once again between her two worlds:

> The enchantment of moonlight . . . upon the city wall and the calm waters of the moat outside is still in my memory, half unreal, and it was in this little northern town that I first felt the strange beauty of Chinese streets at night. The dusty streets were wide and unpaved . . . lined with low one-story buildings of brick or earth, little shops and industries, blacksmiths and tinsmiths, bakeries and hot-water shops, dry-goods and sweetmeat shops, all the life of a people confined geographically and therefore mentally and spiritually to an old and remote area. I walked the dim streets, gazing into the open doors where families gathered around their supper tables, lit only by thick candles or a bean oil lamp, and I felt closer to the Chinese people than I had since childhood.

She made friends with her immediate neighbors, matriarchs and their daughters-in-law from the town's cultivated and ultraconservative leading families. She and Marian gave a highly successful tea party for the ladies of the Chou family, hosts and guests each treating the other with exquisite courtesy, the one laying out an elegant American dinner table with silverware and starched white linens, the other exclaiming in delight and astonishment over strange contraptions like salt cellars and exotic delicacies like bread and butter. Pearl's greatest friend was the head of the Chang family, a widow who lived with her children and grandchildren farther along the same cobbled street in a spacious old house with many courtyards and a curving tiled roof, protected by high walls and a doorman to guard its imposing carved gateway. Madame Chang was considerably older than Pearl, "a tall and ample figure dressed in a full skirt and knee-length coat . . . hair drawn tightly back from her round kind face." A powerful personality, energetic and active in spite of six-inch-long bound feet ("when she walked it was as though she went on pegs"), Madame Chang knew everyone and was relied on for practical advice by the whole town. She was a diplomat and a peacemaker, generous, broadminded, even-handed, a Buddhist and a practicing Christian (she told Pearl she had joined the Church out of politeness to the foreigners, whose good works she approved of and wished to encourage).

Pearl learned by her example how to run a large, complicated, orderly household in the Confucian way, "by being kind, courteous, temperate and deferential," without impatience or anger. "Madame Chang remains as one of the greatest women I have ever known," Pearl wrote more than thirty years later (by which time her international circle of friends provided a wide field for comparison, headed by Eleanor Roosevelt). As a young woman confronting often intractable problems with no one to consult or depend on, Pearl turned to her neighbor for comfort: "when my own heart ached for reasons I could not reveal it did me good just to lay my head down on her broad soft shoulder and be still for a bit."

Next door to the Bucks lived another formidable widow, Madame Wu, autocratic and elegant, still beautiful in old age, immaculately coiffed and painted, robed in rich silks with fine jewels and perfect three-inch feet (Madame Wu came to visit leaning on two young slave girls). She was a harsh disciplinarian to herself and others, imperious and manipulative, ruling her own large extended family with absolute authority. She was said to have married her favorite oldest son to a plain girl on purpose, growing so jealous when the boy fell in love with his wife that she drove her young daughter-in-law to suicide (traditionally the only way out for those without power to change an intolerable situation). When the girl finally hanged herself Pearl was summoned immediately, but although she got there in time to find the body still warm her attempt at first aid was vetoed by Madame Wu: "The Buddhist funeral priests had already arrived and the death chant had begun. I met hostile looks when I persisted, and Madame Chang . . . hurried me away." The son, whose overriding filial duty gave him no option but to go on living in his own courtyard inside the family house, never spoke to his mother again. "If Madame Wu felt this, she gave no sign of it."

Madame Wu was a prototype for the supercilious grande dame

described in Pearl's first published recollections of Nanxuzhou, "a ponderous dowager in plum-colored satin with proud drooping eyelids, opium-stained teeth, and a long bamboo pipe, silver-tipped, which she uses as a cane." Hers was a draconian response to an unforgiving and rigidly repressive environment. But she showed another side in her friendship with Pearl, whose untapped potential and still unformed imaginative sensibility perhaps reflected something of Madame Wu's own early history. Like all Chinese women in her day, she was illiterate ("none of my friends knew how to read and write," said Pearl), but she had learned much as a girl from a father who recognized and prized his only daughter's intelligence. He gave her a wide knowledge of Chinese poetry, which she passed on, together with her sense of style and some useful instruction in local etiquette, to this unexpectedly receptive young foreigner. "She taught me a great deal," wrote Pearl.

Between them these two remarkable women completed the Confucian education begun by Teacher Kung. Each in her different way provided the kind of role model Pearl had never had before, and needed more than ever now that her own mother was preoccupied by other worries far away in Zhenjiang. She learned from her two neighbors the courtesy and calm, the unassertive authority, the unexpected reticence and often astonishing sexual frankness, the broad and impartial vision recognized all her life by everyone who knew her as her Chinese inheritance. "I myself deliberately departed from American ways and plunged myself deep into China," Pearl wrote of these years. "I . . . spent much of my time in Chinese homes where a white woman had never been before; and there in long quiet talk with women whose lives had been shaped on a pattern totally different from mine, I learned again the inwardness of Chinese homes, as a woman now, and not as I had when I was a child playing with Chinese children."

Anything approaching friendship with young women of her own age was almost impossible because, in this distant part of the interior, they were still strictly enclosed in family houses where their status was so low that they had no scope for independent maneuver. One of the few occasions when Pearl managed to make contact with a contemporary was during a visit to a family named Li, on a field trip with Lossing to an ancient walled town which they were the first foreigners to penetrate. The wife of the youngest son explained, in a snatched conversation behind the locked doors of her bedroom, that she was forbidden to speak unless spoken to, ignored by her in-laws, permitted to talk freely only to servants and slave girls even more ignorant than herself. She was obliged to leave any room entered by her husband and remain silent in his presence except when they were alone in their room at night. The first question she asked was whether it was true that foreign husbands spoke openly to their wives in the company of other people. Like Madame Wu's daughter-in-law, she was clever, helpless, hungry for education, and profoundly depressed.

The seismic changes beginning to shake China came too late for girls like these, but not for the next generation. The granddaughters of both Wu and Chang families were the first in their respective clans to be educated and to escape foot binding. They were pioneers at the only girls' school in the region, founded in Nanxuzhou in 1912 by the South Presbyterian Mission, which refused to accept children with bound feet. The school was opened in defiance of immemorial tradition by Reverend Carter's wife, with help from a Christian convert named Mrs. Hsu (who went on to work with Pearl when she too became a proselytizing missionary in her own right). Pearl's friend Marian Gardner, who arrived fresh from the United States to take over the school in 1916, taught her pupils to read, write, and run relay races on the sound American principle "that they were as good as boys, and had minds and could use them." Pearl included one of these infant revolutionaries in her first account of Nanxuzhou—part memoir, part fable, published in 1924 in the *Atlantic Monthly*—about the transformation of a girl from the Hsu family at boarding school in Shanghai. The shy, silent child with downcast eyes who left town hobbling on bandaged feet returns a year later as a cheerful and talkative teenager, still wearing a Chinese outfit of delicate brocaded satin but complacently displaying beneath it her fashionably unbound feet in a pair of sturdy square-toed black leather lace-ups ("they looked like shoes for a very rough little American boy, and they had steel taps on the heels"). Fearless young Hsu Pei-yun belongs to the future. "A small-footed girl can get an old-fashioned husband and a big-footed girl, if educated, can get a new-fashioned husband," was Madame Chang's characteristic summing-up, "but small feet or schooling she must have, one or the other."

Marian Gardner was precisely the kind of companion Pearl needed at this point. Intelligent, highly educated, practical, and outgoing, she liked and looked up to Pearl (who was four years younger), recognizing not only her greater knowledge and experience but a penetration and sense of perspective highly unusual in someone still in her early twenties: "She had a great ability in those early days at seeing things objectively. She would go from the particular to the general with no difficulty. It wasn't easy for me to do that, but she did it remarkably, as though it were part of her heritage." Marian was Pearl's first audience, the person for whom she opened up the closed Chinese world despised or ignored by most Westerners. Marian's memories of the year they spent together at Nanxuzhou were full of excitement and a sense of discovery. The two young women turned the hardship, and often the horrors, they encountered into a sharp, vivid serial comedy. Pearl loved her Chinese friends' instinct for drama, the toughness and lack of hypocrisy that underlay their uninhibited jokes about local characters such as the schoolmaster and the town's only rich man, the head of the Hsu family, whose home life was a battlefield between his wife and three intensely competitive concubines. She made a good story out of her own houseboy, a devout church member who married a recalcitrant slave girl—"I played the wedding march but I never played for so mournful or unwilling a bride"—only to find himself mercilessly bullied and shamed by his wife for trying to treat her in a spirit of Christian meekness and forbearance.

The humorous case histories Pearl relayed to Marian or in letters home had a fearful underside. The two women had been thrown together initially because, when they first met, there was no one else to run the station. Lossing was fully occupied setting up his farming program, and the Carters were absent on sick leave. The Hoods were also away on furlough and when they got back remained preoccupied by their severely disabled new baby. Dr. Wiltsie's wife, who had just lost her first child to meningitis, was struggling with grief and anger against the desperately primitive conditions that made human life in China so precarious. When Mrs. Wiltsie was too depressed to leave her house, her husband had to depend on Pearl or Marian to act as his anesthetist and surgical assistant in emergency operations performed in dirty, overcrowded huts, often reeking with smoke from an open fire on the beaten earth floor. Pearl learned on the job how to sterilize instruments in a tin can of water boiled on a fire of sticks and drip chloroform from a bottle onto a cotton pad laid over the patient's nose. "Once the breathing stopped. 'She's dead,' I whispered. The doctor reached for a hypodermic and stabbed her arm and she began to breathe again unwillingly." These operations commonly took place in front of a silent hostile press of relatives and neighbors scrutinizing every move made by the foreign doctor, who was only ever called in as a last resort to treat cases already despaired of by Chinese practitioners. Pearl described working as Wiltsie's anesthetist on a dying woman, who pulled through and showed signs of recovery after two or three days' treatment but refused to allow the foreigners near her again as soon as she regained full consciousness ("the last we heard she was much worse again, and I suppose of course she will die").

Retrospective accounts of episodes like this in Pearl's memoirs are generally less brutal and raw than the descriptions in her letters at the time, where her cheerful composure risked slipping. She said that repeated exposure to misery the onlooker could do little or nothing about bred a thick skin and a hard heart, or alternatively an oversensitivity liable to end in nervous collapse. The only effective response was to fall back on survival by laughter. "We had to," said Marian. "So much was tragic and sad, so poverty-stricken, in the famine area. If there was a drought, it hit us. *The Good Earth* is laid in Nanxuzhou. I recognized the people. . . . You were on the ragged edge of a famine permanently. It would rain till you were inundated. I have seen it when there would be water over the entire land. And despair. Everything was patched. Even the boat sails were made up of patches, hundreds of them."

Marian was engaged to a fellow missionary, whom she married in the summer of 1918, leaving Pearl as the only member of the mission personnel assigned to women and children. Pearl supervised the girls' school, ran her own Sunday school class, set up a refresher course for recent converts, a girls' club, and a young mothers' group to teach basic hygiene and child care. She also started regular "calling" with Mrs. Hsu, going on foot four afternoons a week from one village to the next to preach the gospel and distribute religious tracts. Pearl's entry into a village always followed the same pattern. Before she could begin to point out to the women that they were worshipping the wrong gods, let alone put them in touch with the right one, she had to allow a settling-down period for them to stare at her huge feet and mountainous nose, finger her clothes, interrogate her in intimate detail about her personal habits and private life, and get over the shock of comprehension when she replied. "How strange! We can understand English, it's the same as Chinese!"

One of the things that had always separated Pearl from the rest of the mission community was her prosaic acceptance of a world almost inconceivably strange to her American colleagues. All of them were taken aback at first sight by Nanxuzhou: "flat and dirty and small . . . just a mud hole," Marian said long afterward. "The whole place stank. . . . The streets were absolutely filthy." The stench was always what struck newcomers to China most forcibly. After forty years as a missionary Pearl's own mother never got used to the smell of human excrement applied daily as fertilizer to the fields in the valley beyond her house. In Nanxuzhou people dried dung for fuel by plastering it over the outside of their houses, pigs roamed freely in streets ankle-deep in mud when it rained, and each bullock was followed by a small boy with a large basket to catch its copious, steaming droppings. Pearl listed the successive shocks—"the lack of sanitation, the congestion, the foul streets, the filthy and diseased beggars . . . the mangy dogs"— that drove visitors to distraction, sometimes to the point of hysteria. The standard American attitude was exemplified by one of her college friends from Randolph-Macon, Ruth Osborn, who never forgot the coating of flies on every surface or the town ponds where people washed themselves and their clothes, dipped water for drinking, and often defecated as well. When she stayed with the Sydenstrickers in Zhenjiang, Ruth was enchanted by Pearl's mother and nauseated by the stinking streets immediately outside the compound gate. She was even more bewildered by the absolute indifference of the Chinese people to the missionaries' message of guilt and atonement ("what we consider sins are nothing to them").

The doctrine of atonement was Pearl's favorite starting point for her village homilies. She would look back afterward on her experience as a mission wife in Nanxuzhou as the period that brought her closest to ordinary Chinese people, especially the women, who treated her as an equal, enrolling her as an honorary member of their ingrained resistance to men in general, and their husbands in particular ("girls knew from the first that they had their own way to make. . . . Chinese women are witty and brave and resourceful, and they have learned to live freely behind their restrictions. They are the most realistic and least sentimental of human beings"). But at the time she wrote grimly to her American parents-in-law about "the terrible degradation and wickedness of a heathen people," hinting at "things one cannot tell because of their unspeakable horror." In her end-of-year report for the New York church that sponsored the Nanxuzhou mission, she itemized these things as idol worship, infanticide, alcoholism, gambling, and opium addiction, adopting the breezy, dismissive tone often used by missionaries to maximize the distance between themselves and their prospective converts. Pearl emphasized the darkness and dirt of the village houses, the smell of "unwashed, garlic-filled humanity," the pernicious ignorance of the women crowding around her to poke and gawk. She referred to them as "natives" rather than as friends or equals. The impossible task of persuading them of their own moral turpitude preyed on her as it had on her father. "I have *sole* charge of the evangelistic work for the women in a district of about two million people!" she wrote to Emma Edmunds, newly married to a missionary herself in 1918. "It is absurd, of course, but it weighs on me terribly at times." Pearl told Marian that she counted any call she paid without preaching the gospel a waste of time. "How can we save her from her own weaknesses?" she wrote, describing China's plight in her report of December 1918. "How can we touch her heart to her own dreadful wickedness and weakness. . . . These are the thoughts that burn in us by day and night."

The terminology of repentance and expiation, nearly always set out in a tone of paranoid self-righteousness, was standard usage for missionaries, and entirely appropriate in a letter intended like this one for circulation among charitable donors. It was a way of thinking Pearl would reject explicitly and unconditionally for the rest of her life, once she finally managed to distance herself from the mission community. But in the winter of 1918, without Marian to make her laugh and reinforce her sense of proportion, she was still capable of stepping right back into her American world and shutting the door. Religious solutions provided the only available means of dealing with constant, intolerable exposure to the consequences of slavery, forced marriage, the murder of female infants, and the suicide of young women the same age as herself. Pearl said that nine out of the eleven members of her women's group admitted to having killed at least one female child at birth. "The average is three or four. One woman had eight daughters one after the other and killed them all as soon as they were born. They strangle them. Often they don't trouble to kill them, but just throw them out to the dogs." In Nanxuzhou Pearl came close to taking the conventional missionary view that pictured Chinese people not as individuals but as a menacing, faceless horde, morally obnoxious and numerically overwhelming: "hard-featured, envious, curious, unsympathetic and ungracious," as the head of U.S. Presbyterian Missions put it on a tour of the Yangtse basin, "they flock to a foreigner and close him in, like ants to a piece of bread."

This was the spirit of the Nanxuzhou mission station from its inception in the aftermath of the 1911 Revolution, when China turned decisively to the West. "It is the supreme moment for the Church to march though these open doors and take possession of these fields," wrote Thomas Carter in his initial bid for sponsorship from New York's wealthy Madison Avenue Presbyterian Church, pointing out that no rival mission had designs on the barren, famine-ridden region of Anhui, a territory the size of the state of Maine, or slightly larger than England. "It is just the sort of mission life I've dreamed of," he reported at the end of his first year, when he was still struggling to master Chinese, and had by his own account little practical experience of the people or the place he had marched into and planned to take over. The chronic flooding that destroyed the spring wheat crop, causing routine food shortages and starvation in winter, rose to epic proportions that year. "We don't measure results yet, but we do hold our breath when we think of possibilities," he explained after another two years, during which the station had made a single local convert. Soldiers had sacked the girls' school, and the people were proving less than cooperative. "No one can get any idea of the task that we are attempting without first realizing something of the depth, the deep-seatedness of the evil that we are fighting," Carter reported, outlining the pernicious tendencies of his potential flock, the persecution of his lone convert, and the demoralization of himself and his staff with "no Christian sentiment in the community, no Christianized civilization, to stand back of us and cooperate with us in working for righteousness." Shortly afterward both Carter and his wife were granted a leave of absence for health reasons. The Bucks' arrival in 1917 brought a fresh injection of hope and energy to the station. "By that time so many people had got sick in Nanxuzhou and left," Marian remembered sadly long afterward.

Pearl's own crisis of disgust and futility came six months after Marian herself left, closely followed by the Wiltsies, who retired defeated to the United States at the end of 1918. "Without the Wiltsies, Pearl got very discouraged," said Marian, who had been dubious about her friend's marriage from the start and whose suspicions were confirmed long afterward, when Pearl herself confided that things had gone wrong quite soon between her and Lossing. The problem was that his preoccupation with his work left little attention for anything or anyone else. Outside his own professional sphere, Lossing's instincts were conservative, conformist, low-key, perfectly in tune with the sober and pragmatic world he came from. He was an undemanding and incurious husband, perfectly satisfied with Pearl, and proud of the energy and drive she put into playing the role of a devoted young mission wife. "We both . . . have the best and finest girl in the World," he wrote a few years later when his younger brother got engaged. "It is a great experience . . . being married. You have wonderful days ahead of you." His religious observance was sincere but perfunctory, which was no help to a wife trying to balance on a tightrope between two worlds and in danger of losing her footing.

An English doctor posted with his young family to replace Dr. Wiltsie, lasted only a few months in Nanxuzhou. Dr. Smith and his wife were repelled by the place, its inhabitants (the Smiths' servants took a traditional revenge by emptying the family chamber pots immediately underneath their windows), and the new house designed by the Wiltsies as part of an ambitious hospital complex built with Rockefeller money. "They just hit the ceiling," said Pearl. By this time she was starting to look through the eyes of outsiders at things she had grown up seeing from inside. Her feelings came to a head in a letter of sick revulsion written to her parents-in-law about yet another girl who managed to get away from a vindictive mother-in-law long enough to hang herself from a beam. This was a common enough drama in any Chinese town, and the whole neighborhood knew exactly what to do. The first step was to cut the body down and bandage the orifices to keep in any remaining breath. The next was to attract the attention of the newly released spirit by beating gongs and shouting for it to come back. Any intervention from foreigners at this stage blocked the spirit's path. Pearl found the hanged girl propped up in a small airless room packed with people and felt her pulse, which was still beating strongly.

To my horror I found they had stopped her eyes, ears and nose and had gagged her so she could not get a breath of air. I told them at once that if she were not already dead she would certainly be smothered to death. I tried to get them to move her out into the yard, or at least stand back and take away the stoppage, and give her a chance, and let me try artificial respiration. . . . I wanted them to let me at least unwrap her face

to see if there were any sign of breath, but they would not. So
I had to go away, knowing that the girl was being murdered.
For murdered she was. . . . There was no reason for her death,
they smothered her. Even the girl's own Mother helped to do
it. . . . I stood there that night and told them they were killing
the girl, but they would not believe it. There is no limit to the
ignorance and superstition of these people. . . . Every day of
my life nearly I hear of or come into contact with some trag-
edy, which if it took place at home would ring over the country, but here is accepted as a matter of course. . . . China . . . is
a country given to the devil.

Pearl's appalled and appalling letter was written on Saturday, March
15, 1919, four days after the girl's death the previous Tuesday. The less
explicit, more clear-headed versions of this and similar episodes in
her published memoirs have none of the immediacy of the letter she
wrote straight away out of pain and anger in short sentences like gasps
of shock, with harsh hammering repetitions as if she still could not
credit what she had seen and tried to stop. The grim underlying realities of ordinary women's lives in China had been familiar to Pearl all
her life through her mother, who listened to the stories they told her
as intently as if their wretchedness were her own. Carie's response
was instinctive where her husband's was doctrinal. "He did not, as
she did, feel on his own flesh and spirit the sufferings of others," Pearl
wrote two years later, by which time she had left Nanxuzhou: "the
voice of human suffering . . . was too often for him the voice of those
who cried out against the just punishment for their sins sent from a
just God." But Pearl was the child of both parents, and uncontrollable
distress drove her back on the punitive teachings she had grown up
hearing from Absalom. "I felt the Calvinism and fundamentalism of
Pearl's father in her 'savage attacks,'" wrote Marian, who recognized
the accuracy of Pearl's account of the farm women but was profoundly
shocked by her reaction. "Her underlying feeling that the people were
sinners who needed to atone for their sins . . . is meaningless to me."
Marian saw rage and despair behind Pearl's attempts to indoctrinate

villagers already brutalized by ignorance and poverty. "I don't think happy people get so angry as she was at conditions which can be quite easily explained. . . . She was miserable, and it certainly shows itself in these letters."

For the moment Pearl had no option but to revert to the fortress mentality instilled by her mother, whose first move in any new place had always been to construct a refuge for her family filled with flowers, books, and pretty curtains to shut out the world beyond the windows. Carie herself, still struggling with pernicious anemia, had finally been forced to accept that she could never again make the voyage home. Absalom alone accompanied Grace when she started college in the United States in the autumn of 1918. He returned dazed and shaken by the wave of bacchic revelry released in America and Europe at the end of World War I, treating Pearl and her mother to hair-raising stories of lewd, raucous, short-skirted, hard-drinking modern youth: "'Everywhere I went they all had their dresses up to their knees.' We stared at him in shocked silence." Mother and daughter exchanged regular visits in these years and spent the summer of 1919 together at Kuling. The Bucks had missed their annual break the year after their honeymoon because of Lossing's inability to tear himself away from his work, but this time Pearl left her husband behind in Nanxuzhou, setting out alone on June 7, three or four weeks before the season began, to spend three months recuperating in her mother's new house in the mountains. She discovered she was pregnant that summer in Kuling.

THE BUCKS WERE next in line after the Wiltsies for a new mission house built to their own design, in which Pearl fully expected to spend the rest of her life. The roof had just gone on when she left for Kuling, and she moved in with Lossing after he came to fetch her home in the autumn. Her Chinese friends, who had known only rambling one-storey family homes constructed around courtyards in the traditional way, were baffled at Pearl's housewarming party by the first flight of stairs they had ever encountered in a private house (they teetered up cautiously, and Madame Chang solved the problem of how to go down by sliding on her backside). They were frankly incredulous when Pearl declared that her husband hoped the new baby would be a girl. "You can't imagine what an impression that made on the women in Nanxuzhou," said Marian. "To think anyone would *want* to have a little daughter." The Bucks had barely settled in when word came that church funding for Lossing's agricultural experiments had been cut off, a crushing blow promptly followed by a job offer from the head of the newly established College of Agriculture and Forestry at the University of Nanjing. The Bucks' housewarming transposed itself into a farewell party, with a fond mutual exchange of gifts, tears, and promises to visit, before Pearl finally departed, once again without her husband, traveling alone in September to Nanjing, where she was to await the birth of her baby in a room in the house of the head of the college, John Reisner and his wife. Some kind of infection had broken out in Nanxuzhou, and Lossing, anxious to avoid any risk to his wife and unborn child, planned to join Pearl in the New Year.

His sponsors at the Madison Avenue Church felt badly let down by his departure, and so did his colleagues on the Nanxuzhou mission team. Although the Carters would leave China themselves two years later, the Hoods (who did in fact spend the rest of their working lives on the station) still hoped to persuade the Bucks to come back. But Nanxuzhou was a chapter that had closed for both Pearl and Lossing. Nearly twenty years later Pearl painted a grisly picture of the future they escaped at this point: "Imagine two, four, five, six— rarely more—white men and women, some married to each other, the others starved without the compensation of being consecrated to celibacy, imagine them thrown together, hit or miss, without regard to natural congeniality of any sort, in a town or city in the interior of China, living together for years on end, without relief, in the enforced intimacy of a mission compound, compelled to work together and unable, from the narrowness of their mental and spiritual outlook, to find escape and release in the civilization round them."

Pearl's doctor, Horton Daniels, Dr. Smith's replacement, had anticipated problems, but in fact her pregnancy went smoothly apart from a mistake in the dates. The baby expected in late December or early January arrived on March 20, 1920. Caroline Grace Buck, named for her grandmother and aunt, impressed all who saw her, especially her mother, with "her unusual beauty and the intelligence of her deep blue eyes." Grace said her sister's ecstatic letter announcing the birth was "like a magnificat of motherhood." But Dr. Daniels, whose suspicions had been correct all along, diagnosed a tumor in his patient's womb and advised immediate surgery. The Bucks returned to the United States with Carol (short for Caroline), a few months old when she crossed the Pacific like her mother before her in a market basket. Fearful for her sister's life, Grace came up from college to look after the baby, who was to be left with her grandparents on the Buck farm in Pleasant Valley, New York. Lossing and Pearl's brother, Edgar, escorted her to the Presbyterian Hospital in New York City, where a benign tumor was successfully removed in early June. Pearl, who had counted on having a large family, was told she would never be able to bear another child. She returned to spend the summer convalescing with her parents-in-law, and making the most of Carol now that there could be no more babies.

The three of them returned to Nanjing in late autumn. Pearl divided her time that winter between her daughter and her mother, pitifully weakened and skeletally thin in Zhenjiang, which was two hours away by train. After a sudden relapse in the spring, Carie's doctor pronounced her case hopeless. Pearl took her for the last time to Kuling, padded in quilts and carried on coolies' backs. Carie fought hard against the knowledge that this time there would be no cure, admitting defeat only at the end of the summer, when she knew she was going back to Zhenjiang to die. Grace arrived home from the United States in early September to find her mother sitting up in bed chewing gum—"I hear chewing gum is the thing in America these days"—and waiting expectantly for the brand new Victrola, with a parcel of records to play on it, which she had ordered from Shanghai. It was a last spurt of defiance. "The poison of the disease had crept through her body and every sense seemed dulled," wrote Grace. "She slept as if in stupor."

One of her last requests was a foxtrot, danced to a jazz record on the Victrola by her nurse, an elderly English ex-prostitute from Shanghai with a ravaged face and died blonde hair, who was an unexpected hit with her patient. Carie told Pearl it had been a mistake to give up dancing as a girl, adding dreamily that, if she could start over again, she would give her life to America. Illness stripped away her faith, and with it her respect for her husband. His presence disturbed her, making her so tense and uneasy that her daughters kept him away. The hymns she had loved and sung all her life now seemed to mock her on the Victrola. "O rest in the Lord / Wait patiently for Him" was an old favorite, but when her daughters played it for her "she said with a quiet and profound bitterness, 'Take that away. I have waited and patiently—for nothing.'" She died in her sleep with Absalom and Grace at her bedside on October 21, 1921.

More than a decade later Pearl described in *The Time Is Noon* a fictional daughter who stays away as if forcibly held back from her mother's deathbed: "Something blinded her—not tears. She was not weeping. Her throat was thick, her eyes fogged, her heart beating all over her body. She was afraid. She turned blindly to the window and stood looking out." In her biography of her mother Pearl saw this as the moment that finally cut her loose from the world of her childhood and the self that had been bound by its constraints. "When I think of her dying I still see that landscape, the bamboos swaying below the window, the valley beyond, the small farmhouses and the tawny fields, the late gleaners moving slowly across them, women and children in their peasant blue, and beyond them again the distant mountains. Those were long minutes in which I felt my very flesh being torn from hers. I longed to go to her and I could not." Pearl's account of Carie's courage and composure at the end echoes the story of Mulan, the folk heroine who had thrilled her as a child, and whose brilliant career owed much to a fearless mother. "Any Chinese who reads this will recall . . . Mulan's mother!" wrote a Chinese critic reviewing *The Exile* on publication. Carie might have relished the comparison. She was buried beside her son Clyde in the foreigners' walled cemetery at Niupipo, down the hill and across the valley from the Sydenstricker house.

"Fiction is a painting," wrote Pearl, "biography is a photograph. Fiction is creation, biography is arrangement." She herself reworked the story of her mother's death in three biographical books and two novels. The first was *The Exile,* an energetic vindication written immediately after Carie died, piecing together her life from her own diaries and from Pearl's recollections, a collaborative and emotional rather than a factual reconstruction, certainly not a biography in Pearl's prosaic and mechanical definition. Two years later she revisited the same subject in her first novel, *East Wind, West Wind,* where the mother's long, slow, stoical dying hangs over the book's last section, putting all other lives on hold as she struggles like someone trying to get rid of a burden, silent, immobile, looking more and more like her daughter, gnawed and savaged by pain that turns her face gray and shortens her breath. At the end, having glimpsed the hard truth of her mother's marriage, the daughter shrinks from looking closer: "I drew the curtain at last, and shut her away, back into the loneliness in which she had lived."

After another decade Pearl removed the concealing curtain in *The Time Is Noon.* She said the book insisted on being written—"I had to get rid of all my life until that moment"—at a time of transition and confusion, when she could see no hope for herself in the future. "In this mood I began to write *The Time is Noon* . . . writing out my thoughts and fears not in my own person, of course, but in a woman I had created out of myself." By far the best and bleakest thing in the book is its frank and angry account of the minister's daughter nursing her mother, whose voice grows hoarse and dry as her flesh swells and her eyes shrink ("death sat, looking out of her eyes, breathing its stenchy breath out of her nostrils"). The horror of physical decay is compounded by shock and incredulity as the daughter finds herself slowly and unwillingly confronted with the sexual coercion and emotional nullity at the core of her parents' marriage. The wife shrinks from her husband's touch, claiming tiredness and refusing to let him near her: "They looked at each other, father, daughter. The daughter cried at him in her heart, 'What have you done to make her so tired?' The father answered with his calm, righteous look. His look said, 'I have done nothing that is not my right to do.'"

The one flicker of genuine feeling between the dying woman and her husband is a moment of mutual savagery when he finds that she has systematically put aside sums from her meager housekeeping allowance for their children. He turns on her, beside himself with fury at having been cheated of funds for his charitable causes, before rifling her trunk and helping himself to her savings. Afterward their daughter finds the contents of the ransacked trunk, family papers, baby clothes and shoes, a lifetime's carefully preserved mementoes, all tipped out as trash on the attic floor. "It darted across her mind that there was nothing there of the man's, nothing of their father at all. He had come and taken all he wanted and he had left nothing behind."

As soon as Pearl got back to Nanjing in the winter of 1921–22 she began to put the story of her mother's life down on paper, refilling that metaphorical trunk, writing out of grief and fury, dashing down her words with no time for correction, driven by the image of her mother that burned in her memory. She wrote without thought of publication, almost without realizing she was writing a book at all. *The Exile* starts with an exuberant image of Carie in her prime, the mother first imprinted on the mind of the infant Pearl, outlined against the sun and holding a trowel in her hand in the garden of the mission house at Tsingkiangpu, radiant, vigorous, all-powerful, at the furthest remove from the sad, shriveled, and defeated woman Pearl had sat with and watched over at the end of a life pointlessly sacrificed to a futile cause. The book ends with an effusive postscript (added fifteen years later, when *The Exile* was finally published), which makes it sound more like a biography of the Statue of Liberty than an actual human being: "Young in spirit to the end, indomitable, swift in generosity, eager after the fine things of life and yet able to live ardently if necessary in poverty, idealistic with the true idealism that is never satisfied with mere idealism not translated into actuality . . . To all of us everywhere who knew her this woman was America." Between these two heroic evocations lies a sober story of rejection, submission, and resistance in which the author catches sight of herself reflected again and again in her mother's mirror.

In the absence of all but the most rudimentary documentation,

Pearl relied in *The Exile* on things her mother had told her backed up by a photographic memory apparently in working order from the day of her birth. But because even Pearl could not remember what had happened before she existed, she shaped her account of her mother's early life on the pattern of her own recent experience. The key turning point for Carie as a young woman—her mother's illness and death—becomes on one level a replay of Pearl's own conscious or unconscious groping toward some still undefined sense of purpose: "She was beginning already to cut her life free, ready for a way to be shown her." Carie rejected the passionate and sensual side of her nature represented by her first lover—"I could see in her eyes her memory hot still with the thought of him"—married Absalom to confirm her rejection, and spent the rest of her life coming to terms with the enormity of her mistake. Pearl, who had married for the opposite reason, found herself as a young wife deep in similar frustration and doubt. At times in *The Exile* she seems to be writing about her own exasperation as much as her mother's, with a husband who makes it painfully clear that no wife can compete in attraction or significance with his work. In her story Absalom provides a focus for her mixed feelings about Lossing. "His somewhat pedantic speech, his slow rare humor, his complete absorption in his task, his inability to face or to understand the practical difficulties in human lives, his own ascetic and rigorous life which had no place for beauty or pleasure, came to repel her."

The Exile is a study of sexual and emotional incompatibility "in an age stern to women," when marriage had no exit. "However two might strain from each other, however barren might be the husks of union between them, however far they dwelt in spirit from each other, the outward bond was not to be broken." In a poignant passage near the end of the book Carie in her fifties finally relinquishes her dream of working alongside her husband, realizes she will never find companionship in her marriage, and accepts that the most she can expect is to live out the rest of her life plodding on foot from one Chinese village to another, giving and getting what comfort she can from the local women. It was the existence Pearl had until recently envisaged for herself in Nanxuzhou.

The Exile is admittedly biased, sometimes factually inaccurate, and in places heavily romanticized, but it takes imaginative possession of its subject with a novelist's aplomb while at the same time retaining a degree of biographical detachment exceedingly difficult for a child to bring to bear on a parent. It is a remarkable achievement, and one that restored Pearl's innate balance and sense of proportion. It also clarified her priorities. For her, as for her brother Edgar, there could be no question of divorce in the lifetime of either of their parents, but with this book she distanced herself from her past, sharpened her understanding of her own predicament, and cleared the way for a very different solution when, like Nora in Ibsen's *Doll's House,* she too would eventually have to confront in her marriage what Hu Shi called the four evils of selfishness, slavery, hypocrisy, and cowardice.

When *The Exile* was finished Pearl showed the manuscript to no one, packing it up and putting it away in a closet, where it lay forgotten for years. Much the same would happen later with *The Time Is Noon,* which spent more than thirty years in a drawer before it was finally published. Both seemed initially too raw and intimate for public consumption. Pearl said she wrote *The Exile* as a family memoir for Carol to read and for her unborn grandchildren. But although she never thought of it at the time as a book, still less as publishable, she must have known it had made her a writer. Judging by what she wrote next, she also realized that her real subject was China—not the China where her mother had lived all her adult life in exile, but the China where Pearl felt at home.

When the Bucks left Nanxuzhou, each of them already had the makings of a book that would shoot them both within twelve months of one another to the top of their respective career ladders. In the two and a half years Lossing spent collecting data from the farmers, Pearl had watched and listened, absorbing into her imagination the shapes and patterns of ordinary Chinese life, the kind of stories that no one had ever written down before and that would have been lost forever if she had not served her time as a solitary witness and confidant for the village women of Nanxuzhou. Her new life in Nanjing marked the start of a process of profound personal change. But it would be nearly another decade before she managed to rid herself completely of the narrow Western vision that could see only grimy, fetid, disease-ridden hovels in the Chinese homes so accurately recreated and inhabited with such warmth and generosity of feeling in *The Good Earth*.

CHAPTER 5

Thinking in Chinese

M<small>RS.</small> J<small>OHN</small> L<small>OSSING</small> Buck on arrival in Nanjing showed no sign of being anything but a typical mission wife. She dressed drably, furnished her house on a shoestring, and put the greater part of her energy into providing backup for her up-and-coming young husband. Almost immediately appointed acting dean of the agricultural college, Lossing replaced John Reisner (on two-year furlough in the United States) as head of what was already well on the way to becoming Nanjing University's largest and most prestigious department. Pearl acted as hostess to a steady stream of international visitors, who landed in Shanghai and stopped off to inspect the department at Nanjing before going on by train north to Beijing or west by Yangtse riverboat into the interior. In the absence of hotels, her guests—scholars, writers, travelers, professors on sabbatical, and young American missionaries studying Chinese at the Language School—often stayed six months or more.

The Bucks' house, conveniently near the university and not far from the center of town, was a standard gray brick faculty building, "too large and somewhat graceless," according to Pearl, who subdued it with characteristic speed and style. Its heart was her hospitable sitting room on the ground floor at the back, looking out through a broad bay window over lawns and flower gardens falling away to a bamboo grove below. She filled the room with odds and ends picked up at bargain prices, capacious basket chairs, low Chinese blackwood tables, glazed ceramic bowls and jars, blue Chinese rugs, yellow curtains, and cushions made from a bale of faded silk that she had dyed herself in different colors. "The living room, large as it was, grew larger while she lived in this home," wrote Grace, who moved in with her sister and married a fellow lodger, a missionary from the Language School. "Porches were taken into it, the south side was pushed out until it became almost an enclosure of a fragment of outdoors, it was so full of sunshine and light and flowers. The colors in the room were rich and warm . . . deep apricot and brilliant Chinese blue and a touch of jade green and the black of ebony." The flowers Pearl planted beneath the window made another luxuriant mass of color. There were lilacs in spring, peach and cherry blossom, jonquils, violets, an orange grove, and a riotous pansy bed. A vine arbor led to the rose garden, shaded by big old trees, where sweet-scented China roses grew against the compound wall above beds of snapdragons, poppies, phlox, hollyhocks, and Sweet William. Lunch and dinner parties often took place on the upper terrace, with a view over the garden wall of Purple Mountain, where the first Ming emperor lay buried, rising in the distance beyond the city ramparts.

Pearl looked after her baby, managed her large household, and entertained her husband's guests as well as teaching English courses at both the private, mission-backed Nanjing University and its Chinese-funded rival, National Southeastern University. She made friends with her next-door neighbor, Margaret Thomson, another highly educated faculty wife with literary aspirations and teaching commitments of her own. Their alliance was a comfort to Pearl, who always dreaded being marked down by other women as a misfit. "I admired her, and was sometimes a little awed by her," another faculty wife said of Pearl. "She spoke her mind so clearly even then." Her house was simple and plain but strikingly different from other people's. "It was the most charming home I was ever in," said a third mission wife, "and the most intellectual." Pearl herself maintained afterward that she felt stifled and imprisoned in those early years. Her houseguests remembered her hunched over a book every morning in a corner by the window. One of the rare strangers who came specifically to see Mrs. Buck in her own right at this stage was Alice Tisdale Hobart, another reader and writer, who never forgot the books crammed into the big, comfortable, untidy living room, "not books lining the wall, the furnishings of so many libraries, but books of odd sizes standing on the tables, unusual looking books which gave the impression that somebody with a very unusual taste inhabited the room."

It was a practical working library, dating back to the moment in the summer of 1922 when Pearl took a first tentative step toward cutting her life free. She was in Kuling with her daughter and her sister, spending the season in the Sydenstricker house for the first time without their mother: "I remember quite clearly one August afternoon that I said suddenly, 'This very day I am going to begin to write. I am ready for it at last.'" What she wrote was a couple of magazine articles. It was no accident that she chose them in retrospect to mark her debut as a writer rather than the far more original, book-length typescript she had just finished about her mother. One was a private act of exorcism, the others were thoroughly professional; slick, chatty, formulaic pieces of a type churned out in industrial quantity for the Western market, remarkable in Pearl's case only because of their unusual content. "In China Too" is a first attempt to articulate her experiences in Anhui, written in the first person by a fictionalized version of herself—the mild, inoffensive, prematurely middleaged self she was currently projecting in Nanjing—stationed on the veranda of her old house in Nanxuzhou to watch the passing traffic on the street below:

> In the early morning blue-coated farmers, and sometimes their sturdy barefoot wives, come to town carrying on either end of their shoulderpoles great round baskets of fresh dewy vegetables, or huge bundles of dried grass for fuel; caravans of tiny, neat-footed donkeys patter past, with enormous cylindrical bags of flour or rice crossed upon their backs, swayed down from excessive burdens borne too early. Sometimes their nostrils have been slit so that they may pant more rapidly under the weight of their cruel loads. Wheelbarrows squeak shrilly along . . . [carrying] anything, from a lean, itinerant missionary with a six weeks' supply of bedding, food and tracts, to a double basket of squawking fowls—geese, perhaps, with yards

of neck protruding from the loosely woven reeds, and viewing the passing landscape excitedly.

The tone is light, the material comical and picturesque but sharply observed, an outsider's view of material Pearl would explore from inside in *The Good Earth*. The subject is undercurrents of change beginning to stir even in this remote and stagnant backwater. "In China Too" evokes a world wholly alien to the new breed of Chinese Pearl met for the first time in Nanjing: ultramodern, Western-educated faculty members who lived in carpeted and curtained two-storey houses, go-ahead young men and their fashionable wives with bobbed hair, unbound feet, and short-sleeved, tight-fitting satin dresses, a generation looking firmly to a future that took no account of the intractable realities of rural life. Flood, drought, pestilence, and crop failure had no place in this brave new urban world. In her second winter in Nanjing, the famine winter of 1920–21, Pearl's new friends responded with blank disbelief to talk of starvation in the countryside. None of them could be persuaded to leave their cosmopolitan comfort zone and climb the city wall, where thousands of refugees from the surrounding villages huddled without food in makeshift shelters. "I saw such things in Chicago slums," one young Chinese sociologist told Pearl smugly, "but I am sure they are not here."

"In China Too" was published in the *Atlantic Monthly* in January 1924 and immediately followed by a commission for another article from the editor of *Forum*. "Beauty in China," published two months later, is a second helping of highly colored travelogue containing in the middle a double-sided snapshot of the view from Mount Lushan that looks in retrospect like a statement of intent:

The other day I stood on a mountain top in Kiangsi. I looked over a hundred miles of lovely Chinese country. Streams glittered in the sunshine; the Yangtse wound its leisurely way along, a huge yellow roadway to the sea; clusters of trees cuddled cosily about little thatched villages; the rice fields were clear jade green and laid as neatly as patterns in a puzzle. It seemed a scene of peace and beauty.

And yet I know my country well enough to know that if I could have dropped into the midst of that fair land I should have found the streams polluted, the river's edge crowded with little, wretched, mat-covered boats, the only homes of millions of miserable, underfed water folk. The villages under the trees would be crowded and filthy with flies and garbage rotting in the sun, and the ubiquitous yellow curs would have snarled at my coming. . . . The homes would be small and windowless and as dark within as caverns.

The first of these pieces dramatizes the shock of exposure to sophisticated Nanjing, where Pearl became a professional writer. The second identifies an area of unmapped territory impossible to explore in the stylized and predigested format of a mass-market magazine. Pearl said it was publication of both articles in the United States that gave her confidence to start thinking about something more ambitious. By her own account she kept her project secret—"It was natural to me to tell no one about the novel. . . . I had no friends or relatives to whom I could speak about my writing"—but Lossing seems to have had a shrewd suspicion of where his wife was heading almost before she knew herself. "I am very proud of her," he reported to his parents on February 18, 1923, "and I also am looking forward to the time when she will have a book out on China. It will be different than anything that has ever been published, and I will guarantee it to be interesting." Lossing correctly predicted that the book would need years of preparation before it could actually be written. Pearl began her secret writing life by constructing a work space of her own in the living room, big enough to hold her desk and her upright piano, which now had a redwood screen mounted on the back, carved for her by the local carpenter with handsome and protective dragons.

Nanjing was full of symbolic guardians like these, ranging from the dragons and lions watching over private gateways to the majestic phalanx of stone beasts lining the ceremonial approach to the imperial tomb on Purple Mountain. In spite of the coming of the railway and the modern enclave formed by its two new universities, China's ancient capital, with its decayed palaces, its temples, gardens, and pagodas, still belonged, when Pearl first settled there, to a world moving at the pace of the walker and the wheelbarrow. In five hundred years the city had shrunk inside its imposing wall, twenty-five miles around and sixty feet high, built by the fourteenth-century Ming emperor to be the biggest in the world, and still broad enough for four modern motorcars to drive abreast along the top. For her visitors Pearl organized excursions, boating parties on Lotus Lake, and picnics among the ruined splendors of Purple Mountain. But her own preference was to walk alone at night through narrow, noisy, cobbled streets filled with piles of refuse, goods for sale, and people drinking tea in front of their little, low, close-packed houses lit by bean-oil lamps. She said it was where any true novelist felt happiest: "His place is in the street."

Back in her American world Pearl became an interpreter in Nanjing, as she had been in Nanxuzhou, translating the country and its people for Westerners demoralized as much by the sheer inscrutability of Chinese life as by its sights and smells. "She made things so much easier for us," said Margaret Bear, newly married to Pearl's childhood friend from Zhenjiang, James Bear junior, himself starting out on a mission career by taking a six-month language course from a base in the Bucks' house. "I was a little homesick bride," said Margaret. "James had been born there . . . but the cultural shock for me was just awful." Cholera and smallpox were rife. Waste choked the gutters. The town's vegetable and flower gardens were manured daily with human night soil ("when they watered there, we just thought we would die"). Pearl spent much time sorting out the problems of new arrivals like the Bears, and her old college friend Emma Edmunds, now Mrs. Locke White, who reached Nanjing with her missionary husband and two small children in 1922. Many of their difficulties with the Chinese boiled down to blank incomprehension on each side of the other's expectations and assumptions.

Faculty members who consulted Pearl learned to trust her ingenious and surprisingly effective advice on questions of man management ("We depended on her for solutions that only a Chinese might understand or appreciate," said Helen Daniels, the doctor's wife). She gave talks at the Language School explaining the intricacies of an alien social system and pointing out that what looked to Westerners like filthy local habits had their counterparts in behavior no less disgusting to the Chinese: the loud laughter, braying voices, and indecently tight clothing of Western women; the men's uninhibited expression of bad temper; the used handkerchiefs full of snot kept in their pockets by both sexes. Pearl cut through the layers of ignorance and prejudice that made foreigners routinely stigmatize their Chinese employees as greedy, lazy, or dishonest. "She was always on the side of giving more and more opportunity to the people around her," said Lilliath Bates, another campus wife profoundly impressed by Pearl's insistence on dismantling racial stereotypes. "After you meet people, and learn more about them . . . and realize what they have come through, and how much character there is underneath there, you don't judge them by the same standards. . . . It's a change in us really, in our attitudes towards people."

Pearl had shed forever the categorical certainties of her upbringing. Even her religion now inclined to tolerance and inclusiveness. "Theologically she was miles away from where her parents and the rank and file of the missionaries were," said James Bear, who enjoyed long heretical arguments with Pearl about the historical credentials of the Bible, and whether Jesus Christ could be classed as more than a great teacher, like Confucius. Chinese people had been telling Pearl their stories for as long as she could remember, and in these years she became steadily more attentive. Her American neighbors were often disconcerted not just by her habit of eating peanuts in the street but by her long talks with the peanut seller or the rickshaw puller, whose family lived in a dilapidated shack beyond her house. The vigorous uninhibited kitchen life confined to servants' quarters at the back of other people's houses spilled out, in Pearl's, to a whole settlement of families in her courtyard. "That part of the household was as Chinese as the world beyond the walls," said Margaret Thomson. "I can see the women squatting, sewing or weeding or drying their cabbages." Pearl listened to the family tailor (whose story she eventually published as "The Frill") and to the gardener's wife, struggling to feed a growing family in a mud hut clamped against the Bucks' side wall, with no help from a gambling husband who fathered another unwanted baby every ten or twelve months. At a time when her own small child made her more than usually aware of other mothers, Pearl paid particular attention to malnourished infants, making up bottles of formula for both the gardener's wife and the rickshaw puller's. "I think I never felt so touched and ashamed in my life," said Margaret Thomson, who came back from a summer holiday to find the rickshaw man's new baby—so skeletal and sickly she had thought best to let it die—grown plump and healthy thanks to Pearl's daily bottles.

Pearl even had a single mother in her henhouse, a northerner with bound feet whose absconding husband had been the Bucks' gardener in Nanxuzhou, and who turned up pregnant, destitute and desperate on their doorstep one winter soon after they reached Nanjing. "'I came to you,' the woman said with touching and I must say annoying naiveté, 'I have no one else.'" Stoutly refusing all offers of practical assistance—a hospital delivery, a room in the Bucks' house—Lu Sadze insisted on giving birth alone in the chicken shed, scrubbed out and whitewashed with a new brick floor and basic furnishings supplied by Pearl. She had already borne five babies, all of whom died of tetanus at or soon after birth. The new one, known as Little Meatball on account of his voracious appetite for life, had to be twice nursed back to health by Pearl as a result of his mother's drastic hit-or-miss approach to child rearing (at one point she doused him by mistake in iodine, at another she accidentally inflicted severe ammonia burns). He died anyway as a toddler, and Mrs. Lu's next pregnancy, the result of rape by a soldier from one of the many warlord armies prowling the country in those years, ended in a brutal self-inflicted abortion that almost killed the mother too. Pearl found her just in time for the hospital to save her from death by septicemia. When Mrs. Lu eventually recovered, her destiny was inextricably bound up with Pearl's—at any rate in her own mind: "She declared that her life was mine and, though there were times when I wished it belonged to anyone else but me, for she was an opinionated, devoted, loud-voiced person, yet I knew her loyalty."

It was like being linked to a human tank. Indestructible and unstoppable, Mrs. Lu saw every obstacle as an opportunity to do battle, whether it was occupying the Bucks' henhouse, scouring out their living room, or commandeering their lives. Graduating smoothly from running errands and doing odd jobs to acting as amah and housekeeper, she became the backbone of the Buck household and later, when Pearl finally left China, of the Thomsons' too. "This illiterate woman fast revealed much brain-power, super loyalty and a will of iron," wrote the Harvard historian James C. Thomson, Margaret's youngest child, who was largely brought up by Lu Sadze ("my second mother and Pearl's best legacy to me"). Her inexhaustible reserves of energy and endurance, her inarticulacy, the simplicity and force of her underlying vision fed directly into Olan in *The Good Earth* (whose first childbirth closely reproduces Meatball's home delivery). Memories of her abortion initially inspired *The Mother*, which Pearl began writing immediately afterward.

As a novelist Pearl returned to her roots: "It is the Chinese and not the American novel which has shaped my own efforts in writing. My earliest knowledge of . . . how to tell and write stories came to me in China." The books strewn about the Nanjing living room were the novels she had first encountered as a child and now read or reread as an adult, systematically devouring all the texts she could lay hands on, using their vitality and power to charge the batteries of her own imagination. The novel in China had always been a popular form, "wild stuff," subversive, capricious and capacious, traditionally despised and at times actively prohibited by a powerful literary establishment that excluded fiction from the classical artistic canon. The word for story, *hsiao shuo*, meant something small and worthless ("even a novel was only a *ts'ang p'ien hsiao shuo*, or a longer something which was still slight and useless"), Missionaries, who learned Chinese exclusively by studying the classics, regarded the vernacular novel as crude, degraded, and "notoriously filthy."

Pearl discovered for herself the breadth, diversity, and depth of Chinese novels, their bluntness and vigor, their ability to grip and hold an audience by unselfconsciously reflecting the danger, drama, and the familiar everyday commotion of the world they came from. She said that the greatest novels—*The Dream of the Red Chamber, The Romance of Three Kingdoms,* and *All Men Are Brothers*—contained the imaginative development of a whole people, constantly renewed and kept alive by passing "not so often from hand to hand as from mouth to mouth" through storytellers. Pearl's reading in these years was part of an idiosyncratic creative writing program. "Only a person with a free, untrammeled mind could have prepared herself thus," wrote Alice Hobart, who had been amazed to find Pearl exploring China in the mirror of her fiction. "Mrs. Buck had come to the original, not to say apostate conclusion that the real Chinese is not in the classics. . . . Sitting in her living-room with the cries of the city reaching her faintly over her compound wall . . . she read the novels of China one by one, peering with the keenest pleasure and increasing curiosity into a mass of story stuff accumulated through the ages."

She also read voraciously the latest works by her own contemporaries, short books pouring from small presses in cheap paperback: "I could buy a basketful for a dollar or so and read for days." In the years she had been away, undergoing reeducation from villagers in the country around Nanxuzhou, the language battles had been won. *Pai-hua,* the common speech of ordinary people, had finally achieved government backing as the national language. Contemporary literature was now an open field, no longer fenced off by the scholars who had monopolized and policed the culture because, as Pearl said, "they alone knew how to read and write." What was derisively called the "rickshaw-coolie school" of writers experimented recklessly in all directions, opening up forbidden territory, defying ancient taboos, exploring themselves and their problems with an unprecedented directness that appalled and alarmed their elders. Romantic outpourings, based more or less superficially on European models, acquired in China the force of a call to arms. The new school's imitation of Western forms might be shaky and repetitive, but Pearl responded unreservedly to the energy and freshness of their perceptions: "they provided for me the clearest mirror of the world we then shared, and through them and their books I understood what otherwise might have been inexplicable."

Literary revolution was closely linked to political upheaval. Anger at the growing threat of Japanese aggression had exploded at the end of World War I, when former German territories in Shandong were handed over by the victorious European Allies to Japan instead of China. Disillusionment with Western treachery and opportunism produced a spontaneous wave of strikes and student demonstrations, driving dissident young idealists toward the Marxist-Leninist prototype offered by the Russian Revolution. Hope for the future lay with New Youth (the journal of that name became a Communist organ, distributed by the young Mao Zedong in his first job for the Party), New Culture, and a New Language for New People. For most intellectuals it was not the tiny, still amateurish Chinese Communist Party but Sun Yatsen's reorganized and rapidly expanding, Russian-backed Nationalist Party that claimed allegiance. Education became a priority at all levels. Nanjing's Southeastern University was a former teacher-training college relaunched as a government flagship school in 1921. Bold, forward-looking, and fiercely competitive, Southeastern became the first Chinese university to admit women students, to appoint a woman dean, and to teach natural sciences. Pearl far preferred it to the missionaries' wealthier and better equipped institution, whose comfortable, conservative, all-male student body responded more predictably than the mixed-sex crowd urgently seeking free tuition at Southeastern.

Hungry, cold, hard-up, they packed into her English courses in huge, bare, unheated classrooms with sand sifting on north winds in winter through ill-fitting door frames and around the edges of paper pasted at the unglazed windows. Their English was inadequate, sometimes almost nonexistent, but their keenness often stopped her leaving at the end of class: "I learned far more from them than from the suave and acquiescent men students in the Christian university. I came away frozen with cold in my body but warm in my heart and stimulated in mind because between me and those eager young students, so thinly clad and barely fed, there were no barriers. They wanted to talk about everything in the world, and we talked." Ten years later she put them into *A House Divided,* where one of Wang Lung's grandsons also teaches literature at the same university: "Yuan, wrapped in his great-coat, stood before his shivering pupils and corrected their ill-written essays and with the sandy wind blowing through his hair he set upon the blackboard rules for them on writing poetry. But it was nearly use-less, for all their minds were bent on huddling in their clothes, which were for many too scanty in spite of their huddling." Like Wang Yuan, Pearl came to feel affection as well as respect for these children of small shopkeepers, teachers, or merchants and the few bright village boys who had overcome almost impossible odds to get there, and who now strained to understand texts and concepts hopelessly beyond their level of formal preparation.

Students like these wander in and out of Pearl's early fiction, driven by an often inarticulate hunger for knowledge, some burning with desire for change, others stunned by the hopelessness of trying sin-glehandedly to overthrow cultural taboos entrenched for centuries. All her life Pearl had watched young men desperate for an education coming to her parents' house in Zhenjiang, where her father taught them what he could before sending them on their way to the theologi-cal seminary he had helped found in Nanjing. Absalom Sydenstricker, like his daughter, believed passionately in democratic access to the means of learning and communication. "*Wen-li* is a dead language, like mediaeval Latin, inflexible . . . vague . . . inexact," he wrote, protesting already in 1900 against the continued use of a language 90 percent of the population could neither read nor understand. He angrily refuted charges that the vernacular was intrinsically undignified and degrad-ing. "A form of language spoken by millions of people . . . can surely not be called undignified," he argued, finding "real dignity . . . in the colloquial language of the people, not in the stilted artificial style of books." The same accusations were made in his daughter's day against the "rickshaw-coolie school" by a group of Nanjing professors, whose last-ditch rearguard action was ably demolished by Pearl's old mentor, Hu Shi, himself now one of Beijing's most influential academics. In Pearl's view, Hu's own writing proved that the spoken word could be turned into "a beautifully clear and graceful written language, flexible and alive, expressing the most profound meaning and thought."

Pearl herself said that she spoke and thought in *pai-hua* more readily than she did in English. It was the language of her early stories, which she transposed into English in her head only when she came to put them down on paper. The first story she ever published as Pearl S. Buck—"The Clutch of the Ancients," about a young student bitterly conscious that the knowledge he craves will always be beyond his reach—was subtitled in the *Chinese Recorder* in September 1924, "A Translation and Interpretation from the Chinese." This method, peculiar to Pearl, practiced and perfected during her Nanjing years, made her fiction in some ways closer to that of her Chinese than her American contemporaries. Its strangeness was immediately apparent to Western readers. "The beautiful cadences of *East Wind West Wind*," one critic wrote of her first novel, "are the direct result of Pearl Buck's having *written* in English while *thinking* in *Chinese*."

PEARL WAS BEGINNING to live in her imagination with an intensity that cut her off even from those closest to her. The only person she knew with literary tastes was Margaret Thomson from next door, whose writing was a hobby that aimed no higher than occasional pieces for the local English press. Lossing's enthusiasm was genuine but limited. He knew nothing about books ("Pearl didn't think he read *anything*," said Emma White), and was in any case increasingly preoccupied by the demands of a fast-growing university department that took everything he had to give. Nanjing Agricultural College had been founded specifically to lead the way in the new postrevolutionary China, and Lossing's first move was to draw up with the college head, John Reisner, an ambitious plan for research and rural reconstruction. He published a seed catalogue for distributing improved varieties throughout the country and instituted programs to investigate all relevant factors, from implements and farm size to crop distribution and soil erosion. His hands-on approach, in its way as radical as the parallel literary revolution, astounded students who had grown up with an immemorial gulf fixed between the scholar and any form of manual labor. "They not only knew nothing about their own country people, they did not even know how to talk to them or address them," wrote Pearl, who became increasingly uneasy over the next few years about the automatic, ingrained contempt of young left-wing intellectuals for ordinary workers and peasants.

Lossing taught his students that firsthand practical experience of farm conditions was their only hope of introducing scientific method to farmers who traditionally blamed malevolent spirits for blight or pests, and whose standard recourse was to consult their paper gods. "If you want to improve it, you should understand it," became his catchphrase. He himself regularly visited the country to talk to farmers, inspect their crops, and ask questions about what they planted and how it grew. "He came alone and ate and lived in farmers' homes," said one of his first students, who introduced his teacher to the villagers of his own home region in 1923 and accompanied him on a return visit the year after. "They were surprised that the foreigner seemed to know more about local agriculture than they did themselves." He established China's first Department of Agricultural Economics, which grew from an initial group consisting of Lossing himself and two students in 1921 to a staff that numbered over sixty ten years later, with a team of one hundred working on his nationwide land-use survey. "He introduced the discipline to China in all its aspects: teaching, research and public service," said the *American Journal of Agricultural Economics* in 1976.

From the start he set the pace for other institutions ("They are feeling that we should go out of business and trying to get our men from us," he reported of Southeastern in 1922). He pioneered extension courses for local farmers and set up specialist teams to provide crisis management in times of flood or famine. A windfall grant in 1923, when the China Famine Fund donated two-thirds of a million-dollar surplus to promote Buck's work in Nanjing, was followed by even more substantial funding from American and British sources. By the early 1930s, when the college played an increasingly important role in Nationalist government policy, Buck's long-term vision, practical organizing ability, and gift for teamwork were generally acknowledged as a driving force. He published papers, gave lectures, attended conferences, and spent his vacations traveling to remote rural areas all over China. He was often absent on business or away working in his office, and even when he was there visitors remembered him as a largely silent presence in his own home. "I don't think he had any intimate friends," said his boss's wife, Bertha Reisner. "He was so absorbed in his own interests and his own doings. . . . He did a very good job in his own field, he concentrated on it, that was his whole life."

The lack of common ground between Lossing and his wife was plain to see. "He wasn't Pearl's type at all," said Bertha Reisner. "I think he was really uninterested in her. He didn't understand her, nor she him." "They never should have married," said Lilliath Bates, dismayed by Lossing's insensitivity in dealings with his wife. He treated her as he might have a farmer's wife whose functions were strictly practical—to work hard, save money, and take care of cooking, cleaning, and child rearing—and whose further needs were no concern of his. She responded by withdrawing into herself, ceasing to care what she looked like and putting on weight as she had done in her last year of college. At the time of their courtship and marriage she had been strikingly pretty, with fair skin, blonde hair set off by blue-green eyes, and the kind of curvy figure flattered by the fashions of the day. But by 1922 even Pearl's faithful friend Emma White was taken aback by her size. A young Chinese colleague remembered a large frumpy Mrs. Buck teaching freshman courses at Southeastern. To young Margaret Bear, Pearl looked "like a bag of meal with a string tied round the middle. She was perfectly enormous, and she'd be all curled up in this big chair reading. . . . She just threw her hair up anyhow, and her belt looked like a string tied round a bag."

Pearl was perfectly aware of how she looked to other people, and especially to the Chinese. In "A Chinese Woman Speaks," a long story or novella written in the summer of 1924, the young Chinese narrator catches sight for the first time of a female foreigner, who might well be Pearl herself: "she wore a long cotton gown instead of trousers and had a flat string about her middle. Her hair was . . . smooth and straight, although of an unfortunate yellow color. She also had a very high nose . . . and large hands with short square nails. I looked at her feet and saw that they were like rice-flails for size." The story is full of private jokes with melancholy undertones like this one. The Chinese woman of the title, exquisitely groomed with perfumed hair, polished fingernails, and tiny feet, responds to the foreigner with baffled pity: "How could a man desire such women as that one . . . ? Such light flat eyes and faded hair, such coarse hands and feet?" But she too has a painful history of sexual rejection by a young Chinese husband, scientifically minded and trained as a Western doctor, who accepts the marriage arranged for him by traditionalist parents but devastates his bride by delivering a stern homily on gender equality, and refusing to consummate a union forced on both of them by an unjust and tyrannical society. The fiasco of their wedding night neatly parodies the steamy marital rapes of Western fiction—"I ran to the door, thinking in my wildness that I might escape and return to my mother's home"—ending with the helpless, terrified, and untouched young wife crying herself to sleep alone in the marital bed.

Over the next months she tries unsuccessfully to attract the attention of a husband worn out by his daily battle to impose rational modern solutions on problems caused by China's legacy of superstition and obsolete belief. Her own struggles against bewilderment and neglect take place in a house clearly based on the Bucks' Nanjing home, with china doorknobs she can't turn, steep stairs she can't climb, scratchy unsightly basket chairs impossible to sit in, and thick cumbersome squares of woolen carpet that can't be shaken out or spat on. Accustomed to the padded silk surfaces, protective screens, and subtly filtered lighting of her Chinese home, she feels cruelly exposed in a Western world as bleak and comfortless as the white walls, slippery polished floors, and harsh glaring sunlight pouring through the clear glass windows of her living room. "A Chinese Woman Speaks" is a light-handed comedy of errors, false assumptions, and reversed expectations played out between its Oriental narrator and its Western reader. On another level it is also a poignant projection of Pearl's own marriage, exploring an alternative fictional self who spends long solitary days preparing for her husband's return from work, experimenting with face creams, hair ornaments, and carefully planned outfits: "His eyes escape hastily to other things—his letters upon the table, his book. I am forgotten." She fills the house with flowers he never notices, prepares bowls of fragrant tea he leaves untouched, and serves delicious dishes he doesn't even taste: "I tried no longer therefore. There is nothing that my husband desires of me. He has no need of anything I can give him." Defeat turns to triumph in a final fairy-tale reversal, when the husband turns to his wife in a wonderfully suggestive image, "like the river in spring-time flowing richly into the canals empty with the drought of winter."

Pearl herself found no comparable relief at this point in or outside her marriage. Many of the magazine stories she wrote in the 1920s (collected later in *The First Wife and Other Stories*) end with suicide, sexual bondage, or total loss of hope. The central characters in two of them kill themselves to escape from loveless marriages; in a third an elderly woman unwanted by her family threatens to do the same. Pearl's own dissatisfaction, dimly sensed between the lines of her account of her mother's problems in *The Exile*, seems to have taken clearer shape after her father moved in with the Bucks in 1923. His presence shifted the balance of the household. Absalom Sydenstricker had never thought much of Lossing, and now made sure that his views were public knowledge. "When Dr. Sydenstricker lived with Pearl, we all knew he had considerable contempt for Lossing," said Bertha Reisner. "The whole community knew he had not approved of Pearl's husband." The two met only at meals, where each pointedly avoided speaking to the other. It was a tricky situation, given that Absalom was technically a guest in Lossing's house. Open clashes were avoided, at least to start with, by Pearl's tact and skill in managing her father. "It did not occur to him that he might not be the head of any house in which he lived," she wrote dryly in her memoirs. "The illusion was not lessened by the unfortunate fact that he did not like his son-in-law, and made no bones about letting me know it by considerable I-told-you-so conversation, which only my deepening affection for him and sense of humor made endurable."

The need to bolster his own superiority by sniping at someone else came in part at least from extreme humiliation. Absalom's last eighteen months in Zhenjiang after his wife died had been disastrous. Once Carie was no longer there to reason with him behind the scenes and defend him in public against his critics, the obstinacy and highhandedness that had for decades provoked his colleagues almost beyond bearing proved his undoing. Questions were raised about lack of transparency, chronic mismanagement of funds, and irregularities bordering on fraud. Money donated by an American benefactor for a memorial chapel had been diverted by Sydenstricker to finance projects of his own. Deeds of another chapel on his circuit had mysteriously ended up in the possession of its native pastor. A third had been used as the headquarters of an opium ring. Charges were laid and evidence produced. He could give no coherent explanation of the conduct of his Chinese helpers, who not only hijacked his chapels for unauthorized and sometimes flagrantly illicit purposes, but systematically helped themselves to bonuses in cash and kind. The case against him had been painstakingly built up over many years. "The North Kiangsu Mission has no place for free lancers or free lance work," declared an official report containing, as far back as 1915, an unmistakable warning to Sydenstricker that routine defiance of mission policy would not be tolerated forever. "No mission should grow by the coral reef method, each person adding what he wants, and when and where he wants it. A mission should not permit . . . the determination of a strong-headed man to veer the bark from its true course."

Absalom, who had always considered it beneath him to account for sums entrusted to him by the church, saw no need to change his tactics. "He went his way, serene and confident, secure in the knowledge of his own rightness," wrote Pearl. "I never saw him in undignified argument with others." From the point of view of the younger missionaries trying to repair the damage, he had very nearly wrecked their enterprise through credulity, poor judgment, and the certainty that his own motives were beyond human criticism. "Those meetings at the station were just a sheer agony to me," said his daughter Grace. "I can remember sitting there and hearing him on the verge of being put out . . . but nothing on earth would stop him." Feeling betrayed by his own kind, Absalom relied blindly on his Chinese followers, who had presented him at the start of his seventieth year with a gilded scroll, red silk banners, and a scarlet panoply on a pole. But once again his defective sense of other people let him down. He was definitively outmaneuvered a few days after his birthday by his brother missionaries. A new rule requiring compulsory retirement at the age of seventy—specifically aimed at Sydenstricker, who was the only missionary in North Kiangsu anywhere near this age limit— became official policy at the annual meeting in Kuling in August 1922. In her fictionalized version of her father's downfall in *The Time Is Noon* Pearl described him dragging himself home after his enforced resignation: "His lips were moving, and he made angry futile gestures like weak blows." He passed the winter "in a sort of stupor of dismay." Reviving in time to set out on his annual spring itineration, accompanied by the stout-hearted Ma Pangbo (who had been accused of corruption along with all the rest), he found his chapels and schools closed down, his native preachers dismissed and their congregations scattered. "Everything was gone—his whole life's work swept away." A minor stroke followed, either just before or soon after Pearl moved him with Grace into her house in Nanjing in April 1923.

This uprooting might have finished him off if Pearl had not, by sheer force of personality, obliged the reluctant seminary board to appoint him head of its correspondence department. "It was only by much contriving, infinite resourcefulness and great kindness that the whole thing was accomplished," wrote Grace, who, like Pearl, dreaded seeing their parents' forty years in China end in failure, disgrace, and death. It took diplomacy to persuade the authorities to offer their father a job, and even more to get him to accept it, but Absalom (who had initiated correspondence courses at the seminary many years before) was immediately at home in a university setting. He worked on his New Testament, preached on street corners, and gave the students keen attention, which they returned with interest. "All his life he rather wistfully admired handsome and clever young men," wrote Pearl. "Many handsome and clever young Chinese certainly did what they liked with him." He continued distributing money he couldn't afford, providing textbooks, paying tuition fees, even handing over his own warm clothes to favored students. Pearl darned his woolen underwear, patched his threadbare overcoat, and rescued him from scrapes as her mother had done before her with a patience that amazed her friends. All the neighbors grew familiar with Absalom's tall bony figure in a long black minister's coat, passing their houses every day without looking to left or right. "He wouldn't even see you," said Pearl's friend Ray Kelsey, whose husband, Dean, had been at Cornell with Lossing (it was at a picnic given by the Kelseys that the Bucks first met in Kuling). "I couldn't stand her father." All of them found him cold, hard, and overbearing. "I don't think anybody could show him affection," said Bertha Reisner. "No one could love *him*," said Ray Kelsey, who had known Carie Sydenstricker at Kuling and hotly resented the way she had been treated by her husband.

But Pearl developed unexpected solidarity with her father in the last ten years of his life. The two found common ground not simply in their mutual stubbornness and pride, nor even in their shared love for the Chinese people and their language. "He spoke Chinese as few white men ever do, with feeling and precision," Pearl wrote. "It came at last to be more native to him than his own tongue—he spoke it far more." Now that her brief uncharacteristic access of religious fervor had passed, leaving her as relaxed and skeptical as on the day she was received into the Church at the age of ten, she enjoyed an intellectual companionship with her father that her husband could not give. Like his daughter, Absalom had loved books all his life. "He had a remarkable mind, not scintillating but steady, penetrating, retentive," she wrote when he died. Pearl took walks with him by day and sat alone with him at night: "He talked more in those hours than he ever had before." According to Grace, who was living in the same house at the time, much of the material for *Fighting Angel* came from the countless evenings when Pearl asked questions and Absalom told her for the first time, with touching shamefaced shyness, stories of his childhood, his young manhood, and his marriage. "I put relentlessly aside Carie's side of the story," said Pearl, already adept at the biographer's bifocal vision. "His own memories . . . were quite unlike Carie's."

Absalom had begun his new life in Nanjing with a ruthless purge. Rejecting the big sunny room prepared for him by Pearl, he threw out curtains, cushions, and soft furnishings, together with his wife's picture and every other personal memento intended to make him feel at home, ending up with an iron bedstead in a small bare monk-like cell above the kitchen. He extended the same frugality to the memoirs he wrote at Pearl's suggestion. The two of them were the writers of the household—"I used to hear his old typewriter tapping uncertainly during hot afternoon hours when everyone else was sleeping"—but she was taken aback when he handed her twenty-five pages of typescript containing all that he considered worth recording. *Our Life and Work in China* is a factual record of his religious journey in the service of the Church, stripped of human interest and omitting all but perfunctory passing references to his wife and children (Carie's favorite son, Clyde, doesn't even rate a mention). Pearl could still be repelled by her father's dysfunctional otherworldliness. Lilliath Bates remembered her anger and distress over a chilling incident in Shanghai, when he announced that he had found the grave of his son Arthur and was puzzled by Pearl's question about the other two graves, having forgotten altogether the existence of his daughters Maude and Edith.

In time Pearl came to admire, perhaps even to envy her father's singleness of purpose: "He espoused early a cause in which he believed all his life without a shadow of doubt. Not even his own mind betrayed him. He had his mind in inexorable control." But what touched her was the serenity, even gaiety of his old age—"Being always perfectly happy, he had a charm about him"—and his fondness for disconcertingly simpleminded jokes, something he had always shared more readily with colleagues than he could with his own family ("Kill Sydenstricker!" went a favorite one-liner passed round the missionaries of North Kiangsu. "That is the only way to stop his jokes"). Pearl discovered in these years aspects of her father she had never previously suspected, and it changed her attitude to him as well as insidiously affecting her view of her husband. She understood the defensive origins of Absalom's fearful rigidity, while his childishness and helpless dependence appealed to the same maternal instincts aroused by her own little daughter.

Carol Buck had grown from an exceptionally beautiful baby into a boisterous child, sturdy and big for her age but restless and demanding, slow to learn, uncoordinated, and lacking in physical control. She played wild games with the neighbors' children, and she loved roughhousing with her father, rolling over and over, laughing and squealing on the sloping lawn below the house. She expressed her wants with jabbering and grunts, sniffing at visitors or jumping up at them like a dog. She had dry itchy skin, suffering from eczema so badly as a small child that her hands had to be bandaged night and day to stop her from scratching. Carol couldn't speak, and she responded blankly to things that made other children laugh or cry, but she knew enough to be fiercely jealous of the writing that drew her mother's attention like a magnet. The Bears remembered her throwing porridge or scooping earth from the potted plants in the living room to clog the keys of her mother's typewriter.

Lossing sometimes tried to control the child, but Pearl could not bear to see her disciplined, nor was she convinced by her husband's cheerful insistence that he and his three brothers had all been late talkers. Pragmatic and unflappable, he accepted his daughter's limitations more easily than was possible for Pearl, who compared Carol to her friends' babies and was cruelly conscious that some mothers kept their children away from hers. Even Emma White found being with Pearl's daughter too upsetting for her two children, who were almost the same age. The young Thomsons and Reisners fooled about happily with Carol, but their mothers could not give the reassurance Pearl longed to hear. All her Nanjing friends recognized long before she did that something was seriously wrong. "I was to have nearly four years of happy ignorance about her," wrote Pearl, who had learned very young how to ignore warning signals and look away from things too dreadful to contemplate. "She was three years old when I first began to wonder."

It took yet more time before Pearl could bring herself to go into action. "I was reluctant and unbelieving until the last." The Bucks rented a beach house in the summer of 1924 at the popular seaside resort of Peitaho (Beidaihe) on China's northern coast so that Lossing could visit farmers in Manchuria while his wife and child swam or paddled and hired ponies to ride along the sand. At a talk given by a visiting American pediatrician from Beijing, Pearl recognized her daughter's symptoms and arranged for the lecturer and two other doctors to examine Carol at her house the next day. She retained forever a mental snapshot of Carol coming in from the beach that morning, sturdy and brown in a white swimsuit with a bucket in her hand, outlined against the sun like Carie on the first page of *The Exile*. "In spite of my terror, I was proud of my child as she stood before the doctors." They refused to make a specific diagnosis but advised an immediate return to the United States for consultations. The Bucks went back to Nanjing, where Ray Kelsey remembered Pearl clinging to her in tears, unable to say anything but "What am I going to do? Oh God, God! *What am I going to do?*"

The family crossed the Pacific by Empress liner in late summer. It was on this ship that Pearl wrote "A Chinese Woman Speaks," dashing it down quickly in free moments in the dining salon on fifty sheets of ship's notepaper. The story was a way of escaping from her own predicament, while at the same time reflecting one aspect of it in a Chinese looking-glass, and on arrival she forgot all about her manuscript. They headed for Ithaca, New York, where Lossing, who was on sabbatical, planned to take a master's degree in agricultural economics at Cornell. He got down to work in lodgings near the campus, while Pearl set out alone with their daughter on a round of visits to specialists in every discipline that might conceivably be relevant. The verdict eventually delivered after exhaustive tests at the Mayo Clinic in Rochester, Minnesota, was that the child was physically in good shape but mentally impaired for no known reason, and that nothing could be done to help her. The consultant advised Pearl kindly not to give up trying. She was thankful ever after to a small, unprepossessing clinician speaking broken English who intercepted her on the way out to urge her not to fool herself: "You will wear out your life and beggar your family unless you give up hope and face the truth. This child will be a burden to you all your life. Get ready to bear that burden."

She never forgot his words—"I suppose the shock photographed them upon my memory"—which shaped her future, both as a woman and as a writer. It would be another quarter of a century before scientists finally identified Carol's condition (she was suffering from phenylketonuria, or PKU, brain degeneration caused by inability in the newborn child to process a chemical called phenyl, a deficiency that can be treated only if detected in its early stages). Pearl said that, although she struggled against the knowledge, she recognized deep down that the man was right because she had already unconsciously given up hope. Long afterward she compared the impact of this blow to deep internal bleeding, tearing flesh, a "monstrous ache of the heart which becomes physical and permeates bone and muscle." In her fictional account in *The Time Is Noon* she wrote that at bedtime on that first night she felt "as though she were laying herself down to die by her own hand."

Pearl rejoined her husband in two small rented rooms in a minister's house in Ithaca. Irrational guilt and a sense of her own failure as a mother gave a kind of dreary horror to the unfamiliar landscape of gray water and snow-covered hills, heightened by American Indian legends that the lakes around Ithaca were bottomless. She sought oblivion in punitive, mind-numbing drudgery. Looking after Carol for the first time without an amah, cooking, cleaning, washing, and shopping for a family of three on the single modest salary that was all they had now that she herself was no longer teaching, meant hard physical labor and stringent economy. The budget could be stretched to cover a single small cheap weekly cut of meat on top of their staple diet: a loaf of bread, a quart of milk, and one egg a day each for Carol and Lossing. A local farmer stocked the cellar with a cartload of potatoes, onions, carrots, and apples that had to last the winter. Otherwise their only other regular expense was the money paid to a neighbor to take care of Carol in the hours when Pearl was away, attending classes in English literature. "I felt it wise to plunge into some sort of absorbing mental effort that would leave me no time to think of myself," she wrote, explaining her decision to enroll in a master's degree program like her husband. She fit her studying into free hours in the college library late at night, after Carol had been put to bed.

Everything she did or planned from now on was subordinate to Carol's needs. Even her longing for another child reawakened only when a doctor suggested that a companion might help to stimulate her daughter. She persuaded Lossing that they should adopt a baby from a small private orphanage attached to the church that acted as his sponsor, the Second Presbyterian of Troy, New York. From the twenty babies available, laid out in their dormitory in rows of cribs, Pearl chose a tiny, bald, severely malnourished infant with a misshapen ear (pushed forward rather than flat against the skull because the child had lain for weeks on the same side), who refused to eat and had added nothing in three months to her birth weight of seven pounds. Ignoring professional advice not to waste time on a dying child, Pearl recognized stubbornness in her new daughter as well as a neediness that matched her own. Janice repaid her by taking to the bottle as soon as they got home, starting the long, slow, uneven process of rebuilding Pearl's confidence in herself as a mother. The despair she felt did not lessen, but it became more manageable as she filled her life with barriers against it—studying for a degree, housekeeping on a shoestring with no human or mechanical help, the full-time care of two difficult and damaged children under five.

She started writing again for the same reason, driven by the family's precarious finances. Lossing taught Sunday school in lieu of rent, but tuition, fees, winter clothes, and mounting bills were more than he could manage. Pearl got out her shipboard story, tidied it up, and sent it to the editor of *Asia* magazine, who wrote back in June 1925, offering a fee of one hundred dollars and publication the following spring. Acceptance of "A Chinese Woman Speaks" launched her professionally as a fiction writer, but without the thrill produced by her articles in the *Atlantic* and *Forum* the year before. Success was now no more than a side effect of financial desperation. She attempted a sequel but abandoned it to concentrate on the Laura L. Messenger Memorial Prize, awarded for the best historical essay "in the field of human progress" and worth $250 to the winner, always in practice if not in theory a male history major. An experienced strategist ever since her days as a child prize-winner on the Shanghai *Mercury,* Pearl had researched the student award situation shrewdly—"Quite cold-bloodedly I asked which was the largest"—and her assessment of what the Messenger judges wanted was spot on. She won with a long, scholarly, cogently argued analysis, "China and the West," which articulated for the first time the hard-hitting positions she would take later on the achievements and failures of the mission movement, and the imperialist and racist implications of American foreign and domestic policy. It gave her the impetus to finish her second story, which *Asia* immediately accepted. "I got back my faith in myself, which was all but gone in the sorry circumstances of my life."

"Endurance is only the beginning," Pearl wrote long afterward, explaining that learning to bear grief that cannot at first be borne has to be done alone. It was an atrocious education. In retrospect she divided it into stages, beginning with devastation and disintegration: "Despair so profound and absorbing poisons the whole system and destroys thought and energy." For Pearl it remained the underlying reality of her life long after the family left Cornell to return to China in the autumn of 1925. She could not share her feelings with Lossing, whose matter-of-fact acceptance of Carol's situation seemed only to intensify Pearl's guilt and apprehension. She tried to offload them instead by blaming him for not telling her about a history of similar problems in his family (in fact PKU can be inherited only from two parents each carrying the recessive gene, which means that both Pearl and Lossing must have been carriers). Her schedule became hectic. Every moment had to be accounted for: "guests always leaving or just coming, special meals, something always *doing,*" said Grace, who found it tiring even to contemplate the pressures of her sister's life.

Pearl could no longer listen to music. Routine claims on her attention—house, garden, plants, books, students, the company of friends—seemed null and pointless. "None of it meant anything," she said. She existed on the surface, struggling, like the dowager empress in a fictional biography she wrote thirty years later, to contain feelings that threatened to overwhelm her: "She was frantic with anger and anxiety and the discipline she enforced upon herself to hide what she felt, drained the strength from her very bones." Apart from her first outburst in Ray Kelsey's kitchen, none of her friends, not even Grace, saw her break down in tears. She said she kept her weeping for the hours she spent alone with Carol, which were also the only times when she felt herself truly alive. Absalom remained oblivious as usual. Ray felt it was Pearl's brother Edgar—by now an experienced statistician, invited by Lossing to accompany the Bucks back to Nanjing as a visiting lecturer—who became at this point "more like a father to Pearl."

The surface pleasures gradually returned—"Books, I remember, were the first"—but it was another fifteen years before Pearl recognized almost with surprise that rebellion had given way to a kind of resignation. "Agony has become static," she wrote grimly. It took longer still for her to be able to explore dispassionately the meaning of her daughter's life, and its impact on her own. "It is not shame at all," she told Emma, explaining why for years she could not talk about Carol, or even admit her existence to anyone but old friends. "I am sore to the touch there, and I cannot endure even the touch of sympathy."

The process of acceptance took place so deep within her that it left only faint external traces, even on her novels. Carol stands behind Wang Lung's disabled daughter in *The Good Earth,* and the girl in *The Mother* whose ceaseless scratching, whimpering, and red-rimmed eyes are discounted by her family until her mother realizes too late that the child has gone blind. Pearl's own state of mind is reflected as always most directly in the mother of the brain-damaged baby in *The Time Is Noon:* "She would sleep a little and wake in the morning stifled, as one might wake in a dense smoke, or under a heavy weight. Before she was well awake, dragging her mind upward out of sleep, she knew something was wrong—terror waited. Then she was awake and there the terror was, fresh and sharp and new with the morning."

INNER PERTURBATION WAS compounded by external tension in China in those years. When the Bucks received their degrees from Cornell in June 1925 the situation was too volatile for them to think of going straight home. The unexpected death of Sun Yatsen in March had sparked a gathering wave of protest and police repression. Perennially simmering fury against foreign economic and military domination erupted in extended strikes, trade boycotts, riots, and student demonstrations suppressed with extreme government brutality backed by Western battleships and machine guns. Hope and apprehension focused on the Nationalist headquarters in Guangzhou, where systematic preparations for armed conflict were in progress under a bold general and prime contender for the party's vacant leadership, Chiang Kaishek. The foreign community watched uneasily. "My own sympathies were entirely with the Chinese," wrote Pearl, who had set out in her Messenger prize essay the long history of coercion and aggression that lay behind the current turmoil. "The driving force . . . was a passionate desire to get rid of the foreigners who had fastened themselves upon China through trade and religion and war, and set up a government for the reform and modernization of their country."

Idealistic students from all over China poured into Guangzhou to join Chiang Kaishek's model army. The Nationalist Party, or Kuomintang, funded from Moscow and reorganized by Russian advisers along Soviet lines—"the same discipline, the same techniques of propaganda, and the same ruthless political commissars"—joined forces with the Chinese Communist Party in fragile, fractious alliance for the sole purpose of seizing power. The Bucks returned that autumn to a country once again on the verge of revolution. In November Nanjing became the capital of the eastern warlord General Sun Chuanfang, who would be defeated by the Nationalists a year later. Pearl sowed larkspur and snapdragons in her garden, and taught courses at Ginling Women's College as well as at both universities. Intellectually she felt closer to her earnest, argumentative Chinese students than to her American compatriots: "I was increasingly conscious of the years of separation from my own people. My childhood had not been theirs, nor theirs mine. . . . Under the life of everyday I knew that the old cleavage was deepening. My worlds were dividing, and the time would come when I would have to make a final choice between them."

In the sweltering summer of 1926 the Bucks did not join the general exodus of foreigners to Kuling. Lossing had farms to visit, and Pearl, always acutely aware of the gossip provoked in any new environment by her two small daughters, preferred to remain behind in her familiar Chinese world. This was the last of what she called the "Waiting Summers," when everyone knew that change was inevitable but no one could tell exactly when or how it would come. "It was difficult to know what was going on except from the Chinese newspapers which printed brief undigested items which had somehow to be connected by pondering and guessing, and then connected again with the grapevine of students' confidences and complaints." Pearl, who taught an extramural English course at home in the evenings, remembered sitting out on the terrace with her students to watch the moon rise over the pagoda beyond the garden wall. Temperatures of well over 100 were normal in these steamy, mosquito-ridden Yangtse lowlands. "You take Washington DC, and raise the temperatures several degrees, and you have Nanjing," said one of Lossing's colleagues. "You'd feel as if you had an iron band round your head and someone screwing it tighter every minute." In July the National Revolutionary Army began marching north from Guangzhou, invading one province after another, capturing cities and recruiting soldiers from the defeated or defecting troops of provincial warlords. Rumors of their legendary exploits preceded them. Chiang Kaishek's campaign relied as much on propaganda and psychological warfare as on military strategy: "all about the country and into every city there ran ahead of them and behind them and on every side of them the tales of their power and strength and never-failing victories," Pearl wrote years later in *A House Divided.* "The soldiers of the rulers, who were hirelings, ran before them like leaves before a bitter wind."

For all the difficulties between husband and wife, Pearl and Lossing agreed that China's best hope lay with the Nationalists. As civil war drew closer to Nanjing, both filled their time with work on their prospective books. Lossing had incorporated farm surveys as a core element in his students' practical training program, and was beginning to shape the resulting data into the text subsequently published as *Chinese Farm Economy*. Pearl, who had just published a short story called "Lao Wang, the Farmer," dramatizing the clash between ancient rural China and the modern Western world, was thinking about the kind of material that would eventually find its outlet in *The Good Earth*. She had been working on and off on a novel of one sort or another ever since she first read chapters to the literary club at Miss Jewell's School in Shanghai. Now she signaled more serious intentions by taking over a room of her own, under the gable in the attic with a window looking out over the garden, and the roofs of the city within its curving wall, to the double-crested peak of Purple Mountain. Here she retreated in spare moments snatched from her students and her household to work steadily all winter on a novel.

Westerners were warned to prepare for siege or flight. Bertha Reisner said she had already had her bags packed for a year or more. By December Nationalist armies controlled five key provinces in southern and central China. The two factions within their ranks split into rival camps, the Communists dominating a civilian government established at Wuhan in Hubei province, while Chiang Kaishek in Nanchang, nearly two hundred miles to the southeast, prepared to challenge Sun Chuanfang by marching on Nanjing and Shanghai. Refugees packed the Yangtse riverboats. Many missionaries headed for the coast, and some left China altogether. By the end of the winter there were nearly two dozen Western warships ready for action in the river at Shanghai. Lossing, who dreaded American military intervention more than Chinese battles — "we are living . . . in fear of what our own home government will do" — persuaded 127 Nanking missionaries to sign a telegram advising Washington that any use of force would be counterproductive. At the beginning of February 1927 the Bucks took in the family of Pearl's sister Grace, who had married a missionary three years earlier and moved to Yueyang in rural Hunan, one of the first provinces to be taken over by Communist cadres within the

Nationalist coalition. Grace and her husband, Jesse Yaukey, with one young baby and another on the way, had escaped like all the other foreigners, with only as much as they could carry. They brought reports of school closures, mass meetings, mob violence, the forcible redistribution of land, and the persecution of any Chinese caught associating with foreign imperialists. Militant students commandeered the Yaukeys' house, and the man who had helped transport their luggage to the river was paraded through the streets and jailed.

The rout of Sun Chuanfang, with the fall of Hangzhou later the same month, put Nanjing next in line as a battlefield for the northern warlords, united only by opposition to the southern armies. Security was tightened within the city. Actual or suspected revolutionaries disappeared from Pearl's classes at Southeastern. Lossing said his students were afraid to be seen on the streets for fear of having their heads chopped off. "All Bolshevist propaganda in Nanking has been put down with a firm hand by the government," a British missionary reported with approval on February 15. "A few student agitators from the government's Southeastern University have been executed and their heads have adorned the city gates." Pearl put these heads into another story, this time about a farmer named Wang Lung, bewildered by his first contact with young revolutionaries as he watches a jeering crowd collect on the Bridge of the Three Sisters in Nanjing: "There at the bridge, on seven bamboo poles, were seven bleeding heads, bent on ragged, severed necks; heads with fringes of black hair hanging over their dull, half-closed eyes. One head had its mouth open and its tongue thrust out, half-bitten off between set white teeth. . . . They were all the heads of very young men."

On the last day of February Nanjing was overrun by the soldiers of General Chang Chung Chang, a former bandit chief, currently military governor of Shandong, who took over the city and its hinterland from the defeated General Sun with an army fifty thousand strong. These were rough, fierce, dirty fighters living by ransack and pillage, "bandits in uniform," said Lossing. They came down from the north on foot, muleback, or shaggy little ponies, armed with whips, guns, swords, and sabers. Lossing watched a company of fifty foot soldiers marching down a narrow cobbled lane carrying long red-tasseled spears. Stalls vanished, shops closed, and streets emptied as they passed. "As soon as the people of Nanking surmised the change last Monday from Sun to Chang, the whole city was in a frenzy of fear of looting," wrote Lossing on March 6. "It is generally believed that the Nationalists will be here within a week or two. . . . With the coming of the Northern soldiers under General Chang Chung Chang anyone in Nanjing who was neutral or opposed to the Nationalists has turned in favor of them." The Nationalists were disciplined, highly motivated, and reasonably paid and could be counted on to restore order if they won the battle. Their leader had promised to protect foreign lives and property. The worst threat was the havoc likely to be caused by the defeated northerners being driven back through the city. "The people fear the Northern army as if they were great grey wolves," wrote one of Pearl's friends, Lillian Williams, wife of the vice president of Nanjing University, "because they loot and destroy and do unspeakable things. . . . The streets are full of these strange-looking Northern men, in grey clothes, with fur caps, with knives and bayonets and guns."

Pearl and Lossing debated whether to stay or go. Most other women with children had already left. By March 21 cannon could be heard booming in the distance. The U.S. consul warned all foreigners for the last time to leave the city. In the end the Bucks stayed put because Absalom, who had no intention of escorting his children and grandchildren to safety, fell ill at the last minute. "It was not conscious pretence—it was an actual disturbance caused by the distress of not having his own way," wrote Pearl. By the afternoon, when he felt well enough to leave his bed, the city gates had finally been locked. The roar of cannon fire came closer. That night the Bucks' attic and basement filled up with Chinese friends, servants, and tradespeople, bringing their relatives and neighbors with them for shelter. Foreigners' houses, protected by gunboats and diplomatic treaties, were safer than Chinese homes in wartime. "I . . . laughed, and told my sister that the cellar was so full of people I felt as though the floors were heaving," wrote Pearl: "the subdued noise gathered and mounted to the very roof in a stilled roar."

The battle lasted three days. When the guns fell silent in the early hours of March 24 the northerners fled without stopping even for plunder. The family woke that morning to an empty house. The people crammed into it from attic to cellar had slipped away noiselessly by night. "It did not occur to me even then that they were afraid to be found with us," wrote Pearl. The family of eight—Pearl with her husband, father, and two children, Grace with her husband and small son—gathered for breakfast, relieved that all danger had passed. Pearl picked the first spring daffodils in her garden. "It was a strange night," Grace wrote in *The Exile's Daughter*. "The battle was over. The city had fallen. In the streets everything was utterly silent with that fearful stillness which falls on a Chinese city whenever there is fear." Absalom had just left for work at the seminary and Lossing was preparing to head off for the university when they were interrupted just after eight o'clock by the family tailor. "His hands were shaking and he seemed scarcely able to speak," wrote Grace. "'Run, run!' he was saying. 'They are killing the foreigners.'" The university's vice president, Jack Williams, Lillian's husband, had been shot dead by a soldier on a nearby street. Parties of soldiers were searching foreign houses and hunting down their occupants. Pearl sent the gateman to stop her father's rickshaw and bring him back, by force if necessary. The servants urged the family to hide, but no one could suggest where until Lu Sadze, now living in a mud house beyond the compound wall, arrived at a run to fetch them. "Her sun-browned hair was uncombed, her jacket half-fastened, her face grey," wrote Grace. "Already there was banging and howling at the main gate."

All of them ran, carrying the two younger children, through the back gate over rough paths between vegetable plots, fish ponds, and grave mounds to a little clutch of huts built against a tiled brick wall. The Chinese inhabitants watched silently as the fugitives packed into Mrs. Lu's low, dark rented room, ten feet by eight, furnished with a chair, a stool, a quilt, a plank bed, and a pot for sanitation. In the distance the individual shrieks and screams of people on the street fused into a collective roar. Inside the hut no one spoke. None of the children cried. They could hear the crowd burst through their garden gate a few hundred yards away and smash down their heavy front door. "I cannot well describe to you the horror of that moment," Pearl reported three weeks later to the Mission Board. She put something very like it into *The Good Earth,* in the scene where Wang Lung finds himself caught up by a mob preparing to sack a city house: "howling together the deep tigerish howl that he had heard rising and swelling out of the streets . . . people pressed forward so tightly packed together that foot was on foot and body wedged tightly against body so that the whole mass moved together as one."

All day the five adults and three children stood or sat in silence, listening to the shooting, the splintering of wood, and the crash of falling masonry, knowing that at any moment someone could give away their hiding place. The doctor's house opposite theirs was fired. Other neighbors' houses followed. Absalom, peering through a single small opening under the roof, reported the seminary burning. This was a replay of stories Pearl had heard at the time of the Boxer uprising as a child of eight, only a year older than her own daughter was now. Carol's seventh birthday had been the day before the fighting started. Janice was almost two, the same age as Richard Yaukey. All of them seemed to understand their situation. Carol behaved with adult gravity; the others sat still and watchful on their mothers' laps. When Pearl and Grace compared notes afterward each found that the other had been planning to see their children killed before their own lives were taken: "Worse than death would be the realization that the children were in the hands of those maddened men."

Soldiers crowded past the hut. By afternoon Lossing reckoned there were five hundred of them in the lane outside. The uproar reached a climax in late afternoon—"we had given ourselves up for lost, since we were just about to be discovered and killed"—when, after a sudden burst of shellfire, the noise stopped. The family waited, still without speaking, for another four hours. At intervals throughout the day Chinese friends had slipped in with food, clothing, bedding, or promises to intercede with the commanding officers. By evening the chance of rescue or remaining undiscovered seemed slim. A red glow of burning buildings filtered through the hole. A young Chinese teacher from the university arrived in tears to warn them that they were to be killed before midnight: "He . . . fell at once upon his knees and he made the ancient kotow." About nine o'clock he returned, bringing a Nationalist officer with an escort of soldiers, who ordered the family to leave. They came out of the hut—"each thinking that now, this, was the moment of death for which they had been waiting all day"—and were taken back toward the university, past wrecked and burning houses between lines of soldiers. "They were all young, every face was young . . . ignorant faces, drunken faces, red and wild-eyed. . . . They glared back at us, and they grinned with a dreadful laughter, for what they saw was the downfall and the humiliation of the white people who had for so long been their oppressors."

The Buck party arrived intact at the building that housed the Agricultural College to find its upper floor filled with refugees from the university like themselves. Some were wounded, all had lost everything they possessed. The Thomsons had been held prisoner in their own house while soldiers ransacked their rooms for money or jewels and threatened, when Margaret's aged mother could not remove her wedding ring, to lop off her finger as well. Everyone had suffered similar shocks. The few missionaries who failed to get away in time had been chased by soldiers through the streets, slapped, beaten, robbed, and in some cases stripped to their underwear. Most had been concealed at considerable risk by Chinese neighbors under piles of mats or brushwood, in cisterns, outhouses, coal bins, and storage bunkers. The British harbormaster, the port doctor, and two Catholic priests had been murdered like Dr. Williams. The British consul lay seriously injured. Missionaries had done better than the business and diplomatic community, cut off in their spacious compound near the port from contact with ordinary Chinese people, who made no attempt to help them. The men (whose wives and children had already been evacuated) barricaded themselves into one of their own big houses. The shelling at five o'clock came from gunboats in the river laying down a corridor of fire to provide sufficient cover for forty or fifty businessmen and traders to lower themselves on knotted sheets over the city wall.

Almost immediately the general commanding the Nationalists' Sixth Army intervened to stop the looting. Nationalist propaganda claimed later that what was gingerly called "the Nanjing Incident" had been accidental, spontaneous, and no fault of theirs, blaming Northern soldiers, Communist infiltrators, and civilian thugs, but contemporary eyewitness accounts agree that the perpetrators were soldiers speaking southern dialects, wearing the southerners' brown uniforms, controlled by southern officers, and following a concerted plan to single out foreigners, break into their houses, and incite local people to help themselves to the contents. These were the kinds of terror tactics explicitly endorsed that spring by Mao Zedong and others on the left of the Nationalist spectrum. Chiang Kaishek, who seized Shanghai with Communist support in a double-pronged offensive at the same time as Nanjing, declared a Nationalist government in April. Its first move was to unleash a brutal purge aimed at systematically eliminating Communists from Nationalist Party ranks. Western recognition of the new regime required a total break with its former allies. The Nanjing Incident, conveniently downplayed at the time, is remembered today, if at all in China, as yet another instance of unprovoked attack by Western gunboats.

The people who lived through it got the underlying message. The majority may have found shelter with sympathizers like Mrs. Lu, but the pillage feared by the Chinese from the Northern army had in fact been directed against Westerners and carried out by the citizens of Nanjing themselves, consumed by resentment and rage as much as greed. They had hacked up doors, banisters, window frames, and floorboards for firewood, but they had also torn down pipes and fittings, ripped out iron grates, smashed bathtubs and pianos for which they had no use, leaving their former masters' homes, as one missionary put it, "looted clean as a Chinese rice bowl." The departure of the occupants took place on the afternoon of Friday, March 25. Dazed, disheveled, exhausted, and comprehensively humiliated, the remnants of Nanjing's foreign community withdrew on foot, walking the seven miles from the university to the river, watched by the city's silent populace, and passing as they went the luckless remainder of the Northern army, heading for captivity in the opposite direction. The two-way traffic on the road that day was a fairly accurate foretaste of what the future held for China.

The few remaining women with small children, such as Pearl and her sister, went in carriages supplied by the Red Cross. Sailors on the American destroyer that took them onboard served an evening meal of bread and meat that made the passengers violently sick with ptomaine poisoning. Unable either to eat or sleep, Pearl sat up all night reading a stray copy of Herman Melville's great hymn to alienation and displacement, *Moby-Dick*. "My roots were abruptly pulled up," she wrote, "and never again was I able to put them down so deeply." It gave her an exhilarating sense of freedom when they landed next day in Shanghai, owning nothing but the clothes they had now been wearing for three days and two nights. The only thing the Bucks brought with them was the typescript of Lossing's book. He had had the foresight to sleep with it in a briefcase beside the bed and the presence of mind to grab it as the family fled the house ("It was a godsend in a way," he said in retrospect, explaining that expulsion gave him time at last to finish writing up his research). The script of Pearl's novel, lying newly completed on her desk in the attic, disappeared forever, along with a mass of other books and papers stolen or destroyed in the Nanjing Incident.

She would be thirty-five years old that summer. Her life had been drastically cut loose by no choice of her own and, whatever miserable complications lay ahead, her immediate response was a thrill of release and recklessness. "I fret sometimes over the years between 25 and 35, which were largely wasted," she told her sister long afterward. "What was I doing in those years? And why didn't I get to work? I see now that I was in a queer submerged state. It was like living in a solitary cell, nothing and no one came in and I seemed unable to communicate with anyone. . . . remembering it, I have the feelings of one having spent part of his life in jail."

CHAPTER 6

In the Mirror of Her Fiction

A FTER TEN HECTIC days in a refugee shelter in Shanghai with the
foreign community close to panic, the family escaped in a buck-
eting little steamer that took twenty-six hours to cross the Yellow Sea
to Nagasaki in Japan, where they split up. Grace, whose baby was due
in a month's time, headed north with her husband and son to Kobe
in search of the nearest Western doctor. Absalom, reluctant to waste
a day that could be given to his work, set off to inspect the mission
field in Korea. The Bucks rented an out-of-season holiday cottage in a
pine forest in the mountain resort of Unzen, a three hours' drive from
Nagasaki. It was cherry blossom time but still too cold for summer visitors, and at first (although the Thomsons joined them later) they were
the only residents. Their small flimsy wooden house had cracks in the
walls, no provision for heating, and paper screens dividing up the different rooms so that, as Pearl said, you couldn't even whisper without
everybody hearing. All of them jumped at small noises and were badly
startled in their first week by a hunter shooting in the woods. "Almost
every night we dream of some kind of attack by soldiers with knives
or guns," Lossing wrote to his parents on April 15. Pearl told Bertha
Reisner that the stillness, safety, and silence of the forest made her
hope they might wake one day to find everything that had happened in
Nanjing had been a nightmare. "But the longer time goes on the more
I begin to feel *that* part of our lives is chopped off short."

With no servants, no one for company, and no money except a
small loan from the Mission Board, the family settled back into their
old Ithaca routine. Lossing got out his papers and Pearl did the housework, cooking rice and fish on a portable charcoal stove on the back

porch, baking her own bread, and washing their few clothes in the stream. "I keep very busy cooking, cleaning and looking after the children," she told Bertha. "Lossing keeps regular work hours, and we don't speak to him between the hours of 8 and 12, and 1 and 5." Pearl organized day trips to local beauty spots, where the girls could picnic, play, and boil eggs in hot springs in the woods. Within a few weeks Lu Sadze tracked them down again, having followed the family to Shanghai and traveled steerage across the sea to reach the mountains without directions, and without a word of Japanese, because, in her view, Pearl needed help. "When I saw her standing there on the back porch in her blue cotton jacket and trousers," wrote Pearl, "I suddenly knew that I did need her, and that I was glad to see her. We fell into one another's arms and within minutes she was managing everything as usual." Cranky, fierce, and obdurate as ever, Mrs. Lu was interrogated three times in her first week by the Japanese police for littering, starting illegal fires, and traveling without a passport.

Shortly after she moved in the Yaukeys arrived too, with their new baby, making nine people altogether in a space designed for half that number. "The little cottage was crowded," Grace wrote. "The paper partitions grew damp and the paper blew off in the night leaving the entire house one room. [The baby] howled. It rained, it poured. The older children played in the mud for there was nothing else they could play in since the world was mud except for the tiny house." Pearl took her two daughters and left, taking trains at random, traveling third-class, buying food on station platforms, and sleeping in village inns. She claimed later to have no memory of what lay behind her departure. All she could remember about her impromptu expedition was the reassuring sense of order and control she got from the Japanese: their cleanliness and courtesy, the neatness of their packed lunches, and the stony simplicity of the tiny moonlit gardens she gazed at through her bedroom window night after sleepless night. "I can't imagine why I was alone," she said, when asked long afterward what had happened to Lossing at this point, "but that shows how unimportant my marriage had already become to me. He had his own life and was living it. I was preparing for mine."

Forgetfulness was a useful mechanism for Pearl, a discipline she worked at from her earliest years until it became instinctive. "I have the habit of forgetting what I do not care to remember," she wrote toward the end of her life. Her autobiography is full of references to canceled or obliterated episodes, nearly always periods of anxiety and disruption that led to major turning points. She forgot what happened after her family's expulsion from Zhenjiang in the summer of the Boxer uprising—"for the next few months, I think it was almost a year, my memory falters"—just as she forgot the second great uprooting ten years later when she left for college: "My memories of China grow suddenly dim on that day we left our compound." She blanked out her unhappiness at Randolph Macon ("Of my college days I remember shamefully little"), the summer she spent with Carol at Peitaho ("I forget it unconsciously since it was the place where I first knew that my child could never grow"), and the year at Ithaca that followed ("I had almost forgotten to mention it because it seems to have no relevance in my life").

When the family returned from Unzen to Shanghai in the autumn of 1927 Pearl tried hard to forget what followed. Her own longing to escape to the United States, at least for a few years, had been overruled by Lossing, who remained unbudgeably determined to pursue a career in China. The political situation was still chaotic. Chiang Kaishek's bloody campaign to exterminate the Communists had reached a temporary lull that summer with the Party's Russian advisers recalled to Moscow, Chiang himself in strategic retreat, and the eastern warlord Sun Chuanfang on the march once more. He was beaten off by the Nationalists in August, but no one could predict the long-term outcome. The Chinese staff of Nanjing University were carrying on business as usual in spite of turmoil in the city, and planning to start the new academic year with a full complement of students at the Agricultural College. Lossing hoped to get back himself as soon as it was safe to do so.

Meanwhile the Bucks moved into a rented house, 1056 Avenue Joffre in the French Concession, shared with the Yaukeys and another refugee family, Pearl's friend Lilliath Bates and her husband and new baby, all of them living on borrowed money until things calmed down sufficiently for them to resume their posts. At Christmas the three young mothers improvised a dinner with a single sprig of holly and homemade toys for the children. "That Shanghai Christmas was the most dismal and wretched I had ever had," Pearl wrote. She retreated into herself and signaled that retreat by rejecting other people's presents, buying herself instead on December 26 a book of essays, a six-foot length of rich soft blue Chinese silk, and a white ceramic bowl, "embossed with a spare branch of budded plum blossom," to mark out her own secret space in "the rented house where nobody noticed anything anyway." She was full of rage—"I was angry to the bottom of my soul"—and fear and foreboding. "And of that winter in Shanghai I can remember nothing else, wilfully of course, for there was plenty in our crowded house."

Pearl, her daughters, and two elderly amahs occupied the top floor. On his return from Korea Absalom moved in below with Grace, perhaps because his long-term grudge against his older son-in-law had broken out that summer in a public spat. Lossing's latest agricultural bulletin, published in the *Chinese Recorder* in July, set out a five-point plan for a self-supporting Chinese Church based on the successful practice of the U.S. Farm Bureau: "We feel that helping the farmer to help himself is a very definite Christian act." He urged the mission movement to scrap its inappropriate church buildings and stop trying to impose an alien system of religious observance, in favor of providing what people actually wanted: access to new seeds and pesticides, provision for cooperative saving schemes, and improvements in public sanitation (starting with church privies). "Few pastors can get self-support in return for words, words, words," he wrote in a rare outburst of exasperation. "None will fail to build a self-supporting church where they make themselves indispensable to the country." Both Buck's general principle and his specific recommendations (less preaching and more specialist training for religious workers) were anathema to Sydenstricker, whose fighting spirit burned as bright as ever at seventy-five. The last piece he ever wrote for the *Chinese Recorder* contains a thumping denunciation of his son-in-law's meddlesome schemes for Chinese farmers. "The farming implements compare favorably with those in use in the U.S. sixty years ago," Absalom wrote tartly. "In fertilizing the land, and getting the best out of it, they certainly excel us. . . . It is thus perfectly clear that there is no need whatever for attempting to improve farming conditions in China. . . . What is needed is not a college graduate with his titles BA, BD etc."

Twenty-five years later Pearl would repeat the same complaints, downgrading her husband's intellectual pretensions and dismissing his professional achievements in terms almost identical to her father's. At the time she remained supportive, but although she never complained about any of her troubles, her close friends were highly critical of Lossing. "I do think she had a bad time," said Lilliath Bates, shocked in those months by his stinginess with money, his lack of interest in the children, his overbearing and paternalistic attitude to his wife. "He made Pearl suffer very much." Pearl accepted, however reluctantly, her husband's refusal to consider leaving China. She did not question that his work came first nor, in spite of her own second salary, that he alone controlled their purse strings. She had stories to write herself that winter, but she still found time in the evenings to work on the typed reports that formed the basis of Lossing's *Chinese Farm Economy*. "She'd go to her room and edit them, make them read well, before going to her own writing," said Lilliath Bates. Grace remembered her sister's steady encouragement and the many suggestions she gave Lossing for his book: "She entered very much into that project, and she did a great deal of editing."

Pearl took pride in putting on a good show in the role of model wife, but the person she was trying hardest to convince at this stage was herself. "I'm not going to fail at anything," as her alter ego puts it in what she claimed to be the most autobiographical of all her novels, *This Proud Heart*. "I can do it all, wife, mother—and myself." The same determination underlies an effusive letter she sent her mother-in-law from Shanghai in 1927. "I should like to tell you that the more the years pass the happier we are together and the more glad that we found each other," she wrote of herself and Lossing: "ours is a real marriage of minds and spirits and we seem to grow more and more happy in it." Over the past ten years Pearl's parents-in-law had received a good few letters like this one, extolling the young Bucks' married bliss, his family's exemplary home life on their New England farm, and the stalwart qualities of Lossing and his brothers ("such splendid good true stock . . . how wise you have been in rearing four such sons. . . . Your daughters have to thank you and Father for that"). There is an element of desperation in Pearl's reassurances, as if on some level she recognized them to be phony. When she finally stopped pretending to herself that nothing had gone wrong in her marriage, she looked back in a very different light. "His house explained so much, when I saw it, of what seemed to me before cruel insensitivity," she wrote to her old friend and Lossing's, Marian Craighill, who had always had her doubts about the two of them as a couple.

There was in fact nothing out of the ordinary about Lossing's parents, strict and abstemious people who had given their lives to running their small, largely self-sufficient Pleasant Valley farm, with a dozen cows (all milked by hand), a hundred hens, and mixed crops of corn, wheat, oats, hay, and apples. Father and sons worked an eighteen-hour day with no hired help and no electricity on the farm. They had no indoor plumbing, and visitors were rare. When Pearl's brother Edgar came to see his sister, the Bucks did not conceal their disapproval of his smoking in the yard. "You'd have to understand my folks, they'd have neither drinking nor smoking, nor coffee or tea," said Lossing's younger brother, Clifford. "He only stayed a night or two." Pearl eventually relieved her feelings about the Buck farm in graphic accounts of the Holm and Pounder farms in two successive novels based, she said, on her marriage to Lossing. The heroine of *Other Gods* marries an undereducated but virile and good-looking New England farmer's son she scarcely knows, only to find to her chagrin that he is dull, clumsy, unimaginative, and incapable of looking beyond his own immediate concerns. Her fastidious recoil is reinforced on visits to his family by a father-in-law who sweats, smells of cow, and washes at the kitchen sink. "It was Mr. Holm's hands that she dreaded most—those great horrible ham-shaped hands, with the black dirt eternally in the creases. . . . They make her think of roots of trees turned up out of the soil." Perhaps it was Pearl's own earthy Stulting and Sydenstricker roots that threatened to drag her down at this point, as they had once threatened her father.

Worse still in *The Time Is Noon* is the heroine's rash marriage to another caricatural farmer's son, "a tall, thick-necked, oafish young man" with lumpy features, coarse limbs, thick pale wind-cracked lips, and meaty hands that make her shrink from his touch. She feels crushed by his family's bovine physicality and by their stolid, censorious, closed minds. "It's a flesh pander" is their dismissive phrase for every sensual indulgence, from cooking with sugar and wearing pretty clothes to the possibility of their new daughter-in-law spending too much time in bed with her young husband. When her baby turns out to be disabled, her husband's family at first flatly deny that there is a problem, then urge her no less flatly to put the child out of sight in a home without making an embarrassing fuss.

The thing that chilled and alienated Pearl most about Lossing was her conviction that he acquiesced in the same fate for their daughter. She herself had understood on the day they spent in hiding from soldiers in Nanjing that, even if Carol emerged from that hut alive, China's anarchic politics made it impossible to ensure the child's future, and that her only hope of security lay in the United States. It was an intuitive decision that brought the same kind of relief as a rope thrown to someone trying to maintain a footing in shifting sand: "I clung to it and dragged myself out of despair day by day. . . . Knowing what I was going to do, and thinking how to do it did not heal the inescapable sorrow, but it helped me to live with it." It also put paid forever to any prospect of appealing for support to Lossing, who was apparently in favor of committing Carol to a state institution in the United States. The prospect terrified Pearl and underlined more urgently than ever the need to make provisions for her daughter in the years ahead, when she herself would no longer be there to give protection.

In the winter of 1927–28 Lossing began commuting with John Reisner and Lilliath's husband, Searle Bates, from Shanghai to Nanjing, still overrun by soldiers and under threat from hostile armies. The three resumed work at the university more or less clandestinely, concealed on campus by their Chinese colleagues and camping out at night in the Williams' abandoned house. Lossing and Searle returned most weekends to their wives and children in the house on Avenue Joffre, run with her usual efficiency by Lu Sadze from a kitchen in the basement, where she turned out to be keeping a male prisoner under lock and key. Interrogated by Pearl, Mrs. Lu explained that this highly attractive young man had seduced and abandoned her for another woman in Nanjing (it was his defection that made her set out for Japan), so naturally, when she bumped into him again by chance in a Shanghai market, she had no choice but to kidnap him. The irresistible but indecisive Mr. Chu agreed at Pearl's suggestion to marry his jailer, only to escape once more to his other concubine before returning to his bride in the basement, where he settled down finally to cook for the entire household.

Pearl's remarkable power of conciliation was a function of an innate, abundant, emotionally exorbitant ability to enter imaginatively into other people's lives. Her second daughter, Janice, now three years old and an intrepid talker, had grown into a tiny, startlingly pretty child with big brown eyes and a mass of tight golden curls. Her upbringing had its problems on both sides (inhibitions about eating dogged Janice throughout childhood), but although Lossing could never think of her as his own, to her adoptive mother she brought the healing energy and comfort Pearl herself had given to her own mother. "I have never seen the creative power of love more perfectly displayed than in the way Pearl loved this little girl into health and life and beauty," said Margaret Thomson, who had known Janice from her emaciated and unprepossessing start. "I have never seen such absolute, self-giving devotion." No one else could see the point of the two incompetent old peasant women taken on by Pearl as amahs because they had nowhere else to go. Lilliath Bates remembered their incredulous delight a couple of years later when a parcel arrived from Pearl, then in the United States, containing two luxurious wool robes, soft, warm, and feather light, the kind of thing neither had ever touched before, let alone dreamed of possessing: "They hugged them to their bosoms and wept."

But by her own account Pearl was learning slowly and painfully to grow a defensive shell that cut her off from all but superficial contact with other people. "Doubtless they felt the surface bright and shallow, and were perhaps repelled by something hard and cold beneath which they could not reach," she wrote, reviewing in retrospect the profound internal realignment that took place within that protective carapace. "Yet it was necessary to maintain the surface, for it was my own protection, too. It was not possible to share with anyone in those years my inner state." Now that she had found a way to control, or at least contain the violence of her feelings about Carol, she set herself to explore her daughter's mind and understand the extent of the stoppage that had shut down its mental and emotional development. For twelve months in Shanghai Pearl gave her attention unreservedly to Carol, playing with her, singing to her, and teaching her to sing, helping her to talk, showing her how to tell one color from another, coaxing her to read, perhaps even to write. Both Grace and Lilliath were astonished by Pearl's gentleness and perseverance: "Hours every day went into the painstaking work of teaching and training with results so small that only Pearl could see them." After everyone else had gone to bed they could hear Carol calling and clumping about upstairs and her mother getting up to calm her three or four times each night.

This was a period of enforced seclusion. It would be hard to overestimate the stigma attached to any form of abnormality or retardation in the 1920s and 1930s. Schools commonly refused to accept disabled children, neighbors were hostile, and other children responded with mockery and bullying. "It's not a crime, but people . . . can behave as if it were," Pearl wrote, discussing the shame and secrecy imposed on parents like herself. Families were expected to close ranks and shut away the kind of offspring still treated by the public as a village idiot. Shanghai's foreign community was no different from any other group of Westerners. It was impossible for Pearl to take her daughter shopping or even to church on Sundays without reproving people turning to point and stare. Other mothers ostentatiously drew back rather than pass her in the park. "You can hear them almost whispering, 'There's that woman who has that strange child,' " she told Lilliath, who was appalled both by the routine callousness of strangers and by Pearl's determination to confront it.

Pearl said she learned far more than her daughter in the year they spent alone together. Carol made progress, but her lessons had to be abandoned because of the excessive strain they put on a child who understood nothing but her own increasingly desperate desire to please her mother. "She was not really learning anything," Pearl wrote. "It seemed my heart broke all over again. When I could control myself I got up and put away the books forever. Of what use was it to push this mind beyond where it could function?" Pearl realized that it was her own pride and aspiration—her longing for independence, achievement, some kind of fulfillment for her daughter—that had to change. She must school herself to expect nothing and be glad of what she had. She said the experiment taught her humility and patience: "I come of a family impatient with stupidity and slowness, and I absorbed the family intolerance of minds less quick than our own. . . . It was my child who taught me to understand so clearly that all people are equal in their humanity, and all have the same human rights."

Both the Bucks were well aware of China's precarious position that winter. Relations with Moscow had been formally broken off after Nationalist forces ruthlessly suppressed a Communist uprising in December in Guangzhou. Fear of another raised tensions in Shanghai. Soldiers were posted at every entrance to the ancient, insanitary, overcrowded Chinese town. Troops drawn from the fifty thousand White Russian exiles in China stood guard on the bridge. On January 1, 1928, Chiang Kaishek left the city for Nanjing in an armored train. Foreigners could no longer count on special privileges or protection. The Nationalists were planning to advance north on Beijing, and Lossing predicted heavy fighting. Pearl warned Emma, who had taken refuge with her family in the United States, that it was too dangerous to return: "Missionaries in all Nationalist controlled areas must be prepared at any instant to run for their lives." Widespread disillusionment added to the troubles of a government that had made no serious attempt at social or educational reform. "He was a soldier," Pearl wrote of Chiang Kaishek, "and he had the mind of a soldier, and neither by nature nor experience was he fitted to be a civilian ruler of a republic. . . . He knew nothing about modern democratic government." She was dismayed to see how quickly idealistic revolutionaries, once in power, fell back on their country's ancient despotic remedies of repression, corruption, and reckless taxation.

Shanghai gangsters grew extravagantly rich on protection rackets and prostitution. Chiang and his new young wife, the beautiful, bold, American-educated Soong Meiling, presided over a celebrity culture of bobbed hair, slit skirts, and all-night jazz parties, rampant consumerism and sexual excess, underpinned by violence and graft. "I feel as if I were living at the capital of Louis of France before the French revolution broke," Pearl wrote that winter. "This cannot go on for ever. Personally I feel that unless something happens to change it we are in for a *real* revolution here in comparison to which all this so far will be a mere game of ball on a summer's afternoon." She expressed her sense of menace in a powerful image from *A House Divided,* where Wang Yuan, briefly caught up in the nightlife of Shanghai's gilded youth, is haunted by shadows at the edges of his mind, dim figures waiting for the dawn when the party will be over, crouched "like street dogs" ready to infiltrate the houses and snatch the leavings from the tables of the rich: "Against his will he saw them, and . . . even in the midst of the night's pleasure . . . he remembered with great dread the moment when he must go into the grey street and see the cringing figures and the wolfish faces of the poor."

The Shanghai literary scene was full of effete young poets like Yuan's cousin Sheng, who publishes a slim silver-bound volume of derivative symbolist verses ("exquisite and empty, though they were so fluent in their line and sound"), printed on thick ivory paper and featuring moonlight on a dead woman's hair, "an ice-bound fountain in a park, a fairy island in a smooth green sea." This is an accurate if unflattering skit on the vogue for European pastiche among Western-educated intellectuals seeking escape from insoluble political and social problems nearer home. Most of the writers Pearl read and admired in her twenties had moved in the opposite direction, toward active political involvement. Chen Duxiu, whose campaign in *New Youth* alerted a whole generation to the possibility of literary revolution, was overthrown as leader of the Chinese Communist Party in 1927, afterward becoming a Trotskyite and narrowly escaping execution. Lu Xun, picked by Pearl as the first Chinese to write about the ordinary life of his own people (and later generally acknowledged as China's greatest twentieth-century writer), turned to Marxism in those years. So did Pearl's favorite, the poet Kuo Mo-jou ("that brilliant mind, whose habit was the utmost candor and whose passion was truth"), currently pioneering the use of propaganda as a tool of the Left in China. Of Pearl's feminist contemporaries, Hsieh Ping-hsin and Ding Ling—"those two intrepid and fearless women writers who used to make me so proud"—Hsieh acknowledged no political allegiance in her work and faded from public view; Ding joined the Communists and, after fighting many bitter battles for women's liberation, ended up as one of the Party's model writers.

There is nothing to suggest that Pearl actually met any of these handsome and clever young Chinese (a species that touched her heart as, in a different context, it did her father's). The exception was the popular and charismatic poet Xu Zhimo, who seems to have encountered her on a flying visit to Nanjing in May 1924. She said she used him as the model for the aloof young husband in "A Chinese Woman Speaks," which she wrote later that summer. Thirty years afterward she singled Xu out in her memoirs in a dismissive account of the superficiality and "sickening romanticism" of contemporary Chinese writing at that period: "It even became the fashion to ape Western poets in person and one handsome and rather distinguished and certainly much beloved young poet was proud to be called 'the Chinese Shelley.' He used to sit in my drawing-room and talk by the hour and wave his beautiful hands in exquisite and descriptive gestures. . . . He was a northern Chinese, tall and classically beautiful in looks, and his hands were big and perfectly shaped and smooth as a woman's hands. . . . Our Chinese Shelley died young, I am sad to say, for he had a sort of power of his own, and could he have outgrown the Shelley phase he might have become himself."

One of half a dozen Chinese Shelleys, Xu (also known as the Chinese Byron) was the son of a banking family in Zhejiang who had spent time in Paris as well as studying in the United States, and spending a postgraduate year in England at Cambridge University. On his return to China he became an authority on the West and an arbiter of taste, a glamorous and sophisticated role model, founder of *Crescent Moon* and other experimental literary journals, a high-flyer who made a major impact when he left his Beijing base for Shanghai in 1927. Pearl included a second sketch of Xu, or someone very like him, in a bitter passage in her memoirs about the promiscuity of Shanghai intellectuals, "rootless young Chinese, educated abroad, who did not want to involve themselves in anything more trying than art and literature, the artists from the Latin Quarter in Paris, the postgraduates from Cambridge . . . who kept their hands soft and spent their time in literary clubs and poetry-making, who published little decadent magazines in English and pretended that the common Chinese did not exist. In such groups there were also a few American women who had come to China for adventure, women who took Chinese lovers and about whom the Chinese lovers boasted. . . ." The American woman who was sleeping with Xu in Shanghai in the late 1920s was Agnes Smedley, an intrepid traveler, left-wing reporter, and notorious believer in free love, as indeed was Xu himself. Both had broken family ties, repudiated social convention, and taken a daring public stand on freedom and the future in a way impossible for Pearl, who was not only married to a missionary but living on mission funds under the close and prurient surveillance of the mission community.

Pearl was only four years older than Xu, but she still looked drab, middle-aged, and mousy. When she gave a talk at the Shanghai High School the girls were chiefly struck by the gap between her appearance and her aspirations. "She was just the wife of a missionary," said one of them, "and we thought it very interesting that someone like her would actually be publishing stories about the people who were all round us." That winter she began losing weight without premeditation and without conscious effort. By New Year 1928 she had lost forty-five pounds and reported that she looked "more like my old self than I have in years." Previous biographers have assumed that Pearl too was having an affair with Xu, which seems unlikely, if only because he was one of the stars of his literary generation, while she was at best an onlooker on the sidelines, having published no more than a handful of pieces in mission publications and American magazines. None of his biographers has found a shred of evidence for this affair, and the only Chinese witness who knew them both, a young professor at Nanjing's National Southeastern University, categorically denied the possibility that Pearl had been Xu's lover, even if she might have liked to be: "She was stout, rather oldish-looking. . . . He mentioned to me the name of Miss Pearl Buck. My impression was that Miss Buck did not impress him much."

No one in Pearl's circle at the time in China, not even her husband, knew anything about this putative affair, apart from a vague assertion made fifty years later by Lilliath Bates that she had heard gossip linking their two names. Pearl admitted long afterward that, when she wrote "A Chinese Woman Speaks," "she imagined herself . . . marrying a young man such as Xu Zhimo." Like the hero of that story, Xu had been married young by his parents to a girl he'd never met and couldn't love, eventually divorcing his wife to make a much publicized and ultimately disastrous love match in 1926. Pearl also claimed that she put something of Xu into the half-Chinese hero of *Letter from Peking*, who was more closely based on the boy she fell in love with as a schoolgirl. The suggestion that either of these romantic heroes might have been based on more than fantasy originated with Theodore Harris, Pearl's companion in old age, who ghost-wrote her official biography with her collaboration and whose testimony is highly ambivalent. "It is the privilege of a writer to grasp a situation as it stands and complete it in her own mind," he wrote of Pearl's relationship with Xu. "It could have happened. How much actually did is not for us to know." Xu gave a course of lectures at Southeastern University in 1929, commuting from Beijing and resigning after twelve months. His early death in a plane crash the year after made him a legend. All that can be said for sure is that he produced a deep impression on Pearl, as on many of his contemporaries, and that her feelings for him grew in retrospect.

What seems to have restored her confidence in herself toward the end of 1927, when by her own account she went through a crisis of acute loneliness and isolation from her own kind, was that for the first time she was moving toward a position where she could begin to take her life into her own hands. Her decision to remove her daughter to the United States, and partial physical as well as moral separation from her husband, made it possible to envisage a professional future in her own right. All previous bids to establish herself as a writer had failed. The novel completed in March 1927 had been destroyed by looters in Nanjing, and she had apparently forgotten all about the book-length typescript of her mother's life (which was in fact salvaged from its wall closet by her students). "A Chinese Woman Speaks," and the story written as its sequel, packaged together as a novel in response to a request from the New York publishing house Brentano's, had been turned down. The stories she posted off at random to American magazines took up to six months to elicit a response, which, when it came, was more often than not a rejection slip. Of the three U.S. literary agents listed in a writers' directory Pearl found in a Shanghai bookstore, two eventually replied that there was no American market for Chinese material. The third was David Lloyd of the Paget Agency, who agreed to handle her stories and also to try to place the two-part novel, now titled *Winds of Heaven*. It was a small, unexpected check forwarded by Lloyd from a U.S. magazine that Pearl squandered so recklessly that Christmas on blue silk and white porcelain, precious symbols not just of her difference from her housemates, but of a new inner life that would mean more to her than any love affair.

Sex was Pearl Buck's territory as a novelist. One of the prime grievances of her critics from *The Good Earth* onward was the frank sexuality of women as well as men in her novels. Her own sensuous nature was not in question. She said that even the gardenia bushes in her Nanjing garden, opening their fleshy white petals in the early morning, could stir her senses so intensely that their heady perfume woke her from sleep. In her early stories she wrote with particular sensitivity about sexual frustration, thwarted desire, the twin miseries of marital rape and marital rejection. Her fictional Chinese lovers never offer sexual fulfillment; even the mixed-race hero of *Letter from Peking* is an American in bed. The American girl who moves with her Chinese husband into his family home, in the second part of *Winds of Heaven,* reluctantly acknowledges the gap opening up between them: "Locked in behind these high walls I imagine things. . . . He seems to slip back into strangeness. . . . I have always been used to frankness and cheerfulness and speaking straight out. And here it is all silence and bowing and sliding eyes at me." Pearl dramatized her own predicament more clearly in "Repatriated," another story written around this time, about a Frenchwoman married to a Chinese intellectual, who had charmed her as a student in France with his gravity and delicacy, his slender erect carriage, his calm oval face, sleek black hair, and golden skin, but becomes in his own country so elusive and inscrutable that he drives her back reluctantly to her irredeemably coarse and lecherous French lover.

Although Pearl had warned Lossing at the beginning of the year that she had no intention of moving the children from the relative safety of Shanghai, he persuaded her in July to go back with him and their daughters to Nanjing. Beijing had capitulated to the Nationalists that spring, but Chiang Kaishek established his government in the old imperial capital of the Ming emperors. Still medieval in its lack of sanitation and running water, and its one-storey buildings lining a main street barely four feet wide, the city was now scarred by burned-out schools and churches, with trees cut down, and soldiers everywhere, camping out in gutted houses and using the gardens as latrines. The Bucks were the first white family to return. Horses had been stabled in the kitchen of their house, the living-room floorboards had been set on fire, the bay window ripped out, and the garden destroyed. Temporary repairs had made the place habitable for government officials, but for their first month the family stayed with Chinese friends while Pearl hired a team of masons, carpenters, and painters. The entire house, which had been used at one point as an army cholera ward, had to be sanded, scrubbed with strong-smelling disinfectant, and whitewashed. The work went on long after the family moved back, squeezed into two upstairs bedrooms where Pearl cooked on an oil stove. For months she was abnormally sensitive to the sound of unfamiliar voices at the gate and the ghostly presence of absent friends in the empty church. One of the first things she did was to dig up the surviving roots from the violet border in her garden and plant them on Jack Williams's grave. She told Emma there was no way of knowing if she would ever pick the spinach, cabbages, and replacement violets she sowed that winter.

It was a scenario familiar from her rootless childhood, only this time there was no amnesty for foreigners. On a last visit to Zhenjiang Pearl found her parents' house engulfed by the revolution and its garden reduced to beaten earth: "Twenty families of refugees crowded into the rooms . . . and the plaster was stripped to the laths, and the floors were inches deep in human filth, and the starving people looked out of the holes of windows like desperate dogs." Even in Nanjing food was short and prices high. People in the streets were mutinous and bitter. Posters everywhere denounced Chiang and the Kuomintang. Attempts at rural reform had turned out to be halfhearted and impossible to enforce. Outside the city walls bandits had instituted a reign of terror. Lossing estimated that eighty thousand farmers within a twenty-mile radius of Nanjing were paying illegal protection money on top of increased taxes. Pearl feared a popular uprising. The new administration was no match for crooks and grafters. Even the most hopeful government officials—some of them the Bucks' friends and former students—were young, inexperienced, and wholly unprepared for the scale of problems posed by overmanned and inefficient agricultural production, the lack of industry and transport systems, the urgent need for educational expansion and public health initiatives, all exacerbated by a bankrupt economy and the presence of an enormously expanded mercenary army. The regime officially welcomed Westerners, but ordinary people no longer bothered to conceal an ingrained contempt reinforced by the ignominious loss of face so recently inflicted on the white community. Pearl got used again to the curses—"Kill the foreigner!"—she had heard shouted when she was a child. Once a fierce young ideologist preaching revolution on the street broke off to swear and spit at her.

*Pearl's parents, Caroline (Carie) Stulting and
Absalom Sydenstricker, at the time of their
marriage and departure for China in 1880.*

*Absalom and Carie with their three surviving children—
thirteen-year-old Edgar, two-year-old Pearl, and the new
baby, Clyde—after their flight to Shanghai in 1895.*

The Sydenstricker family reunited after the terrorist uprising of 1900:
Pearl, Absalom, and Carie with her seventh and last baby, Grace,
presided over by Wang Amah.

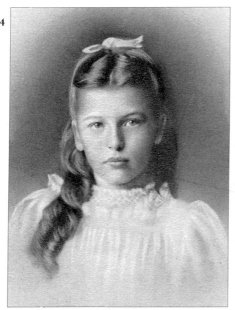

Pearl, aged nine, on her
first visit to America in
1901: "slender face, broad
forehead, pointed chin,
straight, stubborn mouth,
narrow nose, and gray-
green eyes beneath black
brows that contrasted with
the near-fair hair."

A traveler approaching the thousand steps cut into the cliff on the road to Kuling, China's first mountain resort, founded by Pearl's father and others as a life-saving station.

Absalom Sydenstricker in the robes of a Chinese scholar. Six feet tall, red-haired, red-skinned, and blue-eyed with a beaky nose, his appearance astounded and often terrified village people who had never seen a foreigner before.

The scholar, Mr. Kung (Kong), who taught Pearl to write calligraphy and read Confucius: a posthumous portrait by Li Weicheng, president of the National Painting Academy of Zhenjiang.

8

Carie, Grace, and Pearl Sydenstricker in 1910, the year Pearl returned to the United States, entered college, and set about remaking herself for the first time as an American.

9

Pearl as president of her class, standing surrounded by the other girls at Randolph-Macon Woman's College in 1913.

Pearl and John Lossing Buck on their wedding day, May 30, 1917, in the Sydenstrickers' garden with her parents (far left), her sister, Grace (center right), and colleagues from the Zhenjiang and Nanxuzhou mission stations.

Lu Sadze (with her baby and absconding husband): the village woman who saved the lives of the Buck family by hiding them in this hut in Nanjing in 1927.

12

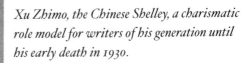

Xu Zhimo, the Chinese Shelley, a charismatic role model for writers of his generation until his early death in 1930.

Xu Zhimo (second from right in front row) when Pearl first met him in May 1924, photographed with a group of young Western-educated intellectuals at Nanjing's Southeastern University during the visit of Rabindranath Tagore, who sits behind Xu with the distinguished Confucian scholar Gu Hongming.

14

Wang Lung the farmer: this photograph was picked by Pearl for reproduction in Asia *(vol. 28, no. 9, Sept. 1928), because she said the man in it looked just like the hero of* The Good Earth.

Richard Walsh, who published The Good Earth, *in China in 1934: "there he was, lean, brown, and handsome, and smoking his old briar pipe."*

Richard and Pearl with the first two of their six adopted children at home in the garden of Green Hills Farm, Pennsylvania.

上海其米茲不拈此攝術增說夾對處中國實具派改片國勵大寫活中有，賓美在華高刊玫查片製幹改事當，，有人地來當騙公米一地成爲周年留珍國南工海各站園勢，員，實局現多尋初情華工電司高時一小朋悲，居珠女超界作公國琴捐成料監拼精經綴加國恐又拍件影將梅，說材村留中安件招北人司露，霜，炬督派加小中反之片，攝人，其影美映，，生以國土家

An MGM film crew shooting The Good Earth *on location near Shanghai in Pearl's final weeks in China in 1934 (from the Shanghai magazine* Liangyou, *May 13, 1934). The footage was destroyed by government officials before it left the country, and Pearl herself never saw China again.*

18

*Pearl in 1938 when she won the Nobel Prize for literature:
"Her beautiful gray-green eyes were as clear as jade, frank,
and sparkling . . . her uneven mouth was cut like a gash in her
expressive face. She was attractive, friendly, natural, easy to
be with, but I had a feeling she had never been young."*

*Pearl as a widow in her seventies, with her
dancing instructor, Ted Harris. She said he
had the looks of a Greek god together with
the glamour of President Kennedy. She set up
a lavishly funded foundation with Harris at
its head until public scandal forced his resignation, but he remained at Pearl's side as her
closest companion to the end of her life.*

The modern world advanced implacably on a city designed to astound contemporaries nearly six hundred years before with a layout and infrastructure essentially unchanged ever since. The general dilapidation, stench, and backwardness of China's new capital was brought home to its more sophisticated inhabitants by the installation of foreign embassies, the arrival of delegations from abroad, and the possibility of state visits. Attempts were made to eliminate rickshaw men, prostitutes, and beggars. Many hundreds of the mat huts adhering like wasps' nests all along the bottom of the city wall were torn down. Mat screens thirty feet high were erected to hide the rest. There was talk of piped water, electricity, sewerage, drainage, department stores, telegraph poles, and tower blocks. Paved streets and even automobiles were already a reality. Pearl left various tragicomical accounts of the long wide straight avenue driven through the center of Nanjing by the first bulldozer the city had ever seen. She watched the machine work methodically down the main street, demolishing a broad swathe of low brick shops and houses first on one side, then the other, supervised by officers from the revolutionary army and watched by a silent crowd, whose livelihood and living quarters turned to rubble before their eyes. "The Communists in China gained their first victory that day," Pearl wrote drily in her memoirs.

She was torn between the horror she felt for the dispossessed people and a kind of pity for their idealistic oppressors, young Nationalists who had learned in the West a corrosive shame that made them desperate to scourge and purify the iniquity and turpitude of their own country and its illiterate people. Pearl recognized the fervor and the fury that had driven her own father nearly mad in face of the inert, uncomprehending indifference of a Chinese crowd. "He was so thin, so intense, so filled with missionary zeal," she wrote of a speaker haranguing passers-by on a street corner: "he was angry with them in his heart because they stood before him unmoved, and laughed when the sweat ran down his poor young cheeks. He was so angry that he could scarcely keep from weeping, and I am sure he would have been glad if lightning had struck them dead." She gave the same bitter rage and pain to Wang Yuan, who sympathizes in *A House Divided* with the stern and single-minded patriots marching back from their training grounds outside the city: "these young men came back silently, and their footsteps were in such solemn unison the sound was like a great single footstep . . . their faces all young, all simple and all grave. These were the new armies. . . . I knew, looking at them, that they can kill as simply as they eat their food."

The students in Pearl's classes were no longer fiery and opinionated. Too many of them had been killed as part of the Nationalists' systematic culling of actual or suspected Communists: "They were arrested for reading liberal magazines, for associating, perhaps accidentally and without knowing it, with a classmate who was a Communist, or for criticizing the new government." Their attitude toward the future emerging from the wreckage of the past was wary and subdued. Throughout that first year Pearl could see from her attic window a white scar spreading across the slopes of Purple Mountain, where a second imperial mausoleum was being constructed as a final resting place for the founder of the Revolution, Sun Yatsen, on a scale to match the Ming emperor's adjacent tomb. The funeral on June 1, 1929, was planned as a state occasion by the new government, celebrating its accession to legitimacy and power with tributes from an international gathering of diplomats and dignitaries. A ceremonial cortege took six hours to process along the specially built new road through the city gates, passing under a triple archway and mounting nearly four hundred white marble steps to a sky-blue tiled gateway and a final white pavilion. After it was over and the crowds had left, Pearl climbed the steps herself in time to see Chiang Kaishek emerge alone from the inner hall and stand in the great gate, oblivious of spectators, gazing out over the countryside below: "I stood near watching his face, so strangely like that of a tiger, the high forehead sloping, the ears flaring backward, the wide mouth seeming always ready to smile and yet always cruel. But his eyes were the most arresting feature. They were large, intensely black and utterly fearless. It was not the fearlessness or composure of intelligence, but the fearlessness, again, of the tiger, who sees no reason to be afraid of any other beast because of its own power."

Within a few weeks of the funeral the Bucks sailed for the United States. Lossing's book *Chinese Farm Economy,* due for publication in 1930, had already persuaded experts at the Institute of Pacific Relations to put his name forward for a more comprehensive survey of land use in China planned by the U.S. Department of Agriculture. Lossing got the job on the grounds that any such survey would be best carried out at first hand in China rather than compiled from published data in Washington. He had been summoned home to consult officials, recruit staff, finalize funding, and negotiate a major grant from the Rockefeller Foundation. It was an impressive coup, one that would transform both his career and the standing of Nanjing's Agricultural College. Pearl planned to use the time to look into the possibility of finding some kind of shelter for their daughter in the United States. She had no immediate family of her own to turn to, and the Bucks had made their disapproval plain. Lossing's refusal to consider leaving China meant that there was little hope of providing a stable and secure environment for Carol, given that country's chaotic present and uncertain future. The current situation intensified the anxiety that had weighed on Pearl for years. Mental health professionals warned parents in those days that it was frivolous to suppose any child with learning or other difficulties could be adequately looked after at home. Pearl blamed herself for dreading the alternative. "I realize I must leave her in some place where she can be trained to the highest of which she is capable, and my heart is wrenched in two at the thought," she had written to Emma White at the beginning of the year. "I can't face it, really, yet."

Lossing's sudden recall forced her to overcome her reluctance. They inspected special schools and care homes, working their way through an ad hoc list with no available guidance, official or unofficial, and no way of contacting other parents in a similar situation. Disability was a taboo subject. Society dealt with it by concealment and coverup, a policy that paid more attention to its own sensibilities than to the needs or wants of the disabled. Pearl was shocked by the impersonal severity of discipline in some of the most expensive and best appointed private schools she visited. Worse was the regimentation in overcrowded state-run institutions, where passive, unresisting children were lined up and made to sit for hours on benches, waiting day after day for nothing. Regarded as unteachable, not even given basic toilet training or shown how to hold a spoon, they were clothed in sacking, fed like animals off cement floors that the staff hosed down two or three times a day, and put to sleep on filthy pallets laid out on the ground. Already vulnerable, depressed, and apprehensive, Pearl was deeply shaken by her encounters with prison-like regimes administered by overworked, underpaid, often callous and desensitized staff, who herded their charges like animals. Twenty years later, when she wrote a book to publicize their predicament, *The Child Who Never Grew,* she told a friend it was "the hardest thing she ever did in her life." Its message in 1950, the year of publication, was sharp and startling. "These too were human beings," she wrote of the children she described, "and many of those who cared for them did not understand it. The children who never grow are human beings and they suffer as human beings, inarticulately but deeply nevertheless. The human creature is always more than an animal. That is the one thing we must never forget."

In the autumn of 1929 Pearl finally picked a small private institution, the Vineland Training School in New Jersey, run by Dr. Edward Johnstone, whose approach she liked and trusted. Each child was treated as a person in his or her own right and given an unusual degree of freedom by staff who were attentive, kind, and gentle. Education and research were central to Johnstone's program ("The only child who can learn is a happy child," he said). Carol was nine years old. Although it was impossible to explain to her what was about to happen, she understood her mother's distress, and the two clung to one another. "We had never been separated, and the time was coming when there would be a separation almost as final as death." At the end of September Pearl agreed to leave her daughter at the school for a trial month, during which she woke night after night, imagining Carol's feelings and knowing there was no way her daughter could make them known. "Only the thought of a future with the child grown old and me gone kept me from hurrying to the railway station." The final parting was excruciating. "If I had known how hard this leaving was going to be, I simply couldn't have done it," she wrote three months later, by which time she was back in China. "Left to my choice, I simply should have given up China absolutely and without question. It has been a dreadful time—having to go back because Lossing felt equally without question that he must go."

Lossing refused to consider leaving his wife behind even temporarily in the United States. He could not have afforded to pay school fees, even if he wanted to, so Pearl borrowed two thousand dollars to cover Carol's first two years from a member of the Mission Board in New York. At the time she had no prospect of repaying the money, except for five hundred dollars offered by the Board for a children's book that would popularize the mission movement. She said she dared not weep for fear that, once started, she could never stop again. Her one comfort was Janice, whose warmth, gaiety, and humor had always consoled and healed her mother. Without her, Pearl said, she wasn't sure she could have endured the company of other children. "I continually marvel at my luck in finding her out of all the world," she wrote to Emma White. "Janice just saves me." Pearl herself told several people that she had been very nearly destroyed by grief and fear for Carol. Grace Yaukey believed that her sister never fully recovered from their enforced separation.

Almost the last thing Pearl had done before leaving for the United States with her daughter was to attend Sun Yatsen's funeral and send a report to the Mission Board that included a characteristic postscript: "it would not be fair to close this letter without some reference to the millions who did not come to the funeral, and who perhaps scarcely knew it was going on. . . . All over this country . . . men and women and children went about their accustomed tasks unmoved and unconscious of any great force gathering about that tomb. These also are China. . . . The common people, the workers had no great share in the day or the hour. . . . They are at once the burden and the strength of the country. They supply the food and the labor and the multiple life of the nation." It was in its own oblique way a statement of intent. Pearl's sympathy for human beings without a voice, the inert silent masses ignored, despised, and stripped of individuality by those who shaped their future, had been confirmed by her experiences in America. "The house in Nanjing was empty without my little elder daughter, and not all the friends and family could fill it. This I decided was the time to begin really to write."

THE LAST LEG of Pearl's return to China in January 1930 is recreated in the closing section of *A House Divided,* where Wang Yuan, himself also a prospective writer, makes the same journey from Shanghai to Nanjing, reading on the train his cousin Sheng's latest book:

> The rains of late winter were begun, and the train drove through the dark day, and the water dripped down the window pane so that he could scarcely see the sodden fields. At every town the streets ran with liquid filth and the stations were empty. . . . Outside the villages slipped past, dark and huddled in the rain. At doorways men looked sullenly into the rains that beat through the thatched roof above their heads. . . . Too many days of rain drove them half-mad with quarrelling and cold misery. . . . Yuan saw the sullen beast-like faces, and he thought, very troubled, "As for me, I can write nothing. If I wrote these things Sheng does, which I can see well enough are exquisite, why, then I remember these dark faces and these hovels and all this deep under-life of which he knows nothing and will not know. And yet I cannot write of such life either." . . . He came down from the train in rain and dusk, and in the rain the old city wall stood grim and black and high. He called a rickshaw and climbed in and sat chilly and lonely while the man dragged the vehicle along the slippery running streets. Once the man stumbled and fell, and while he righted himself and waited for a moment to pant and wipe the rain from his dripping face, Yuan . . . saw the hovels still clinging against the wall. The rains had flooded them and the wretched helpless folk within sat in the flood and waited silently for heaven to change.

The Good Earth, which Pearl started writing almost as soon as she got home, tells the story of a poor farmer who survives, when famine drives him from his village, by pulling a rickshaw to earn a meager living for his family in a mat shelter built against the city wall. It was an attempt to penetrate the deep underlife of ordinary Chinese people that no one else had ever written about before. The Chinese writers who were Pearl's contemporaries had little understanding of or contact with the rural proletariat. Even the iconic central characters in Lu Xun's powerful and sardonic stories of village life are misfits or outsiders. Lao She's "Rickshaw Boy," which had enormous success in the 1930s, was what Pearl called an intellectual performance: "That is, I think a Chinese intellectual who is very far from the common people has written what he thinks a rickshaw boy thinks and feels. But I do not believe it is the way the true rickshaw boy thinks and feels." The traditional Chinese novel, shaped by strong dramatic and structural rhythms, made no attempt to portray the everyday lives of the illiterate fieldworkers who formed its audience, and classical poetry, written exclusively by scholars, ignored their existence altogether. Pearl said her story was already so clear in her mind that all she had to do was set it down: "its energy was the anger I felt for the sake of the peasants and the common folk of China. . . . My material was . . . close at hand, and the people I knew as I knew myself."

The setting is Nanxuzhou and its hinterland, where Pearl came closest to village farmers, especially their wives. As a writer she had been skirting this sort of material for years, testing the ground in articles and stories, including "The Revolutionist," written in the aftermath of the Nanjing Incident, about a farmer called Wang Lung, bewildered by the random violence of the ideological warfare in which he finds himself accidentally caught up. This Wang is clearly a prototype for the farmer of the same name in *The Good Earth*. But Pearl's first tentative exploration of the territory goes back to another sketch of village life, "Lao Wang the Farmer," published two years earlier in the *Chinese Recorder,* where the authors' names are given as Shao Teh-hsing and Pearl S. Buck. Shao was part of Lossing's backup team from his first batch of graduates in 1921, the man who ran the university's experimental farm, a pioneer in rural education and a regional director for the land survey workforce set up in 1930. He was one of very few agricultural students with a practical farming background, having started his working life as a buffalo boy, the child whose job is to mind the beast that serves as his family's transport and tractor. A second story by Shao Teh-hsing, "Lao Wang's Old Cow," a bitter episode from what reads like the author's personal past, was "translated from the Chinese by Mrs. J. L. Buck."

Born in Kiangsu province and sent to school at Wuhu in Anhui, Shao had grown up on the same great northern plain as Nanxuzhou. He was probably the first person Pearl knew who bridged, as she did, the illiterate village world and the cosmopolitan, highly educated Nanjing circle where they met. Perhaps it was talking to and working with Shao that made it possible for her to access the novel that, in her own words, "seemed to be have been in her always waiting to be told." Possibly he supplied material, made suggestions, acted as some kind of consultant. Certainly he went on to become a writer and editor himself, producing agricultural textbooks and editing the college's research journal. If his collaboration provided Pearl with a launchpad, he can hardly have had a hand in the actual composition of the novel, which she wrote at speed in two months flat, thinking in Chinese, translating as she went along into a clear, simple, fast-paced English that "sounds biblical but is pictorial, which is the Chinese way of thinking and writing." An American friend who, like Pearl, spoke Chinese from infancy said that all her early novels had this quality: "If you translated them into Chinese, you would hardly have to make any changes." The accuracy of her idiom, the mind-set of her characters, "her speech presentation in English of the way Chinese people speak in their native language" can be fully appreciated only by bilingual readers, according to Kang Liao, one of China's leading Buck scholars. "One can hardly believe it has been written by a foreign hand," wrote the publisher Zhao Jiabi, an influential voice in China at the time.

Pearl wrote in the mornings, while Janice was at nursery school, on a faulty, battered typewriter at her desk in the attic: "It was all on the tips of my fingers, what I had to say, and it went very fast . . . in spite of the fact that I was in an environment that did not and could not take novel-writing or novels seriously and even I myself came to consider it a secret indulgence." No one in her large household read the book when it was finished. Pearl said her brother (who had returned to China on business and seized the chance to work again with Lossing) was too busy, her father indifferent, and "there was no one else." The impression she gave later of dreamlike ease and speed may have been misleading. Lilliath Bates maintained that Pearl had been working on a book about Wang Lung during the winter they spent in the same house in Shanghai, and although Pearl herself (backed up by her sister Grace) insisted that her novel was written in a matter of weeks in Nanjing, she also claimed it had been "many years planned and pruned many times." Presumably she had been experimenting with similar material in the lost or abandoned novels as well as in the short stories of the previous five years. The typescript of what was then called *Wang Lung* was packed up and posted to her New York agent in late May.

Pearl's first novel came out in the United States that April. *Winds of Heaven* had finally been placed by David Lloyd, after twelve months and more than two dozen rejections, with Richard Walsh, the president of a small, relatively new and struggling publishing firm called John Day. A telegram announcing its acceptance had been sent the year before, traveling from New York to Nanjing, then back to the United States, where it finally caught up with Pearl in September, only to be almost totally eclipsed by the turmoil of her separation from Carol. Both agent and publisher were astonished by Pearl's laid-back approach when she finally turned up in New York to sign a contract for the novel, now retitled at its publisher's suggestion *East Wind, West Wind*. Walsh told Pearl that his firm had been split down the middle, reaching a decision only with his casting vote, which he gave in the book's favor not because he liked it but because he thought her capable of something better. From Pearl's point of view the deal's principal significance was its potential contribution to school fees (no advance was offered, but there would be royalties of 10 percent, rising to 15 percent in the unlikely event of sales above five thousand copies).

Reviews, when they finally reached China that summer, were encouraging. More encouraging still was a cable from Walsh, followed by a letter that took Pearl's breath away. "My publisher sent me a personal letter about my second book which is perfectly astonishing," she wrote to Grace on September 23. "Mr. Walsh is a hard, dry, conservative sort of middle-aged person, so I value this the more. It gives me a wonderful feeling of relief for I feel I can write—I hadn't been sure." Her first thought was that now she could provide for Carol's future, pay for Janice's education, and give presents—"little extra frills that mission salaries don't provide"—to the Yaukeys. Walsh offered the same terms as before, and once again Pearl showed the letter to no one in her family. When the book was selected a few months later by the Book-of-the-Month Club, Pearl received four thousand dollars as her share of payment, and the first print run was increased to ten thousand copies. "We can't afford to think for one moment that this is not going to be a best seller," Walsh told his office.

He suggested taking her subtitle, *The Good Earth,* as the actual title and shortening the text. Pearl consulted two friends, both of whom read the book. One was Margaret Thomson, whose reaction—"admiration, even awe and undoubtedly envy," wrote her son long afterward—became a Thomson family legend: "she was absolutely astounded, as we would say blown out of the water, by its excellence." Pearl's second reader was an unnamed Chinese friend, possibly Shao Teh-hsing (there is nothing to support the supposition, widely assumed to be a fact, that it was Xu Zhimo). Both urged her not to change or take out anything. She wrote firmly to Walsh, promising no cuts, explaining why she could not tone down the book's stylistic strangeness: "When I tried to rewrite it, the people were all wrong as if I had dragged them into a foreign house and they didn't know how to behave." She told him she was about to start on her third novel and had several more lined up at the back of her mind to follow.

Incipient civil war flared again that autumn, with major warlords in the north and Communist insurgents in west and south challenging the central government. There were pitched battles up and down the railway line after rebels took Beijing. Armies circled the capital.

Lossing reported rumors of a plot to burn down Nanjing University together with all mission schools and houses. Three members of his rural survey teams were captured by Communists or bandits ("It's difficult to distinguish between the two"). General Chiang stepped up his campaign of terror, running the regions in his control as a police state and driving the Communists from their established bases into bandit country farther west. Pearl began translating one of the greatest of all Chinese novels, *Shui Hu Chuan,* a hugely popular saga of resistance against a corrupt and unjust government by a band of thirteenth-century outlaws operating in her father's old territory of North Kiangsu from a mountain lair in Shandong. The book was a favorite with the Communist Party, which published its own revolutionary edition in the 1930s, much quoted by Mao Zedong, who used it to legitimize tactics of robbery, kidnapping, extortion, and murder. Pearl's was the first English translation, and she called it *All Men Are Brothers* in preference to its literal title, *The Water Margins*. It took her four years, working in the early afternoons with one or other of two Chinese scholars, Zhao Yanan and the seminary secretary, Long Moxiang, who read passages aloud to her, translating into modern Chinese, while she deciphered the written characters and produced an English text. She knew the kind of northerners depicted in these pages at firsthand and gave their story a powerful immediacy, according to a subsequent review in a Beijing journal: "She could hear them talk, and see them act." She was keenly aware of the story's subversive side: "In the Communists fleeing now into the Northwest, I saw the wild rebels and malcontents who had risen against government in the old days of Empire."

In the mornings Pearl started her next novel—"My mind could not rest after I had finished *The Good Earth*"—and dashed off her children's book for the Mission Board, *The Young Revolutionist*. She invited friends to tea every afternoon and entertained a steady flow of her husband's increasingly distinguished guests, among them in 1930 the English social historian R. H. Tawney, who worked on his *Land and Labour in China* in the Bucks' house, the American philosopher Ernest Hocking, and her brother Edgar Sydenstricker, the director of research at the Millbank Memorial Fund in New York, organizing aid for public health and rural education programs in China. Pearl was still teaching at the university, where her concentration had become so patchy—"It's the papers and grades which oppress me"—that her students complained about her to the president.

Nonstop activity was her defense against thoughts of Carol: "I miss eternally the person she cannot be. I am not resigned, and never will be." She fired off begging letters to Emma, to her sister on furlough in the United States, and to anyone she could think of who might visit the child, enclosing long, loving lists of toys and treats, promising to pay expenses, and always hoping for reports. The novel Pearl was working on was *The Mother,* which includes poignant accounts of a small girl learning painfully to live with disability while the child's mother, a young village woman abandoned by an unsatisfactory husband, works the farm on her own, rears a family, and learns no less painfully to live with frustrated desire. A tough and angry battler, like Lu Sadze (who was Pearl's model for *The Mother*), the nameless heroine finds herself humiliated and betrayed by her own body language ("there was that great, greedy, starving heart of hers showing in her own eyes without her knowledge that it did"), and eventually submits to the casual attentions of the local land agent in a seduction scene of Lawrentian earthiness. The emotion throbbing between the lines is so raw and palpable that Pearl dumped the finished typescript straight into the wastepaper basket. She retrieved it later, but the book remained, like *The Exile,* too blatantly confessional in her view for publication. "It was very specific about sex" was Grace's explanation.

In a time of public prudishness and private inhibition Pearl wrote with extraordinary directness about thwarted sexuality, marital rape, and the physical repulsion felt by women like her alter ego in *The Time Is Noon,* who leaves her husband's bed even before the birth of their only child to sleep alone upstairs in the attic with a trunk pushed against the door. At some point Pearl too moved out of the room she shared with Lossing, explaining to Emma White that she could no longer submit to his sexual demands: "I simply cannot stand it—it's a violation of all that is best in me." Grace said that, when she visited the Bucks in these years, she sometimes woke in the night to find her brother-in-law standing over her own bed. Pearl's fighting mood is clear from a piece she published in February 1930, "China in the Mirror of Her Fiction," pointing out that Chinese novelists accept lust as a routine aspect of ordinary life, taking "open delight in the body and its acts" instead of rejecting them as "abnormal or out of a diseased imagination." For Pearl at this stage the corollary was the visceral flinching vividly described in passages like this one between the young couple in *Other Gods*: "She turned . . . and faced him. Every fibre in her body was quivering and shrinking. Where did the blood go when it left the flesh like this? . . . Little things she had learned not to notice long ago: the thickness of his hands, the way his lips scarcely moved when he spoke, the clumsy farm speech which he could never change so long as he lived, because it was grown into him. . . . Uncontrollable irritation flamed out of her."

Professionally the Bucks were running neck and neck. *Chinese Farm Economy,* published in the United States that autumn with handsome acknowledgments—"For editing I am greatly indebted to my wife"—established Lossing as a leader in his field. He was increasingly in demand as a government consultant, and his land survey scheme attracted not only ample funding but international visiting academics, high-caliber faculty members, and increasing student numbers. "The project brought boom times to the Nanjing campus," wrote Paul B. Trescott, the most recent historian of twentieth-century Chinese economics. The Agricultural College under Reisner and Buck now accounted for more than half the faculty of the entire university and for nearly all the students who completed their education overseas. In 1925 there had been more than four times as many Western staff as Chinese, but five years later the Chinese outnumbered Westerners sixteen to one. Lossing's own departmental staff would soon reach one hundred, more than any other agricultural economics department in the world. The publications, scientific data, and above all the teachers and practitioners emerging from the Nanjing college affected farming at all levels, from Nationalist government policymaking to local village practice all over China.

Pearl reached a low point that winter, missing Carol more than ever after a year away, with another eighteen months to go before the time came to return to the United States on furlough. She ended *The Mother* with the death of the blind daughter from neglect and abuse at the hands of strangers in a far distant valley. "She was always thinking about Carol," said Lossing. In the first week of January 1931 he took her with him on a boat trip south down the coast to investigate the possibility of extending survey work into the country around Guangzhou, where heavy fighting made their progress difficult. Grace and her family, newly back from the United States, returned with considerable reluctance to their post in the Communist stronghold of Hunan. The Bucks got back to Nanjing to find a cable from Pearl's publisher announcing her Book-of-the-Month Club selection (she wrote back innocently that she had never heard of it: "Do they know that I am not a member of their club?"). Janice caught whooping cough, Lossing had several rotten teeth extracted, and Pearl told Emma she was starting a new novel to pass the time. *The Good Earth* was published in New York on March 2. Pearl said nobody at home knew of its existence, "or knowing had forgotten it." When she showed her first copy to her father, he complimented her politely on the jacket but handed the book back after a few days on the grounds that he did not feel up to reading it. Bulletins from the publisher, packages of reviews, and the first fan mail began reaching Nanjing toward the end of the month. Pearl wrote to Emma White that under different circumstances she might have felt excited—"I think I would have been wildly thrilled"— but success mostly mattered to her now because the money it brought made Carol's future safe.

The book's impact was phenomenal. The first prepublication readers responded, like Margaret Thomson, with admiration bordering on awe. Pearl's agent, David Lloyd, had felt that way before she even wrote it, recognizing star quality in the very first parcel delivered to him from China. "That first novel by this girl who could really write," said his daughter, remembering the buzz in the office when she was still at school. "That was pretty thrilling." For Richard Walsh, whose flair, judgment, and publisher's nose for the right book at the right time were exactly what Pearl needed at this point, it was the chance of a lifetime. "He could feel in his hands already the new big book," as Pearl put it in a mildly sardonic portrait of Walsh in *The Long Love.* "He was in the grip of his own private frenzy of creation." Dorothy Canfield Fisher, a literary heavyweight and Book-of-the-Month Club judge, had started by dismissing her unpromising proof copy from a virtually unknown author—"it seemed to be about agriculture in China"—only to sit up reading the book all night, creeping out at dawn the next morning to alert her fellow judges, who unanimously endorsed her choice. Reviewers did the same, and the American public followed suit. The book topped the best-seller charts for two years running, was translated into virtually every language, and has sold steadily ever since. It won its author a Pulitzer Prize in 1932 and the American Academy of Arts' prestigious Howells Medal three years later (the previous winner was Willa Cather). In 1938 Pearl Buck became the first American woman to win the Nobel Prize for literature (the second was Toni Morrison in 1993).

One of the remarkable things about *The Good Earth* is its prosaic acceptance of a brutal world almost unimaginably strange to its Western readership, and the parallel slow growth of trust between writer and reader. The facts of life it depicts, the alien bodily habits and thought patterns, the unfamiliar farming practices and family relations are portrayed with such authority that they seem perfectly natural. Readers identified with these patient, stoical, illiterate people, especially with Wang Lung's mute plain wife, whose character is rooted in gravity and silence: "Words were to her things to be caught one by one and released with difficulty." Olan, the mother who could strangle one girl child at birth and offer to sell another into slavery, became for American readers the moral center of the book and the prime source of its emotional warmth.

It was not simply that the book reversed expectations, although initially these could hardly have been lower. The West in general, and America in particular, operated an unspoken cultural veto against China in these years. "Nobody thought anything by or about China was interesting for the U.S.," said Helen Foster Snow, who with her husband, Edgar, did her best to reverse that implicit prohibition in the 1930s. "You couldn't sell it. Nothing sold but *The Good Earth,* which was the mystery of all time." For a period of just under a century, what Kang Liao calls the Age of Contempt, the Chinese had been systematically restricted, excluded, and penalized by U.S. legislation designed to protect the native workforce from migrant labor flooding into California. The Chinese Exclusion Act of 1882 was the first openly racist law passed by the U.S. government. The popular notion of a Chinaman was either a figure of fun or a monster of depravity. "He is politeness himself," wrote a shrewd and witty young Chinese commentator, Lin Yutang, describing the current literary stereotype in a Shanghai paper in the year *The Good Earth* was published. "The yellowness of his face exactly matches the colour of his teeth. He wears long gowns and long finger-nails. Opium is his favourite smoke, and Fan Tan his favourite game. He never opens his mouth except to grin, he never moves but he shuffles his feet. His name is either Dr. Wu or Fu Man Chu."

Pearl's book eroded the foundations of that wall of ignorance and prejudice. In the early years of the dust bowl and the Great Depression Americans recognized all too well the cycle of prosperity and destitution that overtakes Wang Lung, however hard he struggles by grinding overwork and extreme frugality to keep his family together on a roller coaster of drought, flood, robbers, famine, flight, bandits, and war. Pearl Buck did for the working people of twentieth-century China something of what Dickens had done for London's nineteenth-century poor. Readers saw their own worst fears reflected, magnified, and distorted in her pages in nightmare images of torment and humiliation when Wang is finally forced to find work as a rickshaw puller or join a night shift of men dragging cartloads of heavy goods to the city docks:

> All night through the dark streets he strained against the ropes, his body naked and streaming with sweating, and his bare feet slipping on the cobbles. . . . Each stone he had come to know now as a separate enemy, and he knew each rut by

which he might evade a stone and so use an ounce less of his life. There were times in the black nights, especially when it rained, and the streets were wet . . . that the whole hatred of his heart went out against these stones under his feet, these stones that seemed to cling and to hang to the wheels of his inhuman load.

Accounts of Wang's starving household—"They scarcely rose at all now, any of them. There was no need, and fitful sleep took the place, for a while at least, of the food they had not. The cobs of the corn they had dried and eaten and they stripped the bark from the trees"—and his deserted village—"stillness everywhere, the stillness of inactivity and of people, each in his own house, waiting to die"—run parallel to contemporary reports published in the *New York Herald Tribune* by Edgar Snow. As a young journalist on one of his first assignments in China, he traveled through the northwestern famine region, "a weird landscape swept of every growing thing as if by volcanic ash," where up to half the population in the towns he visited had died within the previous twelve months: "Even the trees had been stripped of their bark and were dying . . . Most of the mud-brick houses were collapsing. . . . Here and there last-ditchers still sat or lay on their doorsteps, scarcely conscious."

Snow's dispatches were ignored and largely unread at the time. He and Pearl Buck would become the two most influential China watchers of their day in the United States, writers of very different character and background whose work probably did more than anything else to alter public perceptions of the country and its people. Snow went on to be singled out by Mao Zedong for special treatment as an apologist and in some sense spokesman for the Communist cause. Pearl had no ideological commitment, but her early novels share the energy and directness that make the literary agenda of her avant-garde Chinese contemporaries so different from the goals of modernism established in the West by Eliot, Joyce, and Kafka. "To educate the masses was a matter of life and death for China, especially in the first half of this century," wrote Professor Liao in 1997, "and so the books were meant to be understood by as many people as possible, but in the U.S. what artists hated most was to lower the level of their works . . . to meet the needs of capitalist commercialisation."

The Good Earth enters into the world documented from the outside in the 1930s by Western travelers, observers, and journalists like Snow. Pearl Buck borrowed techniques from the Chinese novel in episodic sagas covering vast territories and spanning several generations, preoccupied less with individual characterization than with the expressive power of a broad filmic vision and harsh Dickensian imagery, to penetrate the deep underlife of Chinese people, and to draw Western readers in after her. With *The Good Earth* she did for her international readership what she had once done in person for Marian Craighill in Nanxuzhou and Lilliath Bates in Nanjing. "It's a change in us really, in our attitude towards people," as Lilliath put it in retrospect, describing the effect on her of seeing China through Pearl's eyes. She spoke for millions of readers in the years when Pearl Buck's views captured the popular imagination. "She was the first to humanize the Chinese and make them comprehensible," said Helen Foster Snow. *The Good Earth* opened a door between the American and Chinese worlds that had been firmly closed, and for the next four decades Pearl did all she could to stop it shutting again.

CHAPTER 7

The Stink of Condescension

I N NANJING IN the spring of 1931 Pearl's triumph still seemed to her as unreal as a dream. It lifted the barrier that held her back—"Her stories came from her now in a great rush, like the waters of the mighty Yangtze in a flood"—but whatever satisfaction she felt was offset by the horror of an actual flood worse than any known in China for almost a hundred years. Water had been rising for months, seeping out of the land, overflowing the canals, bursting dikes, inundating villages, and melting their earthen houses. By the end of March the wells had been submerged in the upper reaches of the Yangtse, which meant that people were forced to drink floodwaters polluted by refuse, decomposing bodies, and human and animal excrement. Chiang Kaishek, said to have been a river god in a previous incarnation, was blamed for twenty-four inches of torrential rain that fell in two weeks in July, turning a relatively familiar calamity into illimitable, almost unprecedented disaster. There were rumors of cannibalism, and of parents in the country around Nanjing drowning children they could no longer feed. The yellow waters of the river climbed the stone embankment of the port seven miles from the city center to pour across the fields and "come creeping and crawling through the streets." Pearl rode out along the dike wall on horseback and climbed on foot to the top of Purple Mountain, itself now transformed into an island: "lapping at its base, fifty feet deep over farmhouses and fields, were yellow Yangtze waves."

Lossing organized a comprehensive survey of the devastated area, sending out his force of trained investigators to recruit local helpers with backing from the Nationalist government. Madame Chiang Kaishek's brother, the finance minister T. V. Soong, personally authorized the project's funding. Charles Lindbergh, the world-famous American pilot who had crossed the Atlantic in a monoplane, arrived to reconnoiter the devastation from the air after an initial trip in Lossing's sampan. Pearl raised awareness in the United States with magazine stories describing the starving refugees who poured into Nanjing and the desperation of dying people huddled among piles of wreckage protruding from the surrounding waters that stretched in every direction as far as the eye could see. One of her first translators, Hu Zhongchi, cited in his preface to *The Good Earth* a letter from the president of the American Red Cross explaining how much the relief effort owed to the generosity of Americans moved by the sufferings of the Wang family. Twenty-five million people were affected in the flood plains of the Yangtse and Huai Rivers, according to Lossing's final estimate; others put the number at more than twice as many, with half a million drowned.

On August 31 Absalom Sydenstricker died in his eightieth year at Kuling and was buried by his daughter Grace with his Greek New Testament in his hand. Pearl missed the funeral because it was impossible to cross the inland sea, now stretching the whole length of the Yangtse between Nanjing and Kuling. The two sisters paid dignified tribute to their father in obituaries for the *Chinese Recorder* and the *Christian Observer* respectively. "I miss him dreadfully!" Pearl told Grace. "During the past two years his tall ascetic frame had grown more and more frail, his nature more completely the saint," she wrote long afterward in her memoirs, having by that time analyzed with unsparing honesty in *Fighting Angel* the price paid for his saintliness by other people. A stone tablet erected in his honor at the town's south gate after he left Zhenjiang praised his good works, his faithful service over thirty years, and his perseverance in the face of slander and contempt. The text was composed by Ma Pangbo: "We carve this tablet in his honor to show our love just as people long ago expressed their love of Shaobo by cherishing the tree of Gantang" (Shaobo in ancient Chinese legend was a wise and just minister of the Western Zhou dynasty, who liked to sit beneath the tree of Gantang).

The death of her father coincided with the first round in what eventually became a public showdown between Pearl and the mission movement. She still drew her salary as a teacher, but she had stopped going to church when it became clear that she could expect no answer to her passionate prayers for her daughter. Her employers' response to her book was harsh and swift. The first letter Pearl received from a reader in the United States—"several pages of blistering rebuke"—came from the secretary of the Presbyterian Board of Foreign Missions in New York, who threatened her obliquely with public denunciation. His tone was at once so sanctimonious and so squeamish that she did not immediately realize that his main complaint was her sexual frankness. Her friend Emma found herself defending *The Good Earth* against similar objections. "Of course . . . it *isn't* a nice book!" Pearl wrote back cheerfully. "Your friends or whoever they were who said it was a coarse book are perfectly right—it *is* a coarse book from this point of view." She explained that her portrait of Wang Lung was as accurate as she could make it, and that behavior unmentionable in genteel American society—belching, urinating, sexual intercourse—was as natural and unselfconscious for him as for most Chinese. "I like their matter-of-fact attitude to all natural functions of life, including sex. I think it sane and wholesome. . . . They provide for these things as they do for hunger and thirst and there's an end of it." She confided to her brother Edgar her astonishment and initial incredulity over the missionaries' perverse obsession: "sex is the devil to them, and seems to consume a great deal of their attention."

The book's first Chinese reviews were polite rather than enthusiastic. This kind of naturalism had no precedent in classical or contemporary writing ("The study of peasant psychology is . . . practically unknown," wrote a Chinese critic, saluting the book as somber but serious: "The Chinese farmer in his individual element has never yet found proper expression in his own literature"). Olan was the first Chinese woman to be portrayed in fiction as she actually was rather than with the moth eyebrows, porcelain skin, and tiny flowerlike feet of the traditional heroine. The evident authenticity of *The Good*

Earth was a source of aggravation from the start, especially given the book's astonishing popularity. "I was surprised to find how the young Chinese intellectuals hated it," said Helen Foster Snow, who reached China for the first time in 1931: "they were violent about it. . . . Also the missionaries disliked it. In fact, almost nobody living in China liked it at all, for different reasons." The cosmopolitan, Western-educated Chinese community in Shanghai deplored the book's portrayal of insuperable social problems which it was in nobody's interest to spell out so plainly. "They wanted to make a good impression on the foreigners, and also they wanted to avoid facing facts themselves and to avoid doing anything to remedy the situation." The students in Snow's language classes bitterly resented a foreigner exposing their country's poverty and lack of modern amenities in a book that already showed signs of becoming a world-class best seller.

Pearl encountered the same attitude herself, both in China and the United States, in patriotic young people whose experiences of the West had made them bitterly sensitive to racial slights and slurs. She even incorporated their response into the final volume of her *Good Earth* trilogy, in a passage in which Wang Lung's grandson attends a mission fund-raising presentation designed to touch its soft-hearted American audience with slides of beggars, lepers, and starving children in mud huts: "Yuan could not bear it. All through the hour his anger had been rising, mixed with shame and dismay, so to see revealed before this staring, ignorant foreign crowd his country's faults. . . . It seemed to him that this prying priest had searched out every ill that he could find and dragged it forth before the cold eyes of this western world." Over the next half-century Pearl Buck would be heavily criticized and finally banned in China for spreading reactionary imperialist lies about the past in books that wantonly distorted the correct image of Chinese farmers. "The story is set in the benighted period of the Qing dynasty, portraying the Chinese as males with pigtails and females with bound feet in order to depict Chinese society as intrinsically backward," ran a history of Nanjing published in 1985. "It is not hard to see the bad effect produced by *The Good Earth* on American society!"

In September 1931 Japanese troops began systematically seizing territory in Manchuria. There were rumors of Russia mobilizing and Britain proposing to support Japan. In Nanjing six thousand young people took to the streets to protest the Chinese government's inaction. "It is very tense here," Pearl wrote to Emma White on September 24. "Last night the government students gathered around the Japanese consulate and yelled hideously for about three hours, 'Down with the Japanese!' " Four days later they attacked their own foreign ministry. Pressure mounted throughout the winter. In January an advance force of Japanese marines landed in Shanghai backed by a dozen naval destroyers and heavy aerial bombardment. Shells disrupted the rail link to Nanjing, and the government prepared to evacuate inland. Chinese and Japanese armies clashed in February around Shanghai, with fierce fighting inside the city. Roused in the middle of the night, with shells falling and gunboats advancing up the river toward Nanjing, the Bucks and their neighbors packed their bags and left. "We crawled up, dressed and I will confess I was simply terrified and shook life a leaf," Pearl wrote to her sister. Janice, who was seven years old, retained all her life a terror of moonlight on her pillow.

They found temporary shelter in Beijing, where Pearl taught at the language school, spending mornings in the National Library researching illustrations for her translation of *All Men Are Brothers* and afternoons exploring the old city. She attended the Beijing Opera and visited the home of its greatest actor, Mei Linfang. The place that matched her mood most closely was the valley where the crumbling remains of imperial Ming tombs stood in a semicircle against a rocky hillside, "a somber, wild, fierce landscape, the mountains warped and black and craggy against the brilliant sky." All through that cold dry spring when sandy desert winds blew through the city streets, Pearl reviewed her future options: "It was in Peking . . . that I became convinced that sooner or later I must leave China and return permanently to my own country, for such wars and upheavals lay ahead that no white people would be allowed to remain."

War with Japan ended with a cease-fire and suspension of hostilities in early March, and in June the Bucks returned briefly to Nanjing to prepare for their return to the United States on furlough. "I seem not to remember much about the departure," Pearl wrote in her memoirs. Her husband planned to complete his PhD at Cornell, and she was in a fever to get back to Carol. They arranged to take with them Pearl's American secretary, Adeline Bucher, who had turned out to be even more useful looking after Janice. Pearl found a telegram waiting for her in Nanjing with news that *The Good Earth* had won her a Pulitzer. Film rights had already been sold to Metro-Goldwyn-Meyer for fifty thousand dollars, more than any book had ever gotten from Hollywood before. She said she felt "like a common brown hen . . . who has seen a phoenix emerge from what she thought was an ordinary egg." Now that she was in a position to do as she pleased, her plans for Carol and the Vineland School loomed far larger than her publisher's counterplans to unveil his mystery author to the American public. "I shall avoid all publicity stuff, and want to slip in and out of America unnoticed" was the unrealistic scheme Pearl outlined to Emma. "My blood runs cold at the thought of meeting a lot of people."

The secret of Pearl Buck baffled and intrigued American readers, who knew next to nothing about her. Requests for interviews could not be processed. Personal details were unavailable. Some people even doubted her existence. She had just passed her fortieth birthday when she slipped into the United States in July 1932, having landed with her family in Canada to be met by her publisher, who dealt with the demands of journalists, editors, PR mongers, and fans by whittling them down into a highly selective schedule, and delivering her himself to the secluded farm belonging to her parents-in-law in Poughkeepsie. The first the public knew of her arrival was a dinner in the Jade Room of the Waldorf Astoria Hotel in New York on August 3. Two hundred handpicked guests, representing the cream of the city's fashionable intelligentsia in low-cut evening frocks and white tuxedos, were confronted by Pearl, who wore a high V-necked dress with sleeves, little or no makeup, and her hair pulled back in a plain bun, looking so nervous that at least one observer suspected she was about to run away. She made a short shy speech of thanks and captivated her audience by reading from the preface to *All Men Are Brothers*, written three hundred years earlier by its original editor, Shih Nai-an: "How can I know what those who come after me and read my book will think of it? I do not even know if I myself afterwards can even read this book. Why therefore should I care?"

It was a characteristically cool and courteous way of capitalizing on her own ignorance and inexperience in a country where, as she said herself, she didn't understand the first thing about anything, from motion pictures to the banking system. Pearl was courted, fêted, photographed, interviewed by press and radio, and showered with requests that autumn to address literary luncheons, teas, and cocktail parties organized by churches, clubs, and universities. She accepted no more than a handful, including a dinner invitation from Chinese students at Columbia, who urged her for the honor of their country to suppress her translation of *All Men Are Brothers* on the grounds that it made their heritage look barbaric to Western readers. *Sons,* her sequel to *The Good Earth,* was published in September to mixed reviews and escalating sales; eighty thousand copies sold in the first month, preceded by serialization in *Cosmopolitan* for an unheard-of $30,000, bringing Pearl's total earnings in 1932 to roughly $100,000. The book starts with Wang Lung's funeral and explores China's twentieth-century politics through the careers of his three sons, all of whom ruthlessly exploit the land inherited from their father by becoming respectively an idle, venal landlord, a greedy and manipulative merchant, and a bandit chief. Schematic in format and essentially didactic in purpose, the novel's vitality and force lie with the lonely, driven youngest son, Wang the Tiger, a born rebel—stern, disciplined, in some sense a stand-in for his author—who spends his first forty years preparing himself for a campaign that pits him against authority and isolates him more or less completely from weaker, less ambitious contemporaries.

Three months to the day after her first tentative performance at the Waldorf, Pearl initiated a campaign of her own by challenging America's innate racism, bigotry, and cultural imperialism at a fundraising event on November 2 organized by the Presbyterian Church. She was by now an international celebrity, lionized wherever she went and claimed as its own by a mission movement that should have known better than to try to cash in on this Pulitzer-winning outsider, who charmed and disconcerted audiences by looking like a homely Dutch housewife while delivering observations that were anything but reassuring. Pearl had agreed under pressure to report in private to interested members of the Mission Board, over lunch at the Astor Hotel, on her findings in four decades as a mission child, wife, and teacher only to discover on arrival that this was to be a promotional event, staged in the hotel's main ballroom before two thousand paid ticket holders. "I did not know what to do, and yet I didn't know what to say except what I had prepared very carefully for a few people and certainly not for the public. . . . Well, I had to give that speech and I got up and gave it. When I had finished I sat down. Deadly silence fell upon the room. It was appalling to me." A thunderous ovation eventually followed from the hall, but not from the grim-faced religious leaders seated at Pearl's table. "It gave us cold chills as she went along," said the Board's secretary, Dr. Cleland Boyd McAfee, who found himself presiding over a comprehensive indictment of the mission enterprise in theory and practice by an authoritative and devastatingly articulate eyewitness.

If he or any of his colleagues had bothered to glance back over her career beforehand, they might have had a clearer idea of what to expect. Pearl's speech, "Is There a Case for Foreign Missions?" was the final draft of a long, ongoing, internal debate formulated at intervals over the previous ten years in papers published in the *Chinese Recorder.* It began with a talk given to trainee missionaries at the Nanjing language school in 1923, when Pearl as a young woman was still trying to come to terms with her father's expulsion from Zhenjiang. She warned her contemporaries against the intolerance of the previous generation, urging them to understand and make allowances for their elders' stubborn self-righteousness: "It is too much to expect of them in general to get our viewpoint. But we ought to be able to get theirs." She urged them to acknowledge their own aggressive instincts so as to avoid falling into the same trap themselves: "Don't mistake a psychological complex for religious emotion or divine leadership. . . . Don't mistake a wish of your own for the will of God, nor hurt vanity . . . for a call of duty to persist in your own way." It was sensible, practical advice based on painful personal experience. Pearl's recommended strategy was to cultivate a sense of humor and proportion; to recognize the notion of a single, fixed, unalterable truth as superstitious absurdity; and never to be deluded into operating on anything less than a basis of absolute equality: "We simply cannot express the Gospel with any force if we have hidden within us a sense of racial superiority. . . . We are no better than anyone else, any of us."

In an article published four years later under the title "Is There a Place for the Foreign Missionary?," Pearl moved her argument from particular instances to general principles, posing and answering the question she would eventually address before a wider forum in New York. Her lucid, unsentimental analysis concluded that church people's ignorant and hostile dismissal of Chinese philosophy and culture made the missionary position fundamentally untenable, if not actually immoral: "More insidious in its pessimism is . . . the question of whether anyone has the right to impress upon another the forms of his own civilization, whether these forms are religious or not." Pearl foresaw a future of increasing conflict exacerbated by the mission force, whose impact on the country had otherwise been negligible, and whose arrogance masked underlying greed, fear, and insecurity: "Consciously or unconsciously we have come to these foreign countries saying in our hearts that we had all to give and nothing to get. We have not . . . sought to understand the civilizations with which we dealt. . . . We have had the abominable attitude of one who confers a favor. . . . Even though we have spilled our blood and have broken our hearts, it has been a favor." She was fiercer still in a passionate outburst published as a parting shot in the *Recorder*'s letters column as she sailed for the United States in July 1932, repudiating the Calvinist doctrines of sin, guilt, and damnation that had hung over her childhood and filled her with sick revulsion in her teenage years. "I grew up among such as these and I know them," she wrote bitterly, describing an entrenched white community that refused to look beyond its own rigid codes of conduct and belief, and ridiculed any attempt to understand or listen to the people whose lives it proposed taking over.

This long angry letter triggered the text delivered in November at the Astor Hotel, printed in *Harper's Magazine* in January, and published by the John Day company as a best-selling pamphlet. Its tone was judicious, even humorous, but its uncompromising message was memorably driven home by a caustic cartoon of the missionary Pearl claimed to have watched all her life with a mixture of inquisitive affection, reluctant admiration, and downright disgust.

> I have seen the missionary narrow, uncharitable, unappreciative, ignorant. I have seen missionaries . . . so lacking in sympathy for the people they were supposed to be saving, so scornful of any civilization but their own, so harsh in their judgments upon one another, so coarse and insensitive among a sensitive and cultivated people, that my heart has fairly bled with shame. I can never have done with my apologies to the Chinese people that in the name of a gentle Christ we have sent such people to them.

IT TOOK NERVE to stand in front of an audience largely composed of this sort of decent, conventional, well-meaning people and tell them that their smugness and mediocrity had added to the wretchedness of the Chinese poor. Pearl explained firmly that sincerity was not enough. Neither was an individual's solemn conviction that he had heard the call, nor the Church's subsequent assurance that he had officially been consecrated, "that miserable word . . . used to cover so many deficiencies and so much sloppy thinking." Her final constructive plea for the deployment of fewer, more intelligent, and better qualified mission personnel carried none of the conviction of her apocalyptic image of a man with a closed mind, growing steadily emptier and more arid, delivering increasingly mechanical exhortations, failing to establish more than superficial contact with the Chinese and unable to replenish his own dwindling spiritual and intellectual resources from the deep springs of their ancient civilization. "The vast people, the age-old history, the fathomless differences of race, even the enormous opportunity combined with his own apparent lack of success, dwarfed him. He presented, and presents in many cases, the spectacle of a tiny human figure standing among tremendous cliffs and bottomless valleys strange to him. He is lost. . . . He shouts the name of God over and over, lest it lose reality for him."

Initial shock followed by excited applause in the hotel ballroom was reflected in widespread media coverage, which in turn released a flood of letters from all over the country accusing Pearl of atheism, obscenity, material greed, and shameless hunger for publicity. People who had not read her books denounced them as indecent and urged the Church to punish her. One Presbyterian pastor proposed renaming her best-seller *The Dirty Mud*. Another deplored her "ruthless, heartless, insane, bigoted, intelligentsiacal cynicism" and predicted "that Mrs. Buck will pray for her 'good earth' to swallow her up" when physically attacked by what sounds like a lynch mob of enraged fundamentalists. Pearl's speech coincided with the publication of *Re-Thinking Missions: A Laymen's Inquiry after 100 Years,* a report chaired by her old acquaintance Ernest Hocking, who reached conclusions very similar to her own, backed up by hard evidence and statistical tables. Between them the two precipitated a national controversy, with Pearl as its focal point. She had paid generous tribute to her husband in her talk, citing him as an exemplary anonymous "agricultural missionary," eager to learn from local farmers and to provide them with the kind of practical ministry regarded by both Bucks as the only viable future option for the Church. Lossing had stood by his wife at the hotel on November 2 but took no part in the media scrum that followed, returning instead to work on his Cornell thesis in lodgings at Ithaca. Absorbed in gathering material and drumming up recruits for his land survey, suffering from overwork and eye strain, running out of time and energy and reluctant to waste either on any more trips to New York to attend public functions as his wife's sidekick, he was only too happy to devolve escort duty on her publisher.

RICHARD WALSH WAS everything Lossing was not. Witty, urbane, cosmopolitan, and exceedingly well-read, he had been a classmate of Robert Benchley at Harvard and knew everyone who mattered in the New York book world. Pearl's initial impression of him as hard, dry, and conservative melted in the warmth of his easy unassuming charm. He was in his mid-forties, projecting to perfection the image of a comfortable pipe-smoking 1930s bookman in rumpled tweeds and brogues. He lacked the ruthless drive and ego that might have made him a sharper businessman, but he was a natural promoter, fascinated by marketing, publicity, and the art of spin. Pearl said he had a lovely smile, a brilliant intuitive mind, and humorous eyes, "wasted on a man, for they were pure violet with long black lashes." He took over all the things she hated about the celebrity circuit, programming her days, supervising contacts with press and radio, screening out unwanted approaches, and organizing an exclusive contract that made the John Day company responsible for her speaking engagements. In these first hectic months he barely left her side. He took her to fashionable restaurants, introduced her to other literary highflyers, and accompanied her to theaters (a disastrous adaptation of *The Good Earth* with an all-white American cast opened and closed that autumn in New York). In spare moments they worked in her hotel room, going through correspondence, sorting out future commitments, and putting together a first collection of her short stories. Together they edited her two-volume translation of *All Men Are Brothers,* a costly enterprise that drained the firm's resources in spite of selling better than anyone expected on publication at the beginning of 1933. Pearl had never known anything like the quality or quantity of attention Richard gave her. "Sympathy and understanding appreciation are so delightful," she wrote to him on November 3. "I am not used to them—and it is for me wonderful."

For his part he was enchanted by her both professionally and personally. Virtually overnight she had transformed the fortunes of his small, ambitious, desperately hard-up firm, and now her management and protection monopolized him to the exclusion of all his other authors. He made her laugh, and her combination of awkwardness and innocence with highly sophisticated perception took his breath away. The two responded to one another like dancing partners taking to the floor. "He was an impresario of writers and books," she wrote long afterward, "but a man of such tender understanding of the needs and delicacies and shynesses of talented persons that he guided without seeming to do so. . . . he never seemed to lead although he did not follow, he uncovered without shaping." She flowered for him, gaining confidence, dressing better, looking ten years younger, and growing slim again. The change in her was immediately apparent. "Pearl dropped into my office the other day," her brother Edgar wrote to Grace that winter. "I have never seen her looking so pretty. She seems to have the world wrapped round her finger, and yet she is exactly the same. It hasn't touched her at all. I am just beginning to realize what a wonderful girl she is, and she has only just begun."

Walsh was a family man with three teenage children and a devoted wife, all of whom were caught up in the Buck campaign. "He presented her as his star," said Richard's daughter Natalie. For a time the Walshes included Pearl in a relaxed and cheerful domesticity quite different from her own home life. Richard's wife, Ruby, looked after Janice when her mother came to stay for the weekend. Lossing was invited to join Walsh family outings, and the two couples planned holidays together. Pearl had taken a suite of rooms in the Murray Hill Hotel on Park Avenue so that she could commute between New York and the Vineland School in New Jersey, spending a day or two each week with Carol. The child had adapted well to her new life, and Pearl planned a house, Carol's Cottage, specially designed to meet the needs of her daughter and a group of companions the same age. Now that she was no longer tormented by anxiety about the future or distracted by strangers' disapproving stares and whispers, Pearl could relax in Carol's company, taking pride in her happiness and accepting whatever she had to give. These regular visits had to be carefully planned, with security precautions in place at the school to protect the children from intrusive publicity (Richard proved adept at deflecting the glare of media attention). Pearl repaid the borrowed money spent on fees and presented the school's director with a check for forty thousand dollars. Her priority was Carol, but forty years of scrimping made her delight in lavish giving. She bought a Buick for

Lossing and posted parcels off to China: costly woolen wraps for the elderly amahs, toys for her nephews, a whole box of new dresses for Grace. Her parents-in-law got their house repainted and a new porch, a suite of furniture, and shrubbery for the garden. Her farewell gift when she sailed back to China in the summer was to buy their rented farm and sign it over to them for the remainder of their lives, adding a five-thousand-dollar annuity for each of them.

On March 7, 1933, the front page of the *New York Times* featured an unexpected plug by America's most famous cowboy, Will Rogers, who picked *The Good Earth* as the best book of his generation: "So go get this and read it. It will keep you out of some devilment and learn you all about China, and you'll thank me for it." Rogers reached a whole new layer of readers no other critic could. Sales were further boosted in early April by a fresh outbreak of controversy, amounting this time to a public witch hunt spearheaded by a hard-core fundamentalist, Dr. J. Gresham Machen of Westminster Theological Seminary in Philadelphia, who charged the Mission Board with scandalous laxity, identifying Mrs. J. L. Buck as the prime culprit and demanding her immediate dismissal as an unbeliever. Machen's challenge was the signal for a further round of accusation and counteraccusation. There were calls for Lossing as well as his wife to lose their jobs. Pearl escalated the conflict with an article in *Cosmopolitan* questioning the Church's exclusive claim to Jesus Christ, and maintaining that the power of his teaching did not depend on his supposed divinity. The press spoke darkly of lynching, martyrdom, and the Inquisition. Pearl was widely reported to be facing trial by the Church for heresy. Her husband told the press he could not comment. Richard advised her to go into hiding.

The Mission Board, split between opposing factions, stepped up an exercise in damage limitation fronted by Dr. McAfee, who fielded vituperation and abuse, damped down press speculation, and expressed cordial support for Pearl, blandly denying any suggestion that she was a heretic. Reconciliation was his aim, and he pursued it with diplomacy and skill. Some of the harshest criticisms he received came from Absalom Sydenstricker's former colleagues in China, who recognized as clearly as Pearl herself that this was on some level a private reckoning, containing a strong element of personal betrayal. "Everything she has uttered of late tends to discredit her father and the gospel," observed a report submitted to the Board by Rev. James Graham, Absalom's old friend, long-term adversary, and his successor as head of the Zhenjiang station. Graham, who had known Pearl since she was a baby in Tsingkiangpu, denounced her as demented and unwomanly, deliberately pandering to depravity in books based on filthy Chinese novels: "Is it any wonder that we missionaries are perplexed, disturbed, yes *outraged,* that a woman who committed an abomination in a printed book . . . should be quoted on all sides as an authority on what mission work should consist of and the kind of missionary that should be sent to China?"

Strangely enough Pearl agreed with him. She refused to negotiate with McAfee or any of his emissaries on the grounds that the Church's internal feuding was no concern of hers, insisting that she had had enough of the whole preposterous farrago. Her letter of resignation from the mission movement, sent on April 28, raised another storm of protest. Students, liberal church leaders, black people, and women's groups at home and abroad rose to her defense. A Mrs. J. M. Guthrie of North Carolina spoke for many of Pearl's readers in a dignified letter of rebuke, objecting to the spurious respectability lent by the Church to an assault by ignorant fanatics, and saying that for the first time in her life she felt ashamed of her Presbyterian allegiance: "I am only a humble farm woman, but I tell you that there are thousands of other women like me who will rise in indignation against this foolish affair being given further publicity."

Much of the uproar had been caused in the first place by Pearl's increasingly high profile as a speaker on subjects like birth control, race relations, and discrimination against women and black people. She had been appalled by an exhibition in Harlem of black painters whose work depicted lynchings, burnings, ruined families and homes, the desolation caused by segregation in the South. Her feelings surfaced in an address that winter to the National Urban League in New York. "Some of the things my people do make me ashamed of the fact that I am white" was one of her remarks, quoted in the African American *Chicago Defender* with the rider, "from that point forward she was doomed to persecution by her Christian brothers." Reports of her speeches were printed in newspapers around the world. The *Madras Mail* printed Pearl's picture in early May under the headline "eXfh ᗞ bY౩ XeXfl ౩ ha ǧ" with a caption attributing the attacks on her to "her attitude of fairness and justice toward darker races." She shared a platform at Cornell in February with Eleanor Roosevelt, the formidable wife of America's newly elected president, gave the alumnae address at Randolph Macon's commencement in June, and went on to accept an honorary degree from Yale.

In July the Bucks set out by a roundabout route to return to China, traveling via Europe with a large party consisting of Janice and Adeline Bucher, Richard and Ruby Walsh, a recently divorced Edgar Sydenstricker with his new wife, Phyllis, and Ardron B. Lewis, a young Cornell statistician roped in to join Lossing's land utilization team. In England the party divided into two. Lossing's three-man research group (they were joined by another agriculturalist, Charles Stewart of Illinois) set out in the Buick to conduct a scientific survey of farming practices and agricultural departments in England, Wales, Scotland, Ireland, Sweden, Germany, and France. Pearl and Richard led a more leisurely sightseeing tour of cultural sites and publishing houses in Great Britain and Europe. The two parties met up again in Paris at the end of the summer, when the U.S. residents turned back across the Atlantic, leaving the Bucks with Ardron Lewis and Adeline Bucher to take ship from Italy for China. They set off on the long, hot, sticky journey south in an overcrowded car with Lossing at the wheel and a fractious child in the back, oppressed by heavy silent tension between the driver and his wife.

The attraction between Pearl and Richard had come to a head even before they left America and become almost more than they could handle on their foreign holiday, in spite of all the other people present. They had parted in Paris on the understanding that each would at least try to live without the other. Pearl's resolution lasted until the Buick reached Nice, where she finally asked Lossing for a divorce. She claimed afterward that he had suspected nothing: "He was taken by surprise. 'I thought I had made a success of our marriage,' he said." Lossing himself maintained that he knew perfectly well what was going on but had been too preoccupied to stop it; "I was busy, busy, busy, going back with all this Land Utilization data." He was clearly distressed, according to Lewis, who sailed with them from Venice, but phlegmatic and reluctant to talk about what had happened. Pearl confided to Emma halfway through the voyage that, hard as she had tried to save her marriage, she could not endure her husband's touch: "frankly if I am to live in the same house as Lossing I cannot go on with *that.* . . . My whole soul and body turns sick at the thought." They landed on October 2 in Shanghai, where Pearl was fêted for the first and last time by the Chinese in China. She gave interviews before she even left the ship; attended a dinner hosted by the satirical weekly, *The China Critic,* for her to meet its brilliant young columnist, Lin Yutang; and spoke at a reception given in her honor by the city's literary community on the night of the Moon Festival, October 5 (they had done the same in the spring for George Bernard Shaw).

Shortly afterward she returned for the last time to Nanjing, where Lossing had already plunged back into work. His most urgent concern, prompted by the ravages of the Great Depression in Europe and the United States, was to establish a link between China's current monetary problems and the fact that the Chinese yuan was pegged to the rising price of silver. A report on his findings published by the university that winter led directly to Chiang Kaishek's decision to rebalance his country's economy by dismantling the silver standard. "Dr. Buck's prestige with the Chinese Nationalist government was very high," said Ardron Lewis, who coauthored a statistical study, *Silver and Prices,* as well as working on the land utilization survey that had by this time taken over much of the Agricultural College building. In an age before computers, the labor of sorting, filing, and collating fieldwork results collected on an unprecedented scale from all over the country was carried out by teams of statisticians, clerks, and graduate students working at tables set up on the raked tiers of the central lecture theater. "To conceive such a project requires what you might call scientific imagination," Professor Lewis wrote half a century later, assessing in retrospect the audacity of Lossing's vision, his administrative flair, and powerful synthesizing intelligence. "You couldn't conceive it without. . . . It remains the only authoritative picture we've got of the agricultural constitution of China. . . . It must be the benchmark of all measurements in all departments." Lossing himself acknowledged a symbiotic relationship with *The Good Earth* in the first footnote of the first of three monumental volumes of *Land Utilisation in China*. On its publication in 1937 the work was immediately recognized as, according to the *New York Times*, "unquestionably the most detailed study ever made of any aspect of Chinese life." Overtaken by the outbreak of war with Japan that year, set aside during the civil war, and dismissed for decades after the Communists came to power as the elitist product of futile, formalist, bourgeois science, Lossing's survey is only now beginning to be assessed without bias in China. "It laid a solid foundation for China's agricultural development and research," said Cui Zechun, summing up proceedings at a conference held in honor of J. L. Buck at Nanjing University in 2008. "Professor Buck was the founder of China's agricultural economics."

By late autumn of 1933 the two Bucks had parted company in all but the most formal sense. Resuming her old routines as a faculty wife, this time with no job of her own to distract her, Pearl found her situation almost unendurable. "The strain was practically impossible before," she wrote to Emma, "now utterly so. . . . I am quite desperate these days." Her old friends let her know that they would not put up with anything that looked like pretension on her part. "Oh, so we've got a secretary now, have we?" asked Margaret Thomson with a sarcastic intonation that Pearl remembered bitterly for the rest of her life. America receded, becoming once again the exotic unreal dreamland it had been throughout her childhood. She gave up any attempt to work on the novel she had planned to complete the *Good Earth* trilogy, promised for delivery by the end of the year. All she could do was housework and gardening, sunk in the kind of dismal stupor that had overtaken her father when he too saw his own life fall apart.

Her stupor was interrupted by a cable from Richard, who had accepted a second job as editor of *Asia* magazine on condition that his first duty to the paper was an extended tour of his prospective territory, with the Bucks' house in Nanjing as its starting point. He arrived at the end of the year, bringing with him an authentic whiff of Manhattan. Pearl met him in Shanghai, and the two became inseparable again. Back in conventional, conservative Nanjing, their free and easy behavior caused consternation. One of Lossing's closest Chinese colleagues, R. H. Tsui, never forgot the shock of seeing him drive by in the Buick with Pearl and "the publisher Walsh" grinning and chattering side by side together on the back seat. "They were pretty brazen about it," said Lossing, who left on a field trip for Tibet soon after Richard moved into his house. Pearl made it clear that she was planning her departure too. By the time her husband got back, she and Richard had set out alone together to cross Asia (more than thirty years later Pearl remembered pulling off her wedding ring and dropping it overboard from a Chinese riverboat at some point on their travels). They headed south, dropping in to present Richard to Pearl's sister, pottering around the old city of Guangzhou, and exploring the country backtracks of Fukien, before moving on through Vietnam, Cambodia, Thailand, Laos, Burma, India, and back across China to Beijing. "I wanted as little as possible to do with white people," Pearl said of this journey, which was her chance to initiate Richard into the world where she felt at home, just as he had made her free of his literary landscape in New York.

They picked up again a dialogue about writing, politics, historical and cultural connections that spilled out when they got back to the United States into a comprehensive remake of *Asia* magazine. It had coasted along for nearly thirty years as an upmarket, vaguely philanthropical, increasingly ailing travel monthly, kept afloat recently by advertisements for Oriental holidays and luxury cruises. Richard's first editorial, published in his absence in January 1934, signaled a change of course to a more demanding direction with special emphasis on new writing, serious analysis, and objective in-depth reporting by multicultural experts drawn from a broad field. The new management was a joint enterprise from the start. Richard signed up the *Manchester Guardian*'s Asian correspondent, H. J. Timperley, as a talent spotter in Beijing. Pearl, who had already submitted articles by Lin Yutang to *Asia,* now introduced him in person to the new editor. (Lin's book *My Country and My People* would be a runaway bestseller for John Day in 1935.) In Beijing she telephoned a couple of enterprising young American writers, recently returned themselves from a honeymoon voyage of discovery, Edgar and Helen Foster Snow. Both would write for *Asia,* which pulled off a journalistic coup a few years later with prepublication extracts from Edgar's *Red Star over China.* The five of them spent a productive and entertaining day together at the Snows' Beijing home.

An ambitious, energetic loner from Kansas City, Edgar Snow had married a clever, tough-minded, rebellious, runaway Mormon, who became the research end (and some said the brains) of their joint outfit during the ten years they spent together in China. With no previous knowledge of the country or its language, they aimed to educate themselves and undercut the standard Western view of Oriental inscrutability by reading what the Chinese wrote. In a time of widespread disillusion, political tension, and indiscriminate censorship under an increasingly authoritarian government, when more and more writers were being forced to go underground or leave the country, the Snows had built up an extensive collection of books, pamphlets, and periodicals banned as subversive by the Nationalists. Their long-term goal was to persuade America to look at China through Chinese eyes by turning many of these texts into English with the help of hired translators.

When he met Pearl, Edgar was working on the first translation of Lu Xun's alarming allegory, "Story of Ah Q," probably the single best-known and most influential fiction produced by any Chinese writer in its day or since. Lu himself, living at the time in and out of hiding in the French concession in Shanghai, had included a disparaging comment in a letter to a friend soon after Pearl's triumphal reception in that city: "It is always better for the Chinese to write about Chinese subject matter, as that is the only way to get near the truth.

Even with Mrs. Buck . . . what her books reveal is no more than her stand as an American woman missionary who happens to have grown up in China. . . . Only when we Chinese come to do it, can we expect to reveal some truth." Widely circulated after Lu's premature death and formally endorsed as the politically correct view, this passing reference (which Lu seems subsequently to have regretted) irreparably damaged Pearl Buck's reputation in China both before and after the Communist takeover in 1949. For her part she greatly admired his work, going out of her way to mention it in books, articles, and speeches and reviewing *Ah Q and Other Stories* enthusiastically when it finally appeared in the United States.

It was an article by Edgar Snow published in 1935 in *Asia,* followed by translations of two short stories, that first alerted American readers to Lu's existence. Foreigners rarely met contemporary writers of this kind, dissidents with no formal Communist allegiance, critical of their own society and anxious for reform under mounting threat from the Nationalists' fascist regime. Lu was one of many introduced by Lin Yutang to the Snows, who in turn passed them on to the editors of *Asia.* Edgar was as fascinated by contemporary vernacular fiction as Pearl had been at the start of her career, and for the same reason: "It opened many doorways into the thinking of people of my own age in China, and taught me something of the conditions under which writers worked—in constant fear, mixed despair and hope, and nearly always semi-starvation. Pearl Buck and . . . Dick Walsh . . . encouraged me by publishing many of these translated stories."

Helen was deeply struck at that first meeting by the glow of happiness coming from the older couple, whose mutual magnetic field was so strong they could not stop paying one another extravagant, unnecessary compliments. Pearl blushed easily, spoke in a seductive throaty voice "with a cultivated lilt to it," and was enviably well dressed in blue silk crepe with a fashionably draped cowl neck, high heels, and elegant silk stockings (rare in those days in Shanghai). "Her beautiful gray-green eyes were as clear as jade, frank and sparkling. They were not ordinary eyes. You could not say they were without witchcraft. . . . She had presence, a feminine, maternal presence [and] . . . real dignity,

Valkyrean one might say. . . . Her uneven mouth was cut like a gash in her expressive face. She was attractive, friendly, natural, easy to be with, but I had a feeling that she had never been young."

The giddy, careless, rapturous youth Pearl had never really tasted was one of the gifts Richard gave her. She wrote her own account of their courtship twenty years later, recasting it as a comic romance of dreamlike absurdity: "The chase had . . . been a long one. We were past our first youth when we first met, each resigned, we thought, to unsatisfactory marriages. . . . I had firmly refused him in New York, Stockholm, London, Paris and Venice and then had sailed by way of India for home in Nanking, China." Pearl's account skates over their Asian trip together, saying only that she refused him once again in Shanghai, "and this time for ever. I went alone after that to Peking . . . and had been there less than a week when he appeared unexpectedly in the midst of a violent dust storm out of the Gobi desert. We parted again eternally, and he went to Manchuria and I went home again to Nanking to pack my bags for a summer visit to the U.S."

Her plan was to spend the next few months with Carol, returning to China in the winter, but whatever pretext Pearl offered—and whether or not she and Richard were technically yet lovers—she must have known this was in some sense a final break. Still nominally a Christian and a mission wife, Pearl had put herself beyond the pale of the only community she knew. Adultery meant social ostracism as well as theological anathema. Margaret Bear said she nearly fainted when she heard the news that Pearl had run away to India with her publisher. Forty years later Lilliath Bates was still incredulous. When the moment came to leave her house and garden, Pearl took nothing with her, as if pretending to the last that she might one day return. She sailed with Janice and Adeline Bucher on May 30, 1934, boarding a ship that put in at the Japanese port of Yokohama, where Richard turned up without warning. "There he was, lean, brown and handsome, and smoking his old briar pipe. . . . In spite of this I said 'no' every day on board ship and again in Vancouver and all winter in New York. But spring in that magic city was my undoing, and we were married on 11 June."

This time Pearl's fairy-tale account skips a whole year of dire personal and professional problems. The first confronted the couple as they landed in Vancouver, to be met by Richard's assistant with news that his publishing house faced bankruptcy. The worldwide economic crisis, brought home by Roosevelt's surprise closure of the banks, meant that, in spite of Pearl's phenomenal success, John Day had been struggling throughout the previous year. Payment of her substantial royalties had been delayed in four successive quarters, with a further postponement requested at the beginning of 1934. She tried to solve the problem by reluctantly producing the manuscript of *The Mother,* which raised thirty-five thousand dollars from serialization in *Cosmopolitan* and sold eighty thousand copies within three months of publication. But this proved a temporary reprieve, not helped by the head of the firm's absconding for six months to the far side of the world, and in June John Day's accountants issued a final ultimatum.

Richard avoided liquidation by sacking his entire staff except for a single secretary, raising money on his life insurance, taking out a mortgage on the house occupied by his wife and family, and persuading the printer to accept old stock in place of payment. *Asia* magazine, now housed in the John Day offices on Forty-second Street, was also in trouble. The paper's new editorial policy had increased its influence but minimized its advertising without a corresponding boost in circulation. This was the kind of situation that brought out in Pearl her father's fighting spirit. She waived future royalties, offering instead to draw out money from the company only as and when she needed it, and effectively replaced Richard's office staff by taking on their editorial jobs herself under the official title of consultant. Pearl now put in many hours a day in the John Day office on top of a punishing work schedule of her own. She wrote every morning from nine to one, turning out articles and stories on an industrial scale, as well as appearing regularly on widely different platforms as a public speaker.

Between commitments she concentrated with characteristic vigor and decisiveness on a series of family catastrophes. Carol was still thriving at Vineland, growing more stable and talking better, but the school's elderly director seemed to be losing his grip on the verge of retirement. Pearl, who mistrusted his deputy's capacity to replace him, galvanized trustees and parents into organizing the search for a successor. She underlined her backing in a will, leaving everything in trust to her two daughters, with the school as her residual legatee. Next on her list was the third child of her sister Grace, a baby girl whose nervous system had been irremediably damaged in a bungled delivery at birth. "It is Carol all over again so far as I am concerned, Emma, and I must buckle down and make as much money as I can," Pearl wrote, adding ominously, "you may see many more potboilers from now on!" She talked to top American consultants, found out where to get the best palliative treatment, paid for a specially made film demonstrating the recommended techniques to be shipped to China, and encouraged the Yaukeys to return to the United States, even fixing up a prospective career for Grace as an author in her own right. Pearl had long since replaced her mother as the cohesive center of the Sydenstricker family, comforting her sister and spending much time with their brother, whose second marriage was already showing signs of strain exacerbated by Edgar's ill health and a long-term drinking problem.

Already frantically overworked, Pearl was apprehensive about a visit in the winter of 1934 from Lossing, who had been summoned by the U.S. Treasury on the strength of his success as a government adviser in China to discuss the potential role of silver in replacing the gold standard (the consultation ended with Lossing being appointed, to his wife's amazement, personal adviser in China to the secretary of state, Henry Morgenthau). Disconcerted by the size of his office and by the evident respect accorded him in Washington, Pearl took the opportunity to press for a divorce. Lossing agreed on condition—a proviso suggested by Morgenthau—that it was his wife, not he, who sued for dissolution in the divorce courts of Reno, Nevada. Ruby Walsh, who could apparently refuse her husband nothing, did the same. In a bizarre maneuver instigated presumably by Richard to minimize sensationalist press coverage, the two wives took the train together to Reno, where they spent the six weeks necessary to qualify as local residents in the same hotel. Nothing if not methodical,

Pearl used the time to lose all the weight she had put on in the past twelve months, tackling the problem with cabbage soup and a professional masseuse. She and Richard were divorced and remarried in the space of just over an hour on the morning of July 11, 1935. They escaped from a press barrage thanks to Pearl's portly masseuse, who stood behind the honeymoon car in the middle of the road with arms extended, blocking the photographers' exit.

PEARL FOUND HERSELF yet again the subject of nationwide notoriety, and for once unable to claim the moral high ground. When media attention made her feel like an object rather than a person, her remedy was to withdraw. She had bought a house that spring, a plain stone farmhouse just outside Perkasie in Bucks County, Pennsylvania, where her original American ancestor, Philip Sydenstricker—probably a shoemaker from Bavaria—had settled briefly in the 1770s before the family moved on to Virginia. By her own account she built her house first in her imagination, recognizing it instantly from a postage-stamp-size snapshot in an estate agent's office in New York. She insisted that the only successful way of transplanting a person or a tree was to establish new roots straightaway. She planted sycamores to show that she meant to grow old in her new house, choosing them because she said they were an essential adjunct to all Pennsylvania farms, "not the dapper white trees of the city, but great old snarled crooked sycamores, tents of big green leaves in summer and ghostly shapes in winter, their branches twisted and angular, the seedballs swinging at every tip of twig." This was the first home Pearl had ever owned, and over the next thirty years she would transform the property, putting in electricity and running water, building bathrooms and a new kitchen, throwing out a wing, adding offices for herself and Richard (Pearl's opened straight into a conservatory full of camellias), converting the barn, and buying up surrounding farmland. The garden on a sloping hillside with its stream and its clumps of bamboo re-created the view from the Sydenstricker bungalow in Zhenjiang. This was as close as Pearl could get to a China lost forever once she and her sister had sold their family house in Kuling, now the summer capital of Chiang Kaishek, later to become a favored resort of the Communist Party under Chairman Mao, who staged some of the grimmest sessions of his presidium on top of Mount Lu.

Pearl turned Green Hills Farm into an ideal home for the large family of happy, healthy children she had dreamed about in her own childhood. Now she set about realizing that dream too at her usual fast tempo. After due consultation with the eleven-year-old Janice (who had been sent to boarding school), the Walshes adopted two baby boys, both one month old, in the spring of 1936. The year after they adopted two more babies, a boy and a girl. At first the parents looked after their new family entirely by themselves. Pearl had no live-in nanny at Green Hills, only a farm woman who came in to cook at midday and local girls to help with the house and children. The whole family commuted for three days a week to an apartment at 480 Park Avenue, with the four babies laid out in market baskets side by side on the back seat of the Cadillac. They were a source of constant delight and satisfaction. "She was proud of those four laundry baskets," said Richard's grown-up daughter, Natalie: "when they went into the Park Avenue apartment, it was great to have this bunch of kids." Pearl had a natural affinity with babies and often sat in the living room talking unselfconsciously to visitors with a naked infant cradled in her lap, much as she herself used to lie comfortably on Wang Amah's knee. Many years later she and Richard adopted two more daughters, bringing their brood to seven, the same number as the siblings—some ghosts, some not—in her mother's house. Pearl herself sailed serenely on regardless of the doubts of friends and family. "I guess we questioned it some because of her hectic life," Grace said, "but she had everything under control. She usually has."

The first years of rerooting and new growth at Green Hills marked a slow recovery from extreme dislocation. Pearl was in many ways a political innocent when she landed in America, quite unprepared for the impact of the major confrontations she was about to take on. She told Richard the morning after her extraordinary performance at the Astor Hotel that she had twice come close to blacking out in the course of her speech. Her first horrifying glimpse of life in the South, as depicted in the Harlem exhibition, affected her so deeply—"It was a blow from which I could never recover"—that she had to shut herself up alone for several days in order to absorb the shock. The adjustment between her two worlds was too great, the transition had been too sudden and the excision of her past too drastic, for Pearl to find her way easily through chaos and confusion back to any kind of solid footing. Intense activity was an escape from desperation. Its antidote was the peace and isolation of country life. The Walshes knew no one among their neighbors in Perkasie except for local people who came to work in the house or on the grounds. They created from scratch an all-American family with lavish trimmings: mammoth Sunday breakfasts cooked by Pearl in her big new farm kitchen, huge hospitable Christmases for themselves and their houseguests, ponies and a pool for the children. But the only visitors who came to stay at Green Hills were members of their immediate family: Grace and Jesse Yaukey, Edgar and Phyllis Sydenstricker, Richard's mother and his daughter Natalie, together with writers the couple had recruited jointly on their Asian trip, what the family called "John Day Chinese," and the few of Richard's New York friends sufficiently sophisticated to take a double-divorce scandal in their stride. Insofar as she was capable of it, Pearl slowed down her work schedule: "I didn't write any big books in 1935."

What she did write was unpublishable. Pearl told Richard that her missionary speech had opened a door she had never opened before. The novel she started working on after her final return to the United States flung wide many long-locked doors on suppressed anxiety and terror. *The Time Is Noon,* begun in 1935 but not published until 1966, contains harsh and vengeful portraits of Pearl's father, her newly divorced husband, and her Buck in-laws as well as slighter but no less wounding sketches of minor characters. Edgar Sydenstricker was seriously ill when she wrote it (he would die prematurely of heart failure at the beginning of 1936). The heroine's fictional brother in *The Time Is Noon* is a handsome, talented, eager boy who grows up to be an ignominious failure, helplessly dependent on his stronger sister, destroyed by the loss of his mother, his father's inadequacy, and his own fatal attraction to wholly unsuitable women, a compulsion that drives him in the end to suicide. The dim pale younger sister, who rashly tries to follow an imaginary vocation as a missionary, is killed off by revolting heathen rather than forced, like Grace and her husband, to give up and go home. Pearl made short work of complaints that her fiction at this point came too close to fact. "Of my work I must be my own judge," she wrote tartly when Emma objected to a story, "Fool's Sacrifice," about a long-suffering wife who finally manages to cut free from an unworthy husband. "Lossing's type is so average that if I never write about anyone like him I shall be hard put to it. . . . But always I shall write as I please about whom I please."

Arrangements for publication of *The Time Is Noon* went ahead in spite of Richard's misgivings, which remained so insistent that without consulting Pearl he sent a set of galley proofs to Dorothy Canfield Fisher, the Book-of-the-Month Club judge who had launched *The Good Earth* and gone on to become a mutual friend. Fisher confirmed that bringing out the book would seriously damage its author's professional reputation, quite apart from its repercussions on her private life. "I accepted their decision without comment," Pearl wrote, "although I knew the book had to be written for my own sake. I had to get rid of all my life until that moment—not my Chinese life, but my own private years. . . . There was no hope ahead so far as my eyes could see. And I was not sure whether I could enjoy life in my own country or even adjust to it. . . . I confess now to hours, even days and weeks of doubt in those first years in my own country. In this mood I began to write *The Time Is Noon*."

A new Buck bestseller was desperately needed to make the future of the John Day company financially secure. *A House Divided,* the long-awaited final installment of *The Good Earth* trilogy, had come out at last in January to disappointing sales. Its impetus was too obviously educational rather than imaginative. "I conceived the idea of a series of novels, each of which should reveal some fundamental aspect of Chinese life," Pearl wrote of its inception. Begun in a period of turbulent personal transition, abandoned during the acute depression that overtook Pearl on her return to Nanjing, taken up again a year later in an attempt to avert John Day's collapse, the novel suffered more than either of its predecessors from lack of planning. It tells the story of Wang Lung's youngest grandchild, the only son of Wang the Tiger, who rejects his father's militarism in favor of an indeterminate future as a writer. The second of the book's four sections, describing a period of exile in the United States, is a more or less direct transcription of Pearl's own response to the sheer scale, waste, and prodigality, the size and splendor of everything American, from urban skyscrapers to illimitable untouched open space, "fields big enough to be counties and machines struggling like huge beasts to make ready the fertile earth for gigantic harvests." Timid and indecisive, terrified of losing his virginity, accustomed to burst into tears at the first sign of trouble, and still crying himself to sleep in his early twenties, Wang Yuan makes an implausibly girlish romantic hero, but an effective and observant authorial stand-in for what is essentially a firsthand report on the revolutionary turmoil of contemporary China as seen through the eyes of three Wang grandsons: Yuan and his cousins, Sheng the trendy poet, and Meng, an idealistic captain in the revolutionary army. The book ends with the destruction of their family house organized by yet another grandson, this time a young Communist agitator who incites local farmers to ransack and burn private property in the name of the class struggle.

It was Lin Yutang's *My People and My Country*—a first book by an unknown author translated from a foreign language on a subject notoriously impossible to sell—that outstripped John Day's expectations by becoming a best seller in 1935. "Pearl sponsored it and Walsh tailored it for the West," said Helen Foster Snow. "It was a huge success to the total astonishment of Lin Yutang and everyone else—due mostly to Walsh." Richard was a brilliant editor, sensitive, skillful and discreet. "I have seen him take a muddle of a manuscript and make it a unified whole," said Pearl, "he would have been a fine critic . . . he was a genius of his own sort in coaxing books out of writers who did not know they were writers. . . . He had the gift of universal comprehension, an eclectic mind, a synthesizing judgment." His touch was so light that, although the changes he made were sometimes comprehensive, he seemed even to his authors to clarify rather than obstruct or conceal their underlying intentions. He was always the first person to read his wife's manuscripts, and she trusted him implicitly. In her forties and fifties, when stories poured out of her almost without premeditation, Pearl relied heavily on Richard as a kind of artistic conscience, "a screening mind, a critical judgment," as an old friend put it. "He was the *only* one who could criticize her," said one of their three sons.

When her husband finally rejected *The Time Is Noon* Pearl somewhat dubiously offered him instead the biography of her mother she had kept shut up in a drawer for fifteen years. This time Richard had no doubts. Serialization of *The Exile* (for which *Woman's Home Companion* paid twenty-five thousand dollars), followed by its successful publication in January 1936, put the company firmly on its feet again. The book was greeted with such critical and popular acclaim that Pearl promptly produced a parallel life of her father. She herself said that, although she had come to love him in the last ten years of his life, when he lived with her in Nanjing, it was only after her return to the United States that she saw Absalom clearly. Up until then he had been too inextricably bound up with her past for her to be objective. "His outlines remained ghostly to me, even when he ate at my table." Settled now in her new American home, buoyed by the courage and confidence Richard gave her, freed from the bitterness vented in *The Time Is Noon,* she explored her father's deeply divided nature with the honesty, humor, and sense of proportion she had advised her contemporaries to cultivate when dealing with missionaries of an earlier generation. It is the strength of *Fighting Angel* that it somehow manages to see the funny side of a career that was tragic in its protagonist's total failure as much as in its destructive consequences for those closest to him.

The book acknowledges Absalom's qualities as fully as his defects. Pearl inherited her mother's warmth, humanity, and integrity, "her steadfast eye and her firm mouth and her look of something rocklike," the qualities Olan passed on to the boldest of her own children in *The Good Earth.* But in the course of writing *Fighting Angel* she seems to have understood perhaps for the first time her own likeness to her father. She recognized in herself his pride, his dauntlessness, his lofty anger, his secretive withdrawals. She learned to accept and honor the stubborn strength of his vision:

> Nor can I tolerate for a moment any mawkish notion that it was his religion that filled him with that might. Religion had nothing to do with it. Had he been a lesser mind he would have chosen a lesser god, had he been born for today he would have chosen another god but whatever . . . he did he would have done with that swordlike singleness of heart. As it was, born of the times and of that fighting blood, he chose the greatest god he knew and set forth into the universe to make men acknowledge his god to be the one true God before whom all must bow. It was a magnificent imperialism of the spirit, incredible and not to be understood except by those who have been reared in it and have grown beyond it.

Fighting Angel was Pearl's parting present to her father. A second gift (and one he would no doubt have preferred) was a posthumous edition of his Chinese translation of the New Testament, financed by Pearl and produced by the Nanjing Seminary. The two biographies, packaged together in October 1936 under the title *The Flesh and the Spirit* and distributed as a Book-of-the-Month Club double, sold more copies than any of Pearl's previous works except for *The Good Earth*. "I am just *so* happy about the book," Grace had written to her sister when she read *The Exile*. "It does seem as if Mother's life is to count for more than she could ever know." One of the outcomes even Pearl could not have foreseen was the book's impact in the 1970s and 1980s, after the death of Chairman Mao, on a Chinese generation brought up to regard foreign missionaries as tools of cultural oppression. "All the political propaganda, and many years of socialist education, simply went to pieces after people read this little biography," wrote Kang Liao: "young readers were surprised to learn . . . so much that is opposite to what they had been told in class and in the textbooks." *The Exile* set out to right wrongs, both general and particular, but Pearl's brief life of her father goes beyond that relatively narrow remit. *Fighting Angel* has the makings of a twentieth-century classic in its truthfulness and simplicity, the strangeness of its subject, and the lapidary precision of its style. Apart from *The Good Earth*—another work long meditated and written under pressure in a single burst of speed—it is probably the best book Pearl ever wrote in the sense that she never fully recaptured its combination of cool, sharp, scrutinizing intelligence and passionate emotion.

The only dissenting voices came from mission colleagues of the Sydenstrickers, who hotly disputed what they saw as cruel and libelous distortion. "Carie Sydenstricker was . . . a comfortably placid person . . . a devoted wife, admiring her husband, supplementing his dreams with her good sense . . . living in joy and happiness to the end of her life," wrote Nettie du Bose Junkin, whose father had known Pearl's parents from their earliest years in China, and who had been a Kuling neighbor of the Sydenstrickers as a mission wife herself. Junkin's review was not the only one to protest against Pearl's heroic portrait of her mother or to defend Absalom as a model father and husband. James Bear, another mission child who had known the family all his life, insisted that there was nothing out of the ordinary about Carie Sydenstricker ("she was just a good average missionary, not brilliant but she did her work"), and was deeply dismayed by Pearl's "lack of understanding of her father." Some of her closest friends insisted that if anything she had toned down the harsher aspects of both parents. "Her mother was a very, very rigid woman," said Lilliath Bates. "Pearl told a lot of things about her father, but if people had known all they would have been even more startled."

If *The Exile* was written in hot blood as an attempt to exorcise the past, *Fighting Angel* brings to bear the kind of dispassionate lucidity that informs Pearl Buck's articles and speeches but is rarely present in her novels. From now on she would appropriate to herself her father's power as a preacher, applying the breadth and clarity of mind she had inherited from him to interrogate American actuality in the light of the generous idealistic vision instilled in her from infancy by her mother. For three decades hers was a voice of sanity and balance in U.S.

politics. She campaigned for peace, tolerance, and liberal democracy, for the rights of children and minorities, for an end to discrimination on grounds of race or gender. She had no illusions about the nature of Communism in China, and long before the Nationalists' ultimate defeat she delivered a scathing analysis of their failures as a government. Pearl was among the first to recognize that the war inaugurated by Japan's invasion of the Chinese mainland in 1937 would culminate in worldwide conflagration. She struggled tirelessly to raise awareness of China's situation and to swing public opinion in the United States against the Japanese aggressors. But for all her efforts to open minds and alter policy in Washington, it was in the end her novels that did more than any other single factor to humanize the popular American image of the Chinese people. Pearl's efforts to link her two worlds by becoming a human "bridge between the civilizations of the East and West," in the words of Richard Nixon, took up much of the second half of her life.

World War II and the Communist regime established in 1949 ensured that she never returned to China. *The Good Earth* appeared in eight pirated Chinese translations in the 1930s and 1940s, one of them going into twelve successive editions. "No other book by any foreigner has ever achieved such popularity in China," wrote Liu Hai-ping, the leading Chinese authority on Pearl Buck. But Buck's relationship with potential Chinese readers had been clouded from the first by the anger and anxiety she herself identified in Wang Yuan in *A House Divided*. Attempts by the *Good Earth*'s American film crew to shoot actual Chinese villages in the country around Shanghai met with determined resistance from officials, who eventually arranged for the film reels to be x-rayed during a customs inspection on departure. In 1937 Chinese defensiveness combined with Hollywood commercialism to produce a movie with twelve minutes of authentic Yangtse Valley footage, an all-American cast, and a script built round a romantic love interest wholly alien to the original concept.

Chinese critics complained bitterly about Pearl Buck's evenhandedness, her lack of ideological content, and the accurate documentation of rural poverty in her books. Their objections were clearly set out soon after publication of *The Good Earth* in a letter to the *New York Times* by Professor Jiang Kanghu, a distinguished academic moving easily between the United States and China, who had begun his career as a young official at the Manchu court in Beijing. Professor Jiang endorsed Lu Xun's view that China should be left to the Chinese, cast doubt on the existence of the lawlessness and banditry that form the novel's background, and reproved the author for writing with deplorable informality about unimportant, low-grade individuals: "They may form the majority of the Chinese population, but they are certainly not representative of the Chinese people." Pearl responded politely but firmly that she could write only about a world she had known firsthand all her life.

Her frankness, coupled with her refusal to gloss over Nationalist shortcomings, made her an unwelcome advocate. When she won the Nobel Prize for literature in 1938, the Chinese government acknowledged her importance as an independent commentator by withdrawing its official delegation from the ceremony in Stockholm. "The withdrawal heralded a long-term neglect of her in China, Taiwan, and among the Chinese American scholars in the U.S.," wrote Professor Kang Liao. The Communist regime convicted her of conniving at imperialist and capitalist exploitation by failing to mention their existence. "Buck contradicts Marxist theories by regarding China's poor and rich as individuals rather than as members of opposed classes." She was handicapped even by her Chinese name, Sai Zhenzhu. The first part was the family name chosen by her father, the second a literal translation of "pearl," a name with flashy and pretentious overtones in China: the two together sounded like Sai Jinhua, a famous imperial concubine and mistress of an enemy general in the Boxer uprising, signifying to most people a collaborationist tart.

Pearl Buck raised too many awkward questions, exposed too much unpalatable reality, remained essentially too skeptical to suit doctrinaires on the Left or Right. In the 1950s she was stigmatized as a suspected Communist in the United States at the same time as her books were banned in Communist China. By this time she was used to attack from both ends of the ideological spectrum. "Nothing in

Communist theory enrages me more than Trotsky's callous remark that peasants are the 'packhorses' of a nation," she wrote. "Who made them packhorses? . . . in all my years in China I never ceased to feel intolerable pain and anger when I looked into the thin intelligent face of some Chinese peasant twisted into sheer physical agony because on his back he bore a burden too much even for a beast."

Pearl retained to the end the view of China laid out at the start of her career in her Messenger prize essay of 1925: "as the inevitable future leader of Asia, and as a monumental force in herself with her unmeasured resources, both human and material, she will exert a tremendous influence upon the future of the world." She spent the greater part of her life thinking about and speaking for the common man, exploited successively in China by Western capitalism, by the bureaucratic inefficiency and military brutality of the Nationalist regime, and by the Communists' overriding drive for power. Her stance was never ideological. She had known too much too young about ideological campaigns to reeducate other people for their own good, and all such attempts filled her with revulsion. "Yesterday in New York a young Chinese woman . . . told me breathlessly of the great and marvellous changes that the Communists are making in China," she wrote in her memoirs in 1954, remembering perhaps the glorious changes once envisaged by her father and his colleagues. "And in her words, too, I caught the old stink of condescension."

Paper People

W HEN PEARL FINALLY left China to settle in the United
States in 1934, she marked this last great uprooting of her life
with a burst of autobiographical writing, looking backward and forward in the two biographies of her parents and in the three fictional
books she wrote immediately before and after: *The Time Is Noon, This
Proud Heart,* and *Other Gods.* These were her first novels set in America, and in them she rewrote her past and shaped her future, clearing
the ground, establishing control, and getting rid of the heavy, cumbersome, potentially toxic baggage she carried with her.

Storytelling had been an escape for Pearl ever since, as a small
child, she found she could forget her troubles by reading and reread-
ing the collected works of Charles Dickens. She said that every one of
her own novels included a character who was a version of herself, and
that her imaginary world of dreams, projections, and fictional presences came to seem to her as substantial as the real world. Writing
occupied a special compartment in her mind, the mental equivalent
of the attic at the top of her Nanjing house, a safe place "where she
could go and be alone with her people." There she re-created as an
adult the kind of virtual reality she had entered as a child through
other people's stories: "more and more it came about that her only
companionship was in the attic with her people."

This Proud Heart, published in 1938, was for Pearl herself as well as
for those closest to her the nearest she ever came to a deliberate self-
portrait. Its heroine, Susan Gaylord, marries a local college boy and
sets out with high hopes to become a model wife and mother in a small
house exactly like all the others in the small town where she grew up.

Class president and valedictorian of her school year, she sings, plays the piano, and dismays her contemporaries by cooking, cleaning, sewing, and bringing up babies effortlessly, and far more expertly than they can themselves. But Susan's marriage is shadowed from the start by a craving neither her husband nor his suburban world can satisfy. She too leads a secret life in an improvised workroom under the roof of her suburban home: "desire stirred in her, deep and blind, the intolerable, sweet, dark, solitary desire which she knew so well, which she could share with no one else. She rose to her feet and she went slowly upstairs, past the bedroom door, up to the attic."

Susan appeases her blind urge by modeling a clay child. "Up in the attic the thing she had made remained a presence. It was there, a part of herself and yet separate from her." Looking back at the end of her long life, Pearl described the people she created out of words in similar terms: "when I speak the names of my characters, they stand here before me as though they were in this room. . . . Perhaps being surrounded by the people I have created, I don't need other people. . . . They seem real to me. . . . I just don't distinguish between the people in my books and the people outside my books. One is as real as the other to me." On the birth of her first baby, Susan (like her creator) turns away from an activity she sees as dangerously compulsive. For months the attic door remains locked, and dust gathers on the work inside. In the end, overcome by desire in spite of her best efforts to resist, she goes back to the abandoned attic. Working at top speed in a trancelike state without training or preparation, she models a woman out of clay, probing, groping, gouging, feeling the figure take shape and grow beneath her fingers. "Each day when she opened the attic door it was to open it to ecstasy, and when she shut the attic door behind her, it was as upon that secret ecstasy."

Technically speaking, this is absurd. It is not possible to make a freestanding, life-size clay figure on impulse with no kind of external support or internal armature, any more than it would be feasible for a provincial housewife without funding or formal training to carry off a major New York hospital commission and leave for Paris on the proceeds, as Susan Gaylord does, in a bid to turn professional. She studies in the studio of a prize-winning American sculptor—"Beauty was his soul's food"—currently making statues of what he calls his Titans, twenty-one massive males ranging from Galileo, Leonardo, and Napoleon to Thomas Edison, "a gallery of history in stone." In Paris in the era of Brancusi and the young Giacometti, at a time when the aims and means of sculpture itself had been redefined in abstract terms by works in plaster, papier-mâché and wire from Matisse, Picasso, and Julio Gonzalez, Susan Gaylord becomes an academic practitioner, dreaming of monuments in bronze and stone, taking it as a personal slight when told that only very few great men still sculpt in marble. "Her proud heart reared its head like a lion in her woman's body. 'How do you know I am not great?' it demanded."

Susan represents in highly stylized form the hopes and aspirations of a generation of housewives who found any prospect of pursuing a professional career extinguished by domesticity: "She had not enough to do. However busy she was, she knew there was an energy in her still unused, a primary function unperformed." Potential problems—child care, financial dependence, the doubts of family and friends, her husband's lethal feelings of inferiority, Susan's own sense of being a cut above everyone else she has ever met—evaporate as if by magic. Her central dilemma resolves itself when her husband conveniently dies young of typhoid, contracted on the day she receives news of her first major commission. After a brief second marriage to a far more sophisticated New Yorker, she opts for independence and a single life, winning national acclaim for her *American Procession,* a patriotic sequence starting with an enormous black marble statue of her cleaning lady. Like its heroine's most famous work, *This Proud Heart* spoke to and for American womanhood, using an old-fashioned and reassuringly familiar narrative format to convey a new and timely message. It was, by Pearl's own account, a dream come true.

"The book told of the difficulty of being a superior person," her official biographer put it. So did her next American novel. Serialized like *This Proud Heart* in *Good Housekeeping,* and published in January 1940, *Other Gods* explores the penalties of instant fame through its lovely, shy, sensitive, book-loving heroine, the suggestively named

Kit Tallant. Like the central characters of both *The Time Is Noon* and *This Proud Heart,* Kit marries a dull, coarse-grained, well-meaning but thick-witted farmer's son, distantly derived from Lossing Buck. An amateur mountaineer, Bert Holm becomes an international celebrity overnight after accidentally scaling an unclimbed Himalayan peak. Pearl said that her own sudden unexpected fame dehumanized her and made people treat her as an object, a sensation she had known and dreaded as a white child in Zhenjiang, surrounded on the street by Chinese crowds calling out insults about the foreign devil's fair skin, yellow hair, and "wild-beast eyes."

Old terrors resurfaced in these years between the lines of her books. Memories of casual abuse, of being shouted and spat at on the streets after the Revolution, of being forced to flee from murderous looters in 1927—"all that I had purposely forgotten"—lie behind passages like the one in *Other Gods* where Bert finds himself pursued by the press and mobbed by screaming fans at the head of a brass band tickertape parade down Broadway that terrifies his wife: "Madness was about her—something mad and uncontrolled. Her knees began to shake . . . she wet her lips . . . the noise rose into a high wild howling." Kit takes refuge in the peaceful book-lined library of her family's country home. "At once her mind stripped itself. . . . She sat in a long fruitful daydream, shaping her own mood, holding fast her own feeling, until at last she began to feel slowly words in a rhythm, two lines, then another and another. And once this progress began it went on to a completion, whether final or not she could not tell now, but at least to some sort of end, because she felt released and full of ease."

This seems to be a pretty accurate account of the way Pearl worked at Green Hills Farm, where she increasingly retreated from the glare of publicity. As a writer she relied on the knack she had perfected as a child of removing herself from time and place: "once more I found myself withdrawing into my secret habitation. There I am alone. No other enters." She spent every morning at her desk, emerging exhausted, dazed, and stupefied from these sessions with what she called her book people, or sometimes her real people. She wrote in longhand without revision or correction, seldom pausing, covering page after page at phenomenal speed in a small compact script, producing on average 2,500 words at a sitting. "Then I never look at the papers again," she told Helen Foster Snow. "My secretary types them out and my husband edits them. I never have anything more to do with the book until it is published. . . . I cannot stand to read over anything I write. My husband takes care of everything for me except the first draft. He works in the other half of the house."

It was Richard, working with two typists in the next-door office, who applied the critical intelligence Pearl increasingly withheld from the dreamworld of her fiction. He edited her books heavily, and her agent, David Lloyd, did the same for the short stories. "It took two anchors to hold her," said Lloyd's daughter, Andrea. "Father and Walsh . . . It took two men, one couldn't hold her. . . . Her work was always pouring out of her." For four decades she published a book or two a year as well as keeping up a steady flow of magazine stories, articles, and speeches. Her earning power was prodigious. For ten years or more she could count on up to five thousand dollars for a story in magazines like *Cosmopolitan,* the *Saturday Evening Post,* or *Woman's Home Companion,* which meant that, with royalties, translations, and serialization fees, her total income came to $60,000 to $100,000 a year. But her production rate inevitably precluded firsthand contact with the world she wrote about. Pearl had little intrinsic understanding of American idiom or thought patterns. She didn't know how ordinary people behaved, and she had never heard them talking casually among themselves. In Shanghai in 1928 she had been mystified by a stranger who said, pointing at Carol, "The kid is nuts." A decade later in Pennsylvania she depended on Richard to interpret for her ("he said it was fun to be married to me because I was so ignorant that he could tell me all the old American jokes, and they were new to me").

She was isolated in public as a celebrity and secluded at home by the demands of her profession. What little time she did not spend writing was taken up with campaigning, lecturing, traveling, and fundraising for the many causes she vigorously supported. Pearl had long feared the outbreak of World War II, and she expended much energy trying to communicate Asian points of view at all levels both before and after American intervention following the bombing at Pearl Harbor. In 1941 she and Richard set up and ran for the next decade from the John Day offices the East and West Association, a private cross-cultural organization designed to promote friendship, dialogue, and understanding through an extensive program of talks, translations, broadcasts, workshops, and performances. Pearl organized Chinese relief funds and contributed a regular column of book reviews to *Asia* magazine until it closed in 1946. One of the great good turns she did the Chinese people was to help bring about the repeal of the Chinese Exclusion Acts, which had penalized immigrants since before she was born, and which were finally dismantled in wartime after more than sixty years, thanks to another campaign mounted from John Day headquarters.

The day-to-day running of her household at Green Hills was taken care of by secretaries, typists, hired help of one sort or another, and after the first few years by a registered nurse to look after the brood of growing children. She had no intimate friends. Her children found her conscientious and affectionate but as undemonstrative as her own mother had been before her. Sing-alongs at the piano and bed-time stories around the fire took the place of individual contact. Pearl loved and needed the lively presence of young people, the sound of their voices, the energy and clatter they brought into the house, but there were so many of them so close in age that each had to wait in turn for a private interview, by which time the reason for it had often been forgotten or blanked out. "No one really got close to her," said her daughter Janice. "I never really got to know her."

Richard's dual role as publisher and husband was protective and defensive. Marriage to him ensured that Pearl was insulated and kept at one remove from her material. Partnership with Lossing Buck had done the opposite. For all his shortcomings, his insensitivity to anything but his own concerns, and his prosaic insistence on scientific method, he had deepened and enriched her knowledge of the world her imagination explored so confidently in *The Good Earth*. The only equivalent given her by Richard was *The Townsman*, a relatively conventional saga of prairie pioneers set in his home state of Kansas.

Pearl had gone there with him several times to visit relatives, picking up authentic historical detail and local color so readily that, when she published the book under a pseudonym in 1945, the *Kansas City Star* insisted that the real author must be a lifelong Kansas resident.

The novel has the stock characters, episodic structure, upbeat ending, and highly implausible antiracist subplot that had become Buck trademarks. Pearl's sense of humor seldom got the better of her didactic intent. Even her firsthand knowledge of China had gaps and blanks by this time. She faithfully carried out her plan to dispel Western ignorance and prejudice through fictional coverage of China's revolutionary struggles in *The Patriot* (1939) and *Kinfolk* (1949), Japan's war with China in *Dragon Seed* (1941), Japanese attempts to take over Burma in *The Promise* (1943) and to annex Korea in *The Living Reed* (1963). *Letter from Peking* (1957) and *The Three Daughters of Mme. Liang* (1969) gave an alarming and comparatively accurate impression of what little was known at the time about life under Chairman Mao. These books were polemical in their political content, psychologically simplistic, and often sketchy or out of date in their social context, but they opened up an extraordinary and virtually unknown world. Their strength lay in the storyteller's consummate conviction in the essential humanity of her characters. Pearl Buck had set out in the 1930s on what Professor Liao described as "a basically single-handed crusade to change the image of Chinese people in the American mind," a crusade that triumphantly succeeded in dislodging the old visceral antagonism to Chinese immigrants and in shifting public opinion toward support for China's long, grueling resistance to Japanese invasion.

A key factor in making unfamiliar material acceptable to the American public was cultural anachronism, Pearl's habit of importing the alien conventions of Western pulp fiction into an Eastern setting. The tremulous beating hearts of virgin lovers, the stolen kisses, secret trysts, and sacred pacts, the bloodless stereotypes of true romance, already starting to infiltrate the background of *A House Divided,* became more and more blatant in her Asian novels from *Dragon Seed* onward. "Pearl had a very good mind but she didn't use it," said Helen

Foster Snow. Or, to put it another way, she had a powerful imagination, but the audience she wished to reach was not primarily literary. Her aim was always to maximize the number of her readers. She justified her own fiction on much the same grounds as she had once defended the Chinese novel, itself traditionally dismissed by an elitist literary establishment as oral pulp fiction. Pearl's books sold in the millions and were translated into innumerable languages worldwide, not in spite but because of their bland, trite, ingratiating mass-market techniques. "The fact remains that I should not be satisfied if I did not have stories published in the magazines which the mass of people read," she wrote in 1940, uneasily aware that even her former admirers were finding it hard to ignore the grounds she increasingly provided for critical dismissal by the book world. "The finest and most beautiful do not come from those people, but still they are the root and stock of life. A person so secluded as a writer must not lose touch with them. I value their letters, often so foolish. I *feel* them. Their minds reach mine, and I try to make mine reach theirs." It was her strength that people read her whatever the critics said, as she wrote defensively of the blockbusting novelist who is in some sense her alter ego in *The Long Love*.

Her own bestsellers combine hypnotic elements of fantasy and wish fulfillment with glimpses of more disturbing truths secreted beneath the romantic formulae, and occasionally disrupting it, like the scraps of flesh and bone Pearl had collected as a child from the hillside outside her parents' house. Her novels, like her life, incorporate a kind of ongoing amnesia. The reassurance they convey comes in part from both knowing and not knowing where the bodies are buried, simultaneously acknowledging and denying realities too painful to face directly. "She did not think, she did not feel, she would not remember," Pearl wrote in *The Hidden Flower*, describing a desperate young Asian mother who gives birth secretly in a Los Angeles public hospital to the unwanted child of an absconding American father. The book was published in 1952 largely as propaganda for the Welcome House Adoption Agency, an institution set up by Pearl after the war to take in otherwise unadoptable minority and mixed-race children, mostly Amerasians (the word itself was Pearl's coinage), the tens of thousands of rejected babies fathered by American servicemen on Asian women in Japan, and later in Korea. *The Hidden Flower* starts with a lighthearted interracial love affair in a Tokyo of tourist-brochure Oriental charm, and moves the young couple to the darker atmosphere of New York and Virginia, skating over any serious confrontation with southern bigotry, and ducking out altogether with a preposterous messianic happy ending tacked on in its closing pages. But the grim predicament of the Japanese heroine, caught and skewered between two powerful, opposed, and unforgiving cultures, is explored with delicacy and feeling.

Pearl's major self-projections, from Susan Gaylord to the brilliant and powerful Chinese women with whom she identified most easily—Madame Wu in *Pavilion of Women* (1946), the empress dowager in *Imperial Woman* (1956), Madame Liang in *The Three Daughters of Mme. Liang* (1969)—are superlatively intelligent, infinitely resourceful, and impenetrably reserved. They are admired, respected, and obeyed by those around them, but none ever achieves intimacy with any other human being. All possess iron self-control. People who knew Pearl in her prime recognized the serenity and courtesy that had characterized her father in the second half of his life. "He would have been pained and astonished if anyone had ever told him he was arrogant and domineering," she wrote in a passage analyzing the split between his conscious will and the unruly instincts it so rigidly suppressed. "Indeed he did not seem so, his bearing was of such gentleness and dignity, his step quiet, his voice soft, his manner always restrained and controlled except for those rare strange sudden furies, when something he kept curbed deep in him broke for a moment its leash."

The terrifying moments when Absalom hit his children, making them feel they had glimpsed some almost impersonal inner rage briefly let out of captivity, mesmerized Pearl. Half a century later she dramatized the process to macabre effect in *Voices in the House*, a novel whose two central characters represent her own split selves. One is the judicious William Asher, a highly civilized, happily married, wealthy and successful criminal lawyer, who (like Pearl) develops a professional "trick of self-suspension" to protect his inner life from regular exposure to lawlessness and savagery. His is the dull cautious voice of reason that foresees lunacy and chaos unless the workings of the subconscious mind can be safely contained "beneath the routines of daily life." Sure enough the smooth running of his household is disrupted by the daughter of the Ashers' cook and butler, a sensitive, dreamy, and exceptionally pretty child named Jessica, who regularly retreats (like her creator as a girl) into a private world of fairy tale and make-believe.

Jessica's fantasies of being claimed by a gracious, rich, and handsome suitor as his lady wife are grimly parodied when her mother compels her to marry the Ashers' coarse, pasty-faced manservant. After a year of marriage the luckless husband confides to his horrified employer the scene enacted nightly in their bedroom: "what does a man do when a woman never gives in? What does a man do when a woman bites and scratches him so that he had to hold down her hands and thrust his arm against her throat so that she cannot raise her head and then must mount her hard so that her kicking legs and thrusting feet do not wound him in his tenderest parts?" Images like these go back presumably to stories Pearl heard from the unhappy wives she mentored as a young missionary, or even before that, to her memories of girls trafficked into the Shanghai sex trade, who talked to her as a teenager at the Door of Hope. Jessica solves her problem by acquiring a huge, semisavage, red-eyed mastiff dog, which she keeps tied up and straining at the leash in a kennel between her own and her husband's twin beds. One night she unties the maddened animal, by now slavering at the jaws and so far beyond control that its former owner, summoned by the terrified, sex-starved husband, has to choke it to death with his bare hands. Pearl found a potent metaphor for her old terror of being treated as an object rather than a person in the marital rape that follows the dog's death:

> Jessica did not yield. She leaped from bed to floor, she clung to the curtains, struggling to throw herself from the windows,

but he had nailed them shut. The curtains fell about her and she hid in them until he tore them from her. She clung to the table, to the beds, until he wrenched her hands away, pounding upon her knuckles with his clenched fists. He beat her with the rung of a broken chair at last until she fell writhing upon the floor, screaming with pain, and still as tireless, thin as she was, as though she were made of twisted wires. He imprisoned her beneath his vast body there upon the floor and held her down, his hands clutching her wrists, his tight mouth pressed upon her turned cheek, his loins fastened upon hers.

JESSICA SINKS INTO rabid paranoia, barking and biting like a dog, having to be removed in a straitjacket and ending up, after a single catastrophic attempt at rehabilitation, incarcerated for life in an asylum. The Asher family recovers shakily from the destructive impact of her dangerous delusions, "strange voices, disturbing, corrupting, cutting across the human grain of their common life," voices that William recognizes as the dark side of the dreams she had been forbidden to indulge in as a child born into a world that offered no outlet to her secret hopes and longings.

Voices in the House was published in 1953, the year Richard Walsh suffered a stroke from which he only temporarily recovered. It was the first stage in a steady mental and physical disintegration that left him almost blind, half-paralyzed and bedridden, helplessly dependent on other people, unable to respond or eventually even to understand his wife, becoming almost lifeless before he finally died at the age of seventy-three in 1960. The loss of his companionship, more even than his professional advice and backing, was irreparable for Pearl. She missed his warmth, his generosity, his sharp wit, his calming and unfailingly attentive presence. He had been the ideal husband for a writer—"possibly the only one any writer ever had that I can think of," Helen

Foster Snow said sadly—and his rapid decline bitterly recalled the breakdown of her first marriage. "The worst thing any man can do to a woman is to withdraw his love, physically and emotionally, and stay with her," Pearl said the year before Richard died to a young acquaintance, who was appalled: "It came like a cry from the heart, and it was totally unexpected."

Pearl's confidant was the actor Paul Roebling, who played the romantic lead in *Desert Incident,* the most disastrous of the many plays (this one closed after seven performances in 1959) with which she had tried and failed for years to conquer Broadway. Although she sold more rights worldwide than any other living author, her pulling power in the United States was no longer what it had been. John Day still published every book she wrote, and she remained a national figure whose opinions, especially on Asia, carried great weight, but the large-circulation magazines that had always paid her top rates published her less often. The dogmatic right-wing intolerance of postwar America demoralized her and damaged her reputation. The FBI had opened a Buck file in 1937, keeping her under fitful surveillance ever since on suspicion of Communist allegiance because of her outspoken, un-American support for democratic equality and racial justice. She was banned from the pages of *Time* magazine by its proprietor, another old China hand, the virulently anti-Communist Henry Luce, and she figured, like so many well-known authors, on Senator Joseph McCarthy's blacklists. She compounded her troubles in the mid-1950s by leaving the David Lloyd Agency, which had looked after her for nearly a quarter of a century. "When Walsh and Lloyd were gone, there was no anchor," said Lloyd's daughter, who was also his business partner. "Father was a constant steadying influence."

There was no one now in the office to query Pearl's decisions or protect her from herself on either the professional or the human front. Janice had long since grown up and left home. The four teenagers were already in college, or about to be, when Richard's long decline began. Pearl had reared her children to be self-sufficient, insisting that they needed practical skills as well as college educations (the three boys regularly spent vacations working on a plot of land she bought in Vermont, clearing the ground and mixing concrete to build a cabin in the woods that became the family's summer holiday home). She herself had always coped with confusion and calamity in her private life by taking on more to do, and now her response to the prospect of becoming a single parent once again was to adopt another child. A couple of years before Richard first fell ill, the couple had acquired a half-German, half–African American daughter, and in 1957 Pearl completed her family of seven adopted children with a five-year-old Amerasian from Japan. The two girls and their friends brought life back to the house, now mostly empty except for Pearl and the dying Richard with his nurses.

Like her father before her, she found intermittent consolation in the company of the various handsome, hopeful, talented young men who circled around her in these years, acting as her escorts, accompanying her on her travels, and involving her in projects that came to nothing much in spite of her sponsorship. None of these entanglements seems to have involved more than mild flirtation on either side. She even conducted a platonic romance in his final years with her old friend Ernest Hocking, who said she reminded him of both Aristotle and Homer, and whose ardent love letters make him sound more like a wistful adolescent than a distinguished philosopher in his nineties. Pearl maintained that sex took place between them only in the head. She was beginning to imitate her own fiction, taking a leaf out of her book about Madame Wu, who celebrated the onset of middle age in *Pavilion of Women* by retiring from active service in her husband's bed, providing a concubine to take her place, and embarking on an intimate relationship with an unworldly monkish intellectual (he turns out to be a defrocked Catholic priest), an affair consummated only on the astral plane after her lover's death. "She loses her grip on reality," the *New Yorker* said severely of Pearl's handling of this episode, "even Oriental reality."

Her humor and perception, her sharp eye and balanced judgment were increasingly restricted to nonfiction works like *The Child Who Never Grew,* the little book about herself and Carol published in 1950 in aid of the Vineland School. Pearl was one of very few American celebrities prepared to admit publicly in those days to a family member's mental disability, and the book had an impact out of all proportion to its size. It is a concise and lucid plea, at once passionate and marvelously dispassionate, for a ruthless facing of the facts, the opposite of the process that drained the blood out of her fiction. She followed it four years later with *My Several Worlds,* a volume of memoirs that cuts fluently between the author's American present and her Asian past, painting a clear, bright, elegiac, and unsentimental picture of a life inextricably bound up with the turbulent history of twentieth-century China.

Memory for Pearl was an intensely creative faculty. It opened and closed like quicksand over fragments of the past, absorbing and transforming them, sucking them down only to disgorge them once again as much as ten or twenty years later in fictional or nonfictional form, sometimes in both one after the other. During the transitional period marking the collapse of each of her two marriages, the treacherous sands of memory became especially active, swallowing and regurgitating the past as if in readiness for an uncertain future. "I have to make all I do out of my own life," says Susan Gaylord in *This Proud Heart.* "It's my only material." The same was true of Pearl. Even *Imperial Woman,* the fictionalized biography of the dowager empress that occupied her in the first uneasy years of Richard's illness, drew as much on her own personal experience as on the historical and biographical sources she consulted. Like all other portraits of the empress at the time, it relied heavily on a hostile account by J. O. Bland and Edmund Backhouse, whose supposed authenticity was shown to be spurious only after Pearl's death. Her novel paints a relatively reliable picture largely thanks to intuition. "You could see Pearl all through that book," said Andrea Lloyd, "the way she pictured herself anyhow." "She was very much like the old empress," said Sarah Rowe, Pearl's secretary at Green Hills. "Nothing happened there that she didn't know and approve of. . . . when you've had all the success she'd had, maybe your imagination spills over into fact, and I think it became more and more difficult to discern the difference between actuality and the wish."

Of all the bright young men who charmed Pearl and dispelled her loneliness, the most persistent and persuasive was her red-haired dancing master, Theodore Harris. He was a natural courtier, eager, assiduous, and deferential. Pearl said he had the looks of a Greek god together with the glamour of the young President Kennedy. Born Fred L. Hair in rural South Carolina in 1931, he was a school dropout who worked his way up to become an instructor at the Arthur Murray Dance Studios in Jenkintown, Pennsylvania. Pearl hired him in July 1963 to teach her two youngest daughters. They disliked him, but from the first day he captivated their mother, becoming a constant visitor at Green Hills. Within three months he had organized a charity ball in Pearl's barn to raise money for Welcome House. It was the first step in an ambitious nationwide campaign built around grand fund-raising balls held in twenty-one different cities. "Mr. Harris was presenting Pearl just as Richard Walsh had done thirty years before," said Richard's daughter Natalie. Pearl was thrilled by the possibilities he opened up. Harris felt comfortable, as she did, in a world where fantasy merged easily with fact. When his irrepressible energy, lavish spending, and big ideas failed to persuade the Welcome House board members to offer him a job for which he had neither training nor experience, she sidestepped their objections by setting up the Pearl S. Buck Foundation in January 1964, with herself in the chair and Ted Harris as president.

Its aim was to house and educate destitute Amerasian children in their own homelands, starting in Korea, and its staff consisted largely of dance instructors. Ted and his young friends, "the Arthur Murray crew," infiltrated Pearl's personal and professional life at all levels from then on. Financed initially from her own pocket, the Foundation had a star-studded board whose names headed the begging letters circulated in an extensive mailing program. Pearl roped in everyone she could persuade to sign on, from Joan Crawford to Dwight D. Eisenhower and Robert Kennedy. Harris devised a plan for Pearl to sign over her copyrights to the Foundation, which would bank her royalties and provide her in return with whatever income she required. She also made a will leaving her entire estate, including Green Hills Farm, to the Foundation, which meant that (apart from the Amerasian children) Harris was her principal beneficiary. At Pearl's request the board voted him a massive annual salary of forty-five thousand dollars in perpetuity, regardless of whether or not he remained in their employ.

Harris reinvented Pearl by treating her like royalty. "She imagined herself a queen, an empress," said one of her young men, who watched her transformation at Harris's hands into a character from her own fiction. For years Pearl had tended to assume what Margaret Thomson, her tart-tongued old friend from Nanjing, called "aspects of imperial grandeur." Now she had found a trusty henchman who made her feel like the heroine of *Imperial Woman,* "the true ruler, the beautiful powerful woman who feared no one and by whose charm and strength all were subdued." The fund-raising balls became ceremonial occasions, opened by Pearl taking the floor in Ted's arms in elaborate jewels and a full-length pink, white, or silver ball gown. She had a white mink coat with snap-on white fox-fur trim and a Chrysler limousine with her monogram in silver on the door (Ted had a matching one marked with his own initials). Together they installed the Foundation's headquarters in a handsome Philadelphia townhouse with luxury suites on different floors for him and her, and a state room filled with trophies, starting with Pearl's Nobel insignia. Margaret's son, James Thomson, working as assistant to Chester Bowles, the undersecretary of state in Kennedy's first administration, was amazed when Pearl came to call in a personalized limo "that seemed . . . twice as long as the Secretary of State's." He saw Pearl's Philadelphia setup as an unlikely re-creation of the Manchu court, centering round a figure gifted, like the empress in her book, with innate authority, imagination, courage, ambition, and a tiger heart. "Magnificence became her, as always."

Part of Harris's remit was to rewrite Pearl's image. She herself had authorized and edited a short biography, *The Exile's Daughter,* written by her sister and published in 1944 under the name Cornelia Spencer as part of an attempt to launch Grace as a writer. Partly perhaps because of its subject's constant intervention, the book is admiring and insipid, chiefly interesting in retrospect for occasional independent insight into their parents' lives. More problematic are the three books put together by Harris with Pearl's collaboration: *For Spacious Skies,* much of it dictated on their trips together in the back of one or other chauffeur-driven limo, and the two strange, scrappy, confessional volumes of *Pearl S. Buck: A Biography.* Their coverage is uncoordinated and unreliable, especially in passages where Harris attempts to strengthen his own position by denigrating Pearl's second marriage. She was already well into her seventies by the time these books came out, and her memories drift and waver in the disconcerting time warps of old age, clouding over in some areas but startlingly clear in others. Many of her disclosures have the pristine freshness of authentic recollection. Harris's prompting was not malicious or exploitive, but soothing and reassuring. If he was unscrupulous, it is in the sense that he tried to release the locks and censors that controlled Pearl's access to the past, and to console her by relieving its sometimes intolerable emotional pressure. His style was naïvely ingratiating, his judgment biased, and his understanding limited, but his sense of what distressed her was acute.

The first volume of his life of Pearl was published by John Day in 1969, which turned out to be a dreadful year for both of them. An FBI inquiry into Harris's running of the Foundation had been shelved a couple of years earlier, but newspaper allegations now resurfaced, first in Korea, then in the United States. "The Dancing Master," a well-documented, detailed, and damning piece of investigative journalism published in the July number of the monthly magazine *Philadelphia,* accused Harris of mishandling charitable funds and making sexual advances to Korean boys in the Foundation's care. He promptly resigned his post, denied the charges, and disappeared. At least one board member had already left in protest, and more now resigned. Feeling deceived, betrayed, and publicly humiliated like her father before her, Pearl rallied in furious defense, briefly taking charge of the organization herself, flatly rejecting every allegation, and threatening the press with lawsuits. Shortly before her seventy-seventh birthday she decamped, leaving behind everything that had rooted her life in Pennsylvania for more than three decades — her family, her house, garden, farm, and barn, her books and possessions, her beloved stands of sycamore and ash—to settle in Vermont with Ted. "Destiny compelled her onward, and her own she must leave behind," she had written of one of the empress's many flights in *Imperial Woman*.

Pearl spent the last years of her life in self-imposed exile in Vermont, keeping up a certain state in isolation but not obscurity. "She lived alone, this Empress, the walls of her courtesy impregnable and inviolate, and through that wall there was no gate." She and Ted had initially taken refuge in the summer house built by her sons in the Green Mountains, which reminded Pearl of Kuling's Mount Lu. Later they moved into the little neighboring town of Danby, where Pearl bought several rundown properties, setting up Ted and his former dance-instructor friends as antique dealers with a sideline in local crafts, while she lived in rooms over the shop. Their high hopes for the business dwindled in the end, and so did their even more optimistic schemes for transforming the future of Danby and its people. The outfit ended up more like a junkshop selling curios and copies of Buck books, with Pearl herself often seen seated at a window in Chinese silk robes, drawing five or six thousand people each summer as the town's sole tourist attraction. "I take my prestige with me," she had said grandly many years before to a woman who protested that wealthy charitable patrons would never attend balls in unfashionable locations like Philadelphia's Convention Hall. Pearl remained largely cut off from her children, who were liable to find their visits curtailed or barred altogether by their mother's entourage. Ugly disputes about money and access simmered beneath the surface. As Pearl approached her eighties, still in full command but growing frailer, it became hard to get through to her even on the telephone.

She followed, indeed sometimes almost seemed to be directing, world affairs from exile in Danby, emerging occasionally with a small train of attendants for meetings at the Philadelphia offices of her Foundation (now effectively reconstituted after its drastic shake-up, working better than before, and moving toward eventual merger with Welcome House). She gave interviews, wrote articles, and fronted a TV show as guest host for a week in Boston. She told a journalist that she had never gotten used to America and still could not feel at home

there. Her longing to return to her roots, to revisit the country that
had shaped her and to see her parents' graves again, intensified as the
U.S. government seemed to draw closer to the People's Republic. "By
birth and ancestry I am American," she said, ". . . but by sympathy
and feeling, I am Chinese." In February 1972, when President Richard
Nixon announced his intention to visit Beijing, Pearl planned to go
with him, or alternatively to follow in his wake. Proposals were drawn
up for fiction and nonfiction books on the trip, syndicated newspaper
coverage, and a TV documentary. She sent telegrams and letters to
anyone who might assist her, from the president himself to the Chinese prime minister, Zhou Enlai, who came from Tsingkiangpu, where
Pearl grew up. It was a bitter shock when, after months of waiting, a
curt note from a junior Chinese diplomat in Canada turned down her
visa application on the grounds that her works had for years "taken
an attitude of distortion, smear and vilification towards the people of
new China and its leaders." Zhou Enlai sent her a set of nesting lac-
quer boxes as a consolation. Long after her death it turned out that
Zhou had personally signed the memo banning her return.

Pearl retained and if anything increased her power over her readers, who wrote in their thousands year after year to consult her about
prejudice and injustice, confiding their life stories and asking her
advice. "They were the communications of my own people to me,"
she said of these letters to which she scrupulously replied. "They
were my communication with my own people." All her life she had
been able to absent herself, withdrawing from reality, often seeming
to friends and family to be a prisoner of her imagination, present only
in body in the actual outer world. "I could pass her on the sidewalk
and she could go right by without knowing me," said the director of
Welcome House, who worked with her on a daily basis. "She had a
trick sometimes of being completely abstracted, and at times, when
you would meet her, she would be looking right over your shoulder,
as if she didn't know you were there," said Natalie Walsh, who acted
for a few years as Pearl's typist. "It wasn't rudeness, she was just living an interior kind of life, alone." She spent more and more time in
Vermont in that secret place where she could be alone with her peo-

ple. Sometimes she hardly distinguished between her imaginary characters and the letter writers who responded to them, "what I called her 'paper people,'" said her Vermont secretary, Beverly Drake, who remembered Pearl surrounded by ghostly presences, some real, some fictional. "She often spoke of those characters as if they *were* real people. In one sense they *were* real, these creations who reached out and touched her correspondents who in turn reached out and touched her as creator, until the circle was completed, and then repeated over and over again."

Outwardly Pearl grew more and more to resemble the last empress, China's Venerable Ancestor, from whom, as a child, she had believed herself to be descended. James Thomson, who visited her for the last time in her eightieth year, was received by Pearl dressed in brocaded silk and attended by ladies-in-waiting: "As I remember one or two wore pantsuits which seemed out of kilter with . . . her imperial gown." The two sat uncomfortably side by side on large throne-like chairs in a first-floor audience chamber. She was protected, like the empress, who had herself been both cosseted by and ultimately dependent on the shrewd, manipulative eunuchs running her court, controlling her revenues, and channeling contact with her empire. In Pearl's book anger was the empress's driving force, power her goal, and the solitude imposed by power her curse: "Her spirit dwelt in loneliness but to this she was accustomed. It was the price of greatness, and she paid it day after day, and night after night."

In June 1972 Pearl returned briefly to Green Hills Farm to celebrate her eightieth birthday with her sister, her children, and her grandchildren. Shortly afterward she collapsed. Two successive operations meant that she spent much of the autumn in the hospital. By New Year 1973 she was back home in Danby, where she lay dying of lung cancer under heavy medication, refusing visits, slipping in and out of a coma she could not bear even her family to see. She roused herself on February 21, when she sat up in bed, summoned her attendants, and called for paper to dictate what turned out to be the last letter she ever wrote. "The scene was beautiful, wild, incongruous. I wouldn't have believed it if I hadn't seen it myself," wrote Mrs. Drake, one of her waiting women. "In minutes she returned to a helpless state, the brilliant flash of old reality gone. I wish the whole family, the whole world, had seen this incredible lady sitting imperiously on her throne, wrapped in white satin and commanding that her will be done."

She died in Danby on March 6 and was buried as she had wished beneath an ash tree in the garden at Green Hills Farm. Her name on the stone that marks her grave is inscribed in Chinese characters, Sai Zhenzhu: 赛珍珠. One of her last visitors in Vermont had been another old friend from Nanjing, Bertha Reisner, who came with a tourist group to pay homage to America's Venerable Ancestor. "We were told a lot about Pearl S. Buck before she entered. Then at the dramatic moment she came in: very ancient, very dramatic, very immobile. Very oriental, inscrutable. She was there, and very gracious, and yet she was not there. Very distant. You couldn't be quite sure that she wasn't captive."

SOURCES AND
ACKNOWLEDGMENTS

The Los Angeles art critic Edward Goldman described an installation in Beijing in 2007 called *Staring into Amnesia*. Visitors were invited to board a dimly lit, 1950s railroad car to view multiple screens, installed in each of the windows, "projecting black and white documentary footage of twentieth century Chinese history, with special emphasis on the brutality experienced by Chinese people during WW2 and the Cultural Revolution . . . long lines of spectators formed to climb aboard the railroad car of Qiu Anxiong's *Staring into Amnesia*." Writing this book has been in some ways a comparable experience. Pearl Buck left a vast amount of autobiographical writing in the form of memoirs, essays, articles, pamphlets, and prefaces. As a novelist she constantly drew on her past for source material, sometimes so thinly disguised that it is hard to draw a definite line between fact and fiction. She wrote full-length lives of each of her parents and edited or coauthored two biographies of herself. Almost all of these writings are riddled with selective amnesia. I have treated them as the imaginative equivalent of an archaeological find: dense, complex, richly layered, heavily built up in parts, thin and uninformative in others, a treasure trove of images compressed, elided, or distorted by the pressure of subsequent emotions and events.

Pearl's various accounts depend almost entirely on her own memory, always a highly creative faculty and one that can be seen at work over half a century exploring, shaping, and reshaping incidents and exchanges from her past. Her early recollections draw heavily on tales her mother told her, collated with her own vivid but patchy infant memory, which started functioning, by her own account, from the moment she opened her eyes on the day of her birth. Her sense of time was elastic. Two months can expand into ten; several years may be condensed into one or suppressed altogether. She relied scarcely at all on documentation, and most of the few family documents she mentions (her mother's diaries and letters, the newspaper produced by her oldest brother as a child, certain passages from her father's memoirs) seem to have disappeared.

In the more or less complete absence of external evidence relating to Pearl's childhood, I have where possible followed the relatively factual accounts left by her father and sister: a terse but reliable memoir by Absalom Sydenstricker, *Our Life and Work in China*, written in the 1920s and eventually published in 1978 with editorial amendments and additions by his youngest daughter, Pearl's sister Grace Yaukey; and *The Exile's Daughter*, Grace's own brief biography of her sister, heavily edited by Pearl and published in 1945 under the pseudonym Cornelia Spencer. The two volumes of Pearl's official biography were produced in her lifetime and with her collaboration by the companion of her last decade, Theodore Harris, who strung together her published and unpublished reminiscences with a selection of her correspondence, linked by reverential commentaries of his own.

My chronology is based initially on these often contradictory family sources, supplemented, corroborated, or corrected by material from three major archives. The Buck Papers in the Lipscomb Library of Randolph College (formerly Randolph-Macon Woman's College) in Lynchburg, Virginia, proved a rich resource, principally because they include the research files amassed by Pearl's first independent biographer, Nora Stirling, who conducted extraordinarily comprehensive and perceptive interviews with family, friends, assistants, and professional colleagues soon after Pearl's death. The Nora Stirling Collection is unique, and for me especially precious, in its emphasis on firsthand accounts of Pearl in China. Stirling's book, *Pearl Buck: A Woman in Conflict* (1983), is more problematic. Written in the sentimental style of popular fiction, containing copious dialogue with no sources specified and little sense of historical context, it gives the impression of being a great deal less reliable than it actually is. Because the wording of quotations in Stirling's published text frequently differ from her interview typescripts, I have cited the original typed versions as being probably more authentic. My book owes much to the generous and scholarly support of Theodore Hostetler, the library director; Frances E. Webb, the reference librarian; Adrian Broughman, the archives assistant; and Elizabeth Johnston Lipscomb, who catalogued the Buck Papers.

The comprehensive mission records preserved by the Presbyterian Historical Society in Philadelphia made it possible to trace the career of Absalom Sydenstricker in considerable detail through private reports and letters as well as annual records printed for the Southern Presbyterian Mission in Shanghai. I am grateful to the Society for permission to quote from documents in its possession, and to Eileen Sklar and her colleagues for guiding me through the collection's labyrinthine pathways. The archives of Pearl S. Buck International, meticulously preserved in her old home at Green Hills Farm in Pennsylvania, and primarily concerned with her American years (which are beyond the scope of this book), yielded much incidental illumination. My best thanks go to the president, Janet L. Mintzner, and the curator, Donna C. Rhodes. Last I thank Peter Conn, whose authoritative and impeccably researched *Pearl S. Buck: A Cultural Biography* (1996) laid a solid foundation for all subsequent Buck studies. My book could not have been written without constant recourse to Professor Conn's groundbreaking work, and it has had the benefit of his encouragement and advice from start to finish.

I am grateful to Pearl Buck's children, in particular to Janice and Edgar Walsh for so patiently answering my questions, and to Paul Buck for permission to quote from his father's writings. My warmest thanks go to Sue Stephenson, my cultural interpreter and guide in West Virginia, for her insight and hospitality. Also to James E. Talbert, archivist of the Greenbrier Historical Society in Lewisburg; to Lloyd and Elizabeth Lipscomb for introducing me to the Pearl Buck House in Hillsboro, West Virginia; to the house manager, Anita Withrow, for a personal tour; and to Mrs. Betsy Edgar for firsthand recollections of the Stultings, who eventually sold their house to her family.

I owe more than I can say to Prof. Liu Haiping of Nanjing University for moral and practical support. I am grateful for help and instruction to his students Hu Jing, Li Qingshuan, and most particularly to Jiang Qinggang; also to Robert Riggle, Catherine Germond, and Rev. Zemin Chen of Nanjing Union Theological Seminary. My next great debt is to Ye Gongping (Ernie Yeh) of Nanjing Agricultural University for invaluable and indefatigable research, for translating documents, and for sharing with me his extensive knowledge of John Lossing Buck. In Zhenjiang my thanks go to the director of the Pearl S. Buck Research Association, Madame Xu Xiaoxia, and to the Association's vice directors: Mr. Li Jingfa, curator of the Pearl S. Buck Museum; Mr. Wang Yuguo, vice director of the Municipal Culture Bureau and director of the Municipal Historic Relics Protection Bureau; and Prof. Zhou Weijing, director of the Pearl S. Buck Research Center, Jiangsu University of Science and Technology. I thank too the Association's general secretary, Mr. Ji Dong. I am greatly indebted to Prof. Shao Tizhong and Prof. Chang Hong of the Pearl S. Buck Research Center, Suzhou College, Anhui, for kindness and hospitality, and to Mr. MU De-hua, vice chairman, Lushan Federation of Literature and Art Circles, Guling, for much information and a guided tour.

My best thanks go to my agent, Bruce Hunter, to my editor, Alice Mayhew, and to Roger Labrie, for encouragement, resourcefulness, and forbearance under provocation.

Finally I should like to thank all those who sheltered me during the writing of this book: Ellen Wagner in New York, Sue Stephenson in Lynchburg, Susie and Nick Reilly in Shanghai, Hilary Tulloch in Westminster, Ian and Lydia Wright in Islington, Ivor and Hilary Cox in Beulah, and, as so often before, Dame Drue Heinz, Dr. Martin Gaskell, and the staff at Hawthornden Castle in Scotland.

Hilary Spurling, Holloway, November 2009

KEY TO SOURCES

All Pearl Buck's books first published by John Day, New York, unless otherwise indicated. Where quotations come from later editions by other publishers, these are cited in square brackets.

AS	Absalom Sydenstricker
BP	*A Bridge for Passing*, 1962
CR	*The Chinese Recorder*, Shanghai
CS	Carie Sydenstricker
CWNG	*The Child Who Never Grew*, Vineland Training School, New Jersey, 1950
ED	*The Exile's Daughter: A Biography of Pearl S. Buck*, by Cornelia Spencer (Grace Yaukey's pseudonym), New York, 1944
EDts	passages deleted by PB from the typescript of *The Exile's Daughter* in the possession of Randolph College Archives
EW	Emma Edmunds White, correspondence with PB in Randolph College Archives
EWWW	*East Wind, West Wind*, 1930 [Moyer Bell, New York, 1993]
Ex	*The Exile*, 1936
FA	*Fighting Angel*, 1936
FW	*The First Wife and Other Stories*, 1933 [Methuen, London, 1933]
GE	*The Good Earth*, 1931 [Pocket Books, 2005]
GY	Grace Yaukey (née Sydenstricker)
HD	*A House Divided*, 1935 [Moyer Bell, New York, 1994]
IW	*Imperial Woman*, 1956 [Moyer Bell, New York, 1951]
JLB	John Lossing Buck
KL	*Pearl S. Buck: A Cultural Bridge across the Pacific*, by Kang Liao, Greenwood Press, Connecticut, 1997

MGC   Marian Gardner Craighill

MO   *The Mother,* 1934 [Moyer Bell, New York, 1993]

MSW   *My Several Worlds,* 1954

NS   *Pearl Buck: A Woman in Conflict,* by Nora Stirling, New York, 1983

NSC   Nora Stirling Collection (typescript interviews conducted by Stirling with Pearl's friends and family, as well as miscellaneous documents), Lipscomb Library, Randolph College Archives

OLW   *Our Life and Work in China,* by Absalom Sydenstricker, West Virginia, 1978

PB   Pearl Buck (née Sydenstricker)

PC   *Pearl S. Buck: A Cultural Biography,* by Peter Conn, Cambridge, UK, 1996

PHS   Presbyterian Historical Society Archives, PCUSA, Philadelphia

PSBI   Archives of the Pearl S. Buck House, Pearl S. Buck International

RCA   Randolph College (formerly Randolph-Macon Woman's College) Archives

Sons   *Sons,* 1932 [Moyer Bell, New York, 1994]

SS   *For Spacious Skies: Journey in Dialogue,* by PB with Theodore F. Harris, 1966

THi and THii   *Pearl S. Buck: A Biography,* by Theodore F. Harris in consultation with Pearl Buck, volume 1, 1969 [London, 1970], Volume 2, 1971, Creativity, Inc. [London, 1972]

TN   *The Time Is Noon,* 1966 [Methuen, London, 1967]

TPH   *This Proud Heart,* 1938 [The Book Club, London, 1939]

VH   *Voices in the House,* 1953, in *American Triptych: Three "John Sedges" Novels,* 1958

Notes

Chapter 1

1   "We looked out over the paddy fields *Ex,* 55–56.

1   "These three who came before *My Mother's House,* by PB, West Virginia, 1965, 8.

2   "I spoke Chinese first THi, 44.

2   "If America was for dreaming about *MSW,* 5.

2   " 'Everything you say is lies THi 69.

2   "Why must we hide it? THi, 44.

2   "Here in the green shadows *MSW,* 25.

3   "That huge empire *The Gentle Inoffensive Chinese,* by Mark Twain, vol. 2, New York, 1872[1992], 318.

3   Sometimes Pearl found bones *MSW,* 19; THi, 74–5.

4   old Chinese novels *MSW,* 57.

4   "wonderful daggers FW, xii; see THi, 33.

4   Wang Amah was wrinkled THi, 89; *ED,* 23.

5   "because you wash yourselves THi, 34–38; see also *Ex,* 135–38; GY in NSC.

6   "a place called Home *ED,* 15; EDts.

6   "I grew up misinformed *MSW,* 63.

7   "He had to himself an area *FA,* 129–30.

7   One of the thrilling stories *Ex,* 156–62.

8   first-rate novelist's training *Ex,* 300.

8   her "two selves" Foreword to *American Triptych: Three "John Sedges" Novels,* by PB, 1945.

9   "people would once have said *VH,* 481.

9   "But I cannot This and the next quote are from "Address to National Education Association," 1938, cited in *ED,* 193.

9   "In China she is admired "Pearl of the Orient," by Mike Meyer, *New York Times Book Review,* March 5, 2006.

9   Henri Matisse said *Matisse the Master: A Life of Henri Matisse,* vol, 2, by Hilary Spurling, New York, 2005, 342.

9   Jawaharlal Nehru read *MSW,* 8.

10 "We had a full cup *OLW,* 25.

10   "the heart-rending bereavements *CR* 31, April 1900, 196.

11   "The deaths of these two children *OLW,* 25.

11   "I shouldn't have listened *BP,* 21.

11   "He went about Europe *FA,* 102.

11   "I never saw so hard a heart *FA,* 100.

11   "irrevocable as death *Ex,* 130.

11   "Had it taken the death *Ex,* 177.

11   "We are by no means overtaking "The Importance of the Direct Phase of Mis-
     sion Work," by AS, *CR* 41, June 1910, 389.

12   "Gospel herald "On the Present Situation," by AS, *CR* 57, August 1926, 603.

12   "His children were merely accidents *FA,* 208.

12   "My father set off on a long trip *OLW,* 22.

13   prisoners in their own houses *Earthen Vessels and Transcendent Power: American
     Presbyterian Missionaries in China, 1837–1952,* by G. Thompson Brown, NY, 1997,
     138. For PB's memories of Tsingkiangpu, see *Ex,* 180–87; *ED,* 13–15.

14   "the other one's, the white one's room *Ex,* 182.

14   "The masses of feathery Passage conflated from descriptions of the same
     autumn landscape in *Ex,* 99; and *FA,* 63.

15   "My memory of his middle years "In Memoriam," PB's obituary of her father,
     typescript, 1931, NSC.

15   "a man very tall *GE,* 133.

16   "almost as devoid All quotes in this paragraph are from "Preaching to the Chi-
     nese by Similarities and Contrasts," by AS, *CR* 20, July 1889, 330.

17   "The people were afraid of us *OLW,* 29. PB's account of Hsuchien in *Ex,* 196–
     98; *FA,* 129–30.

17   "They were living like beasts *The Townsman,* by PB, 1945, in *American Triptych:
     Three "John Sedges" Novels,* 1958, 140.

17   "For neither of them was it a struggle *FA,* 139. For other versions of this con-
     frontation, see *Ex,* 198–99; *Ed,* 17. For AS's escape from and return to Hsuchien,
     see *OLW,* 30–34; *Ex,* 197; *FA,* 88–89.

19   "My father seemed oblivious GY in *OLW,* 29.

20   "No large cities "What I Learned in Shantung," by AS, *CR* 18, July 1887.

20   "the great sprawling opulent city" *GE,* 116. The nameless fictional city in this
     book combines features taken from both Zhenjiang and Nanxuzhou.

21   "They did not even know him well enough *FA,* 151.

21   godowns that smelled of hemp THi, 56.

21   three small rooms. The rooms above a Chinese liquor store rented in Zhenjiang
     in 1896–97, and the Sydenstrickers' dramatic departure from them, are clearly
     described in *ED,* 18–19, 22–25, 32; EDts; THi, 56. PB describes her parents liv-
     ing in what seem to be the same lodgings in 1886–87 in *Ex,* 142–47.

22   "It robbed her of the tiny margin *Ex,* 191.

22   "They snatched at us THi, 46.

23 "if he took a pair of chopsticks *Sons,* 1932, 111–12.

23 "the silk shops flying brilliant banners This and the following quote are from *GE,* 120, 116; sweets, lanterns, and kites from *MSW,* 28–29; THi, 85.

24 I learned to know its every mood THi, 62.

25 the Kuling Mountain Company—Kuling (now Guling) was founded by Edward Selby Little (1864–1939) whose original plan showing the Sydenstricker plot was in the exhibition *Story of Old Villas* at the Guling Museum in 2007. Kuling was the birthplace in 1911 of the English draughtsman and novelist Mervyn Peake, who re-created the mountain as Gormenghast in his *Titus Groan* trilogy.

25 a lifesaving station—*MSW,* 125. See also *MSW* 126–31; *Ex,* 227–31; *OLW,* 41–42; *ED,* 32.

25 Clyde contracted diphtheria—Accounts of Clyde's death in *Ex,* 202–4; *MSW,* 131; *BP,* 67; *ED,* 35; EDts.

25 "I have two little brothers The text of this letter, dated April 5, 1899, is in THi, 86.

26 "But his body is precious *BP,* 67.

26 "I was so happy *CWNG,* 6.

26 "Bred in this sparkling *Ex,* 41.

27 "If it had not been for this other one . . .' *Ex,* p. 120. All quotes in this paragraph are from *Ex,* 119–22 (the storm at sea turns into a hot still moonlit night in *BP,* 21). Maude Sydenstricker died in the arms of Dr. W. A. P. Martin (1827–1916), one of the negotiators of the treaties that opened up China to the West in the 1860s, afterward president of T'ungwen College in Beijing.

27 "remained for Carie to the end of her life *Ex,* 93.

28 "She had to plunge her hand *Ex,* 131; invasive snakes from *The Townsman,* 1945, in *American Triptych: Three "John Sedges" Novels,* 1958, 216.

28 "a small, decrepit brick cottage *Ex,* 209.

28 "Their segments were covered *SS,* 146.

29 "In the year 1900 *OLW,* 27.

30 "Then he looked at us all strangely *FA,* 160.

31 "even Father with his collar off EDts.

31 "The air that summer's day *MSW,* 39; see also *Ex,* 221–22.

31 "I seemed without the body *FA,* 164.

31 "The white people in Shanghai *ED,* 49.

31 "I had never seen her afraid *MSW,* 42.

32 In October Absalom convened—*Minutes of the North Kiangsu Mission of the Southern Presbyterian Church, 1899 and 1900,* American Presbyterian Mission Press, Shanghai, in PHS.

32 "down through the states *FA,* 105.

Chapter 2

33 "thousands of Christians suffered *OLW,* 37.

34 "Did I not see sights *MSW,* 19.

34 "immensely better *OLW,* 42.

34 "for those savage *MSW,* 59.

35 "I knew every tree Grace Stulting Smith interview, NSC; PB's memories in *Ex,* 135–41, 70–72, 175; THi, 82; PB, *My Mother's House, passim.*

35 Throughout her childhood—Stulting family history taken from *The Stulting Family: Dutch Ancestors of Pearl Buck,* by Grace Stulting Smith, Richmond, Virginia, 1974, a privately printed monograph that differs in almost all particulars from PB's folkloric version in *Ex,* 11–25 (the Stultings bought land but never developed it: the original 1848 deed of purchase is on p. 8, and the eventual notice of sale is in the *Greenbrier Independent,* January 18 and May 24, 1883.) Further details from *A Historic and Scenic Tour of Pocahontas County,* by C. A. Curry, West Virginia, 2004, 38–39.

35 "He was a city man This and the following quotes from Grace Stulting Smith interview, NSC.

37 "a harvest of dark, white-clad heathen Passage conflated from PB's fiction and nonfiction accounts in *TN,* 171, and *Ex,* 88.

37 "Must we have the revolution *MSW,* 45.

38 Yankees had horns—*Ex,* 54.

38 "That amah, she raised her—This and the next quote are from Grace Stulting Smith interview, NSC.

39 "Sir, I know *Ex,* 89.

39 He was the youngest but one—Sydenstricker family history based on *FA,* 12, 15–29; *Ex,* 173–74; *OLW,* 2; PB's ts obituary, NSC. Further information from an article by AS's brother, "The Sydenstricker Family," by Rev. Christopher Sydenstricker, in *A History of Greenbrier County,* by J. R. Cole, privately published, 1917, 240–42; the Greenbrier County Census for 1830, 1840, and 1850; Pocahontas County Census, 1880; *Greenbrier County, (West) Virginia: Marriages 1782–1900,* by Larry A. Shuck, Athens, Georgia, n.d. [1991]; *A Genealogy and History of the Kauffman/Coffman Families of North America, 1584–1937,* by Charles F. Kauffman, privately published, 1940; "A Genealogy of the Isaac and Esther Coffman Family Descendants," by Daniel Roy Coffman, 1971, both in Greenbrier Historical Society Archives, Lewisburg, West Virginia.

40 "In that house bursting *FA,* 25.

40 "I saw him an overworked boy *FA,* 18.

40 "his austerities, his shynesses *Ex,* 174.

41 "It was the same sick helplessness *Sons,* 313.

41 "When he came back PB, *My Mother's House;* see also *FA,* 81, 182.

41 demanding to join the church—*FA,* 171–74.

42 "slender face EDts.

42 "with the feeling *FA,* 181.

42 "He was a spirit *FA,* 12–13.

42 Station meetings were stormy affairs —*FA,* 67–70, 75–76; further information from *Minutes of the North Kiangsu Mission of the Southern Presbyterian Church,* printed annually in Shanghai from 1899 in PHS.

43 "We are better judges — Rev. C. W. Mateer in CR 31, January 1900, 18.

43 "I succeeded *FA,* 67.

43 "My memory of that circle *FA,* 76.

43 "On Sunday everyone *FA,* 67–68.

44 "if a little water *FA,* 72.

44 "We sat silent *FA,* 73.

45 "when something he kept curbed *FA,* 55; EDts, 49–50.

45 "I have seen other *FA,* 69.

45 Pearl admitted in private—*ED* 82.

45 "Their language as well as their thought *Light and Shadows of the Mission World in the Far East,* by S. H. Chester, Richmond, Virginia, 1899, chapter 5 (a report on mission work in the Yangtse Valley by the secretary of foreign missions in the U.S. Presbyterian Church).

46 "Assyria, Babylon, Greece Rev. P. F. Price in *CR* 31, September 1900.

46 "Even the smallest children *By My Spirit,* by Rev. Jonathan Goforth [1929], Evangel Pub House, 2004, chapter 3 (report on a revivalist campaign in Manchuria in 1908).

46 "so hopeful and encouraging—AS, "The Importance of the Direct Phase of Mission Work," *CR* 41, June 1910, 391.

46 "I never stood up *FA,* 137.

47 "There is fire in him *FA,* 98. My account of Ma Pangbo pieced together from *FA passim; OLW,* 36; Thompson Brown, *Earthen Vessels and Transcendent Power,* 111.

47 "Many times I stood there *FA,* 164.

47 "the Pauline spirit—This and the next two quotes come, respectively, from an editorial in *CR* 24, February 1893, and articles by Rev. J. Goforth, *CR* 39, October 1908, and by Rev. Arnold Foster, *CR* 19, 1888, 528.

48 "The power to work miracles AS, "Jesus as Teacher and Trainer," *CR* 24, September 1893, 197.

48 "into three great types *Between Two Worlds,* by PB, West Virginia 1992, 8.

48 "aggressive evangelistic work"—*CR* 41, June 1910, 411.

48 "The effrontery of all this *MSW,* 49.

48 "a stinging conviction of sin" "Preaching to the Chinese by Similarities and Contrasts," *CR* 20, July 1889, 328.

49 "all the essentials of Salvation" *FA,* 92.

49 "in anger and indignation" This and the next quote from *Is There a Case for Foreign Missions?,* by PB, John Day, New York, 1933, 10–11.

49 "Somehow I had learned from Thoreau *MSW,* 51.

50 "in his beautiful polished Peking Mandarin"—*MSW,* 50.

50 "I became mentally bifocal *MSW,* 52.

51 "His favorite text *MSW,* 53.

51 "When I was in the Chinese world *MSW,* 10.

51 "so strangely called *MSW,* 49.

52 "Gradually the workers disappeared This and the next quote are from ED, 85–86.

53 "a brilliant figure"—*Kinfolk,* by PB, 1945, Moyer Bell, 1996, 4.

53 "I decided well before I was ten *MSW,* 76.

53 "Such books poison the thoughts *IW,* 19.

54 "And there quite alone This and the next quote are from THii, 229; see also *FA,* 35; *MSW,* 62.

55 "plaguing everyone with questions *MSW,* 62.

56 "and in His images" *MSW,* 70.

56 "I heard talk about this *MSW,* 48.

56 "They grew up with me THi, 51. The next quote is from THi, 4. For the story of Tsai Yun, see *Ex,* 12, 13–15, 300; *The Chinese Children Next Door*, by PB, New York, 1942; *MSW,* 5–7; THi, 45–55. PB gave her adoptive sister different names, origins, ages, even generations in these four versions of her story, which grow progressively less romanticized. Passing references elsewhere (*ED,* 129; *SS,* 30) confirm that she did actually exist, and I have followed the last and fullest of these accounts, which seems the most authentic.

56 "A first girl they accepted *MSW,* 7.

57 "She rocked back and forth EDts, 76–77.

57 "I used as a small child THii, 224.

57 At regular intervals—*BP,* 150.

57 Wang Amah developed symptoms—*Ex,* 224 sets this in 1900, but I have followed ED, 83, which gives the date as 1903.

57 annual general meeting —The meeting at Hsuchowfu took place on October 3–7, 1903; James Bear died on October 9. *Minutes of the North Kiangsu Mission,* 1903; *OLW,* 39.

58 The road wound around *MSW,* 114–15.

59 "the tall white Madonna lilies *MSW,* 113.

59 "Mr. Lu said *MSW,* 61.

59 "Peace covered China *MSW,* 69.

60 "Not until justice—*MSW,* 50. For the death of Mr. Kung, see *MSW,* 60.

60 Longden sisters—See *MSW,* 64; *ED,* 87–88, 93.

61 "mental infanticide *Analytical Reader,* by Dr. W. A. P. Martin, Presbyterian Mission, Shanghai, 1897. On the Methodist Mission School, see *MSW.* 60; *ED,* 77–80, 89. On PB's Chinese friends, see *ED,* 88, 93–95; THi, 96 (where Dottie becomes Dolly).

62   "dreadful shivering hordes— *Ex,* 246. The next two quotes are from *Ex,* 247, 249. For contemporary reports of the famine, see *CR* 38, January and February, 1907, 57, 121, 124–25, 235, 401.

62   "like a toothless *GE,* 81.

62   "the hue of a liver *Sons,* 231.

62   "not even her avid reading This and the next quote are from *ED*ts.

63   "with bits of tin *GE,* 128.

63   "the normal sounds *ED,* 93.

63   Charles Hancock—*ED,* 89–91; *Minutes of the North Kiangsu Mission,* 1907, 1908.

64   "Mother is angry *ED*ts, 15; the next quote from EDts, 39.

64   "that as Christ was head *MSW,* 90.

64   It did not occur to him *FA,* 140.

64   "and I must say *MSW,* 90.

64   "He was penurious *FA,* 50.

65   "incredible pinchings *FA,* 197.

65   "Absalom's New Testament *ED,* 81.

65   "upstairs with the other white people" *FA* 122. The next three quotes are from *FA,* 123–24.

66   Kuling American School *MSW,* 64, *ED.* 86–87.

66   "She said she read Lewis Carroll's *ED,* 97; for Miss Jewell's School, see *MSW,* 64–70; NSC for interviews with old girls.

66   *Shanghai Mercury*—*ED,* 74; THi, 87.

67   "Religion I was used to *MSW,* 68.

67   "She was expressing—"The Conflict of Viewpoints," by PB, *CR,* 54, September 1923, 540.

67   Door of Hope—*MSW,* 69–70, 73–74; *Ex,* 249.

68   "My mother approved it *MSW,* 90.

68   "There was nothing *OLW,* 46.

69   scathing review—*CR,* October 1912, 591–96; see also *Ex,* 268; *OLW,* 48.

69   naked statues—NS, 23.

69   "grave and bitter look" *MSW,* 71.

69   "Their faces in repose *GE,* 121.

69   "They were always sweating THi, 56.

70   "It is clearly foretold *MSW,* 89. All quotes in this and the next paragraph are from *MSW,* 89–90.

Chapter 3

71   "He never troubled himself *FA,* 241.

72   "She knew she must seem *ED,* 106. My account of PB's college days is based on *MSW,* 91–97; *ED,* 105–26; interviews with alumnae in NSC; information from Sue Stephenson; background materials in RCA.

72 "Girls came in groups *MSW,* 92.

73 "Externally I became an American *MSW,* 93.

75 "No one of them knew This and the next quote from *FA,* 208, 209; see also *CWNG,* 32.

75 "the one against whom This and the next quote are from EDts, 130.

75 Pearl regretted her decision later PB letter to EW, October 10, 1968.

76 "most of them white-haired *FA,* 19–20.

76 "I did all that I could *MSW,* 93.

77 "It meant everything to me PB, letter to EW, April 17, [1917], NSC.

77 "I was trained by Asian Women *SS,* 140.

77 "The shock . . . of the departure *The Hidden Flower,* by PB [1952], Pocket Cardinal, 1954, 172–73.

77 "Of my college days *MSW,* 91, 95, 96.

78 "She never forgot the pity *Ex,* 275.

78 "It was a young man's revolution *FA,* 211.

79 "A little seed of anxiety *ED,* 120. For the Sydenstrickers' new house, see *ED,* 119; *MSW,* 100, *OLW,* 49. This second Sydenstricker house (which no longer exists) stood behind the larger "Paxton house," which is now the Pearl S. Buck Museum in Zhenjiang.

79 "I began again to think in Chinese."—*MSW,* 98.

80 "Why did I never see *HD,* 252.

80 "In all the time *ED,* 126; see also *MSW,* 98–100.

81 "it seemed nothing Pearl could do *ED,* 130.

81 "I was always touched *MSW,* 101.

81 "To other Americans in Zhenjiang *ED,* 130.

81 high school for boys—*Catalogue of the Chinkiang Presbyterian High School,* January 1915, PHS.

81 "It was a wonderful time *MSW,* 118.

81 "He was the crest of a wave *MSW,* 183. The next two quotes are from *MSW,* 184, 185.

82 "The wonder is that none *MSW,* 119.

82 "with the terrible sadness "The Clutch of the Ancients," by PB, *CR* 55, August 1924, 520.

83 "They taught me far more *MSW,* 102.

83 "It seems to me now *MSW,* 107.

83 "far more Chinese in his mentality *MSW,* 109.

83 Her field of sexual experimentation For the mixed-race student, see chapter 2. For the shipboard affair and the Standard Oil boyfriends, see *MSW,* 98, 108; THi, 99–100. Further information from a letter from Emma White to Nora Stirling, November 20, n.d. [1975], and interviews with Emma White, NSC.

84 'He'll never marry you *TN,* 161.

84 "I listened and reflected *MSW,* 109.

84 Cornelia Morgan—Morgan founded the Mid Yunnan Bethel School for the China Inland Mission; see *MSW,* 110, THi, 113.

85 'I know it,' she said *MSW,* 110.

85 "Her flesh fell away . . .' *Ex,* 286.

85 "I studied my Chinese books *MSW,* 115. The next two quotes are from *MSW,* 117, 99.

86 "Born a generation earlier *FA,* 210.

86 "Since those days *Ex,* 283.

86 Neale Carter—See *Ex,* 60, 72–73, 77, 240, 270.

86 "The word 'flesh'—AS's annotations in his copy (in the possession of Nanjing University Library) of *The Person and Work of the Holy Spirit as Revealed in the Scriptures, and in Personal Experience,* by R. A. Torry, New York, 1910, 7, 59.

87 "he did not enjoy whimsy *Ex,* 231.

87 "I sat in horror *EWWW,* 142.

87 "I began what was to be *MSW,* 117.

88 "repressed, strong, vigorous *FA,* 189.

89 "She did the things *Ex,* 292; for Carie's house, see *Ex,* 290–93.

89 "The failure of missions *MSW,* 120.

90 "I think before all others *MSW,* 126.

90 "When in 1916 This and the next two quotes are from *MSW,* 127. *New Youth (Hsin Ch'ing-nien)* published Hu Shi's article "Some Tentative Suggestions for the Reform of Chinese Literature" in January 1917.

91 "vivid, articulate *MSW,* 128.

91 "This was an enormous release *MSW,* 127–28.

Chapter 4

92 a fellow student at Cornell University—Hu Shi (1891–1962) entered the agricultural college at Cornell in 1910, the same year as JLB (1890–1975.)

92 "that darling Mrs. Sydenstricker's daughter JLB, letter to his parents, July 23, 1916, NSC. The next two quotes are from his letter of September 19, 1916.

92 "She was worth it," JLB interview, NSC. JLB said they had met four or five times, and PB confirmed it in THi, 112.

92 "like a nice big overgrown farmboy,"—This and the next quote from MCG interview, NSC.

92 Sunday school teaching —JLB interview, NSC.

93 "He was not at all religious *MSW,* 129.

93 "I am happier every day," PB, letter to EW, April 17, [1917], NSC.

93 "downright ugliness" This and the next quote from *MSW,* 135; see MGC interview NSC.

93 "The bare willow trees *MSW,* 136.

94 "the garden seemed part *MSW,* 135; further information from PB, letter to Grace and Vincent Buck, JLB's parents, October 14, [1917], NSC.

94 "My new housekeeper JLB, letter to Clifford Buck, September 7, 1917, NSC.

95 "the economic salvation This and the next quote from T. F. Carter, letter to Mr. Henry, New York, October 15, 1914, PHS.

95 "Poor devil Paul Buck interview, June 26, 1975, NSC.

95 "He had no idea *GE,* 115.

96 "They would bend down *MSW,* 144.

96 "literally hundreds This and the next quote from PB, letter to Bucks, April 8, 1918, NSC.

96 "They were having fun This and the next two quotes from MCG interview, November 29, 1975, NSC.

97 "You see, she understood MCG, letter to Nora Stirling, July 19, 1977, NSC.

97 "a world as distant *MSW,* 129. The next quote is *MSW,* from 140.

98 "people spoke in syllables *GE,* 113. For descriptions of Anhui home life, see JLB, letter to Bucks, February 28, 1916, NSC.

98 "The land stretched out *HD,* 19, 22.

98 His two monumental statistical surveys—*Chinese Farm Economy,* Chicago, 1930; *Land Utilisation in China: A study of 16,786 Farms in 168 Localities, and 38,256 Farm Families in 22 Provinces in China, 1929–33,* 3 vols., University of Nanking, 1937. Statistics and quotes in this paragraph come from *Chinese Farm Economy,* 357, 332, 375, 395, 402, 404, 414, 415.

99 "There was something eloquent *Sons,* 156.

100 "so charming, so virile *MSW,* 255. The next quote is from *MSW,* 146.

100 "He has a great future PB, letter to Bucks, April 8, 1918, NSC.

100 "situations which limit or affect This and the next quote are from JLB, *Chinese Farm Economy,* 427.

100 Honan-Shandung Education Association See JLB, letter to Bucks, December 1, 1919, NSC; "Practical Plans for the Introduction of Agriculture into a Middle and Primary School," by T. L. Buck, *CR* 50, May 1919 (the initial "T" was clearly a misprint since this paper was given at the Honan-Shandung Education Association, of which JLB was chairman, and the author identifies himself as having worked in Nanxuzhou since 1916.)

101 Lossing's questionnaires—*MSW,* 215; JLB had learned this method as a student from his Cornell professor, George Warren, see *Agricultural Economics at Cornell: A History, 1900–1990,* by Bernard F. Stanton, Ithaca, New York, 2001, 20–22.

101 "the elders, merchants and teachers T. E. Carter, letter to Dr. Henry Sloane Coffin, minister of the Madison Avenue church sponsoring Nanxuzhou station, December 5, 1912, PHS.

101 "the testing of new grains From JLB, "Practical Plans."

101 "Mr. Wang the farmer—JLB, letter to Bucks, January 12, 1919, NSC; and see

"Agricultural Work of the American Presbyterian Mission at Nanhsuchou, Anhwei, China, 1919," by JLB, *CR* 51, June 1920, 415.

101 "idle, reckless PB, letter to Bucks, September 17, 1917, NSC.

102 "filling the street *GE*, 344–45.

102 one of these battles JLB, letter to Bucks, October 8, 1918, NSC.

102 "At least once or twice a year *MSW*, 149.

102 "This does not tell This and the next quote are from *ED*, 140.

103 "I defy any bandit PB, report to Mrs. Coffin, the minister's wife, at Madison Avenue church, December 12, 1918, NSC.

103 "He seems so busy PB, letter to Bucks, February 2, 1918, NSC.

103 "Agriculture was his life MGC interview, NSC.

103 "an endless stream *ED*, 138.

104 The enchantment of moonlight *MSW*, 136.

104 "a tall and ample figure *MSW*, 140.

105 "by being kind Confucius, *Analects*, 1:10.

105 "Madame Chang remains *MSW*, 140. The next quote is from *MSW*, 141.

105 "The Buddhist funeral priests *MSW*, 151; see also THi, 115.

105 "If Madame Wu felt this *MSW*, 141.

106 "a ponderous dowager "In China Too," by PB, *Atlantic Monthly*, January 1924, reprinted in *MSW*, 163.

106 "none of my friends *MSW*, 140. The next quote is from *MSW*, 141.

106 "I myself deliberately *Of Men and Women*, by PB (New York, 1941; Methuen, London, 1942), 26.

107 a family named Li—*MSW*, 144–45.

107 "that they were as good as boys *The Craighills of China*, by Marian G. Craighill, Ambler, Pennsylvania 1972, 26.

107 "they looked like shoes *MSW*, 165. The next quote is from MSW, 147.

108 "She had a great ability MGC interview, NSC.

108 "I played the wedding march PB, letter to parents, October 14, 1917 (the sequel is in a letter dated November 18, 1917), NSC. For the Hsu wives, see *MSW*, 150.

109 "Once the breathing stopped *MSW*, 138.

109 "the last we heard PB, letter to Bucks, February 2, 1918, NSC.

109 "We had to," said Marian MGC interview, NSC.

110 "How strange! PB, letter to Mrs. Coffin, December 12, 1918, NSC.

110 "flat and dirty and small MGC interview, NSC.

110 "the lack of sanitation *MSW*, 171.

111 "what we consider sins Ruth Osborn interview, NSC.

111 "girls knew from the first *MSW*, 151–52.

111 "the terrible degradation PB, letter to Bucks, February 2, 1918, NSC.

111 "unwashed, garlic-filled humanity PB, letter to Mrs. Coffin, December 12, 1918, NSC.

111 "I have *sole* charge PB, letter to EW, August 29, [1918].

III   "How can we save her PB, letter to Mrs. Coffin, December 12, 1918, NSC.

112   "The average is three or four PB, letter to Bucks, March 15, 1919, NSC; see also *MSW,* 146.

112   "hard-featured, envious, curious Chester, *Light and Shadows of the Mission World,* 49.

112   "It is the supreme moment "A Brief Statement concerning the Need of a New Station in the Province of Anhwei, China," by Thomas Carter n.d. [1911], PHS.

113   "It is just the sort of mission life T. Carter, letter to Dr. Coffin, December 5, 1912, PHS. The next two quotes are from letters of March 30, 1914 and December 10, 1914.

113   "By that time so many people This and the next quote are from MGC interview, NSC.

114   "We both . . . have the best JLB, letter to Clifford Buck, July 27, 1922, NSC.

114   "They just hit the ceiling MGC interview, NSC; JLB, letter to Bucks, January 12, 1919, NSC.

114   "To my horror PB letter to Bucks, March 15, 1919, NSC.

115   "He did not, as she did *Ex,* 152.

115   "I felt the Calvinism This and the next two quotes are from MGC, letter to Nora Stirling, February 14, 1976, NSC.

116   " 'Everywhere I went *FA,* 155.

117   "You can't imagine MGC interview, NSC.

117   The Bucks had barely settled in—JLB, letters to Bucks, June 29, 1919, and January 27, 1921, NSC; *MSW,* 152–53.

117   "Imagine two, four *FA,* 53.

118   "her unusual beauty *CWNG,* 8.

118   "like a magnificat *ED,* 141. For the return to the United States in summer 1920, see *ED,* 142, *MSW,* 213.

118   "I hear chewing gum This and the next quote are from *ED,* 146.

119   "she said with a quiet *Ex,* 307; for CS on America, and her rejection of AS, see *Ex,* 310.

119   "Something blinded her *TN,* 117.

119   "When I think of her dying *MSW,* 160.

119   "Any Chinese who reads this John C. H. Wu in *T'ien Hsia Monthly,* Shanghai, vol. 2, no. 4, April 1936, 394.

120   "Fiction is a painting *THi,* 204.

120   "I drew the curtain at last *EWWW,* 246.

120   "I had to get rid of *SS,* 191.

120   "death sat *TN,* 110. The next two quotes are *TN,* 96, 129.

121   "Young in spirit to the end *Ex,* 314–15. On the writing of *The Exile,* see *MSW,* 161–62; *ED,* 149; *THi,* 203.

122   "She was beginning already *Ex,* 78. The next four quotes are from *Ex,* 72, 278, 281, 279–82.

Chapter 5

All quotes not otherwise attributed in this chapter come from interviews with Nora Stirling, NSC.

125   "too large and somewhat graceless *MSW,* 176.

125   "The living room, large as it was *ED,* 144. My account of the house and garden is based on *MSW,* 157, 176, 189, 204; PB, letter to Bucks, November 18, 1920; Margaret Bear's letters home: October 22, 1923, April 13, 1923, May 25, 1924, all in NSC.

126   "I admired her This and the next quote come from interviews with Margaret Bear and Lilliath Bates, NSC.

126   "not books lining the wall Review of *The Good Earth,* by Alice Tisdale Hobart; *Saturday Review,* July 20, 1931. The encounter described here took place in 1926.

127   "I remember quite clearly *MSW,* 162.

127   In the early morning *MSW,* 163, from *"In China Too,"* (reprinted in *MSW,* 162–67).

128   "I saw such things *MSW,* 154.

128   The other day I stood *MSW,* 171, from "Beauty in China," by PB, *Forum,* March 1924 (reprinted in *MSW,* 167–175).

129   "It was natural to me *MSW,* 17.

129   "I am very proud of her JLB, letter to Bucks, February 18, 1923, NSC.

129   a work space of her own GY interview, NSC; "Pearl S. Buck," by EW, Randolph-Macon Woman's College Alumni Bulletin, February 1939, 7.

130   "His place is in the street." From PB's 1938 Nobel lecture, "The Chinese Novel," in THi, 238.

130   "She made things so much easier This and the next quote are from Margaret Bear interview, NSC.

131   "We depended on her for solutions This and the next two quotes are from interviews with Lilliath Bates and James Bear respectively, NSC.

131   "That part of the household This and the next quote are from *ED,* 157. For the gardener, see *MSW,* 157–58.

132   "'I came to you,' the woman said *MSW,* 194. For the child's birth and subsequent misfortunes, see *MSW* 195–96.

132   "She declared that her life *MSW,* 222. See also pp. 221, 223, and 232–33. Mrs. Lu was apparently the same person as Li Sao-tse (Sao-tse, Sadze, or—in current Pinyin transliteration—Saozi means wife), who later married as her second husband the cook Li Hua (alternatively known as Chu) and went to work for the Thomson family, who called her Tsu Sadze or Ch'u Sao-tse (James Thomson and Nancy Thomson Waller interviews, NSC). She was forty-four in 1927, according to a letter from PB to JLB's mother, 23.8.28, NSC.

133   "This illiterate woman "Pearl S. Buck and the American Quest for China," by James C. Thomson, in *The Several Worlds of Pearl S. Buck: Essays Produced at a Symposium, Randolph Macon Woman's College, March 26–28, 1992,* ed. Elizabeth

Johnston Lipscomb, Frances E. Webb, and Peter Conn, Greenwood Press, Connecticut, 1994, 11.

133 "It is the Chinese THi, 218; the next quote is from THi, 236.

133 "notoriously filthy Rev. James Graham, Zhenjiang, letter to Presbyterian Mission Board, February 4, 1933, PHS.

134 "not so often from THi, 226. *All Men Are Brothers* was the title PB gave to her translation of *Shui Hu Chuan,* or *The Water Margins.*

134 "Only a person Alice Hobart, *Saturday Review,* July 26, 1931, 13.

134 "I could buy a basketful *MSW,* 179.

134 "they alone knew THi, 218.

135 "they provided for me *MSW,* 179.

135 "I learned far more *MSW,* 177.

136 "Yuan, wrapped in his greatcoat *HD,* 300.

136 "*Wen-li* is a dead language Review by AS of the bishop of Shanghai's *Wen-li* Bible, CR 31, June 1900; the next quote is from his review of the Revised Mandarin New Testament, CR 39, 1908, 268.

137 "a beautifully clear and graceful *MSW,* 178. See also *MSW,* 152. Opposition came from the *Critical Review,* founded in 1922 by conservatives at Nanjing's Higher Normal College.

137 spoke and thought in *pei-hua MSW,* 275.

137 "The beautiful cadences SS, 138,

137 Nanjing Agricultural College "Blueprint for Nanjing Agricultural College" by Joseph Bailie and J. E. Williams, University of Nanking, October 16, 1912, PHS; for JLB, see *Development of Agricultural Economics at the University of Nanking, 1922–46,* by JLB, Ithaca, New York, 1973; "John Lossing Buck and Agricultural Economics at Nanjing University," chapter 9 in *Jingji Xue: The History of the Introduction of Western Economic Ideas to China, 1850–1950,* by Paul B. Trescott, Hong Kong, 2007.

138 "They not only knew nothing *MSW,* 188.

138 "If you want to improve it This and the next two quotes are from "In Memory of Professor Buck," typescript, by R. H. Tsui (Cui Yujun in current transliteration), kindly translated for me by Ye Gongping, Nanjing University, 1991.

138 "They are feeling JLB, letter to Bucks, January 4, 1922, NSC.

139 A young Chinese colleague Liang Shih-chiu, letter to Nora Stirling, January 12, 1978, NSC; EW interview, NSC.

140 "she wore a long cotton gown *EWWW* 104; the following quotes from *EWWW,* 151, 38, 32, 51, 94.

141 Dr. Sydenstricker AS had an honorary doctorate from Washington and Lee.

141 "It did not occur to him *MSW,* 187.

142 "The North Kiangsu Mission *Half Our Burden: Report of North Kiangsu Mission,* Shanghai, 1915, 25, PHS.

142 "He went his way *FA,* 53–54.

143 "His lips were moving TN, 201.

143 "In a sort of stupor *FA*, 252; the next quote is from *FA*, 254. PB's reconstruction of this affair in *FA*, 162–68, 170–71, is powerful but biased and full of inaccuracies corrected by James Bear's eyewitness account in "The Mission Work of the Presbyterian Church in China, 1567–1952," unpublished ms., vol. 5, 156, 167, Union Theological Seminary, Richmond, Virginia, and James Bear interview, NSC. For the retirement rule, see *Minutes of the Annual Meeting of the North Kiangsu Mission,* Shanghai, 1922, 13, PHS.

143 "It was only by much contriving *ED*, 147. For the seminary correspondence course, see *FA*, 256–59, 263–64; *OLW,* 53; *History of Nanjing Theological Seminary, 1911–61,* by Frank Wilson Price, New York, 1961, 10.

144 "All his life *MSW*, 54–56.

144 "He spoke Chinese as few *FA*, 51–52.

144 "He had a remarkable mind Typescript obituary by PB, 1931, NSC.

144 "He talked more *FA*, 43; preface by GY to *OLW.*

145 "I put relentlessly aside *FA*, 47. The next quote is from *FA*, 10.

145 "He espoused early a cause *FA*, 56.

145 "Kill Sydenstricker!" Review of *The Exile* by Nettie du Bose, The *Presbyterian,* November 4, 1936.

146 Carol Buck See *CWNG*, 31 *et passim;* interviews with James and Margaret Bear, Lilliath Bates, Helen Daniels, John Reisner Jr., Nancy Thomson, and Emma White, NSC.

146 "I was to have nearly four years *MSW*, 158.

147 "She was three years old CWNG, 8–9; the next quote is from CWNG, 10.

147 "In spite of my terror *CWNG*, 12.

147 "A Chinese Woman Speaks," See preface to *FW; MSW,* 201 (where this story is confused with its sequel).

148 "You will wear out your life *CWNG*, 19. The next two quotes are from *CWNG,* 19, 18.

148 "as though she were laying *TN*, 296. For Ithaca, see *MSW,* 201–2; the next quote is from *MSW,* 201. On adopting a baby, see *MSW,* 203; THi 125.

150 "Quite coldbloodedly I asked *MSW*, 202. For "China and the West," see *The Annals of the American Academy of Political and Social Science,* vol. 168, July 1933, Philadelphia, 1933, 119–31. The original prize-winning essay was submitted under the pseudonym "David Barnes."

150 "I got back my faith *MSW*, 203.

150 "Endurance is only *CWNG*, 1. The next quote is from *CWNG*, 28.

151 "None of it meant anything *CWNG*, 27.

151 "She was frantic *IW,* 141.

151 "Books, I remember *CWNG*, 29.

151 "Agony has become static Note dated April 1940 in THi, 279.

151 "It is not shame PB, letter to EW, July 29, 1931, NSC.

151 "She would sleep a little *TN,* 296.

152 "My own sympathies *MSW,* 198–99. The next three quotes from *MSW,* 186, 192, 196.

153 "You take Washington DC—A. B. Lewis interview, NSC.

153 "all about the country *HD,* 122.

154 "Lao Wang, the Farmer," CR, 57, April 1926, 237–44. For the novel, see THi, 128.

154 "we are living . . . in fear JLB, letter to Mission Board, March 6, 1927, NSC. Texts of telegrams sent to the U.S. government and the Church Council by JLB's Fellowship of Reconciliation, organized with J. Reisner, Claude Thomson, and Searle Bates, in JLB, letter to Bucks, February 12, 1927; see also B. Reisner interview, NSC.

155 Grace and her husband JLB, letter to Bucks, February 12, 1927, NSC.

155 his students were afraid JLB, letter to Mission Board, March 6, 1927, NSC.

155 "All Bolshevist propaganda W. J. Drummond, letter to J. Addison Henry, Memorial Church, Overbrook, Philadelphia, February 15, 1927, PHS.

155 "There at the bridge "The Revolutionist," by PB, *Asia,* vol, 28, no. 9, September 1928 (reprinted as "Wang Lung" in *FW*).

155 "bandits in uniform—This and the next quote are from JLB, letter to Mission Board, March 6, 1927, NSC.

156 "The people fear the Northern army Mrs. J. E. Williams, letter to Mrs. Dimmock, Mission Board, March 9, 1927.

156 "It was not conscious pretence *FA,* 274.

156 "I . . . laughed *MSW,* 210; the next quote is from *MSW,* 211.

157 "It was a strange night *ED,* 159. My account of the Nanjing incident is based on eyewitness testimony in JLB's letters to his parents (February 12 and April 15, 1927) and to the Mission Board (March 6 and April 15, 1927), and PB's Mission Board report (April 13, 1927), PHS; contemporary typescript reports by W. J. Drummond, "The Nanjing Incident of March 24, 1927"; C. Stanley Smith; and A. R. Kepler, "Nanjing—Four Months After," PHS; 1970s interviews with JLB, the Thomson family, and others, NSC; *MSW,* 210–17; *ED,* 158–62.

158 "I cannot well describe PB, letter to Mission Board, April 13, 1927, NSC.

158 "howling together *GE,* 144.

158 "Worse than death *ED,* 161.

158 "we had given ourselves up PB, letter to EW, May 19, 1927, NSC.

159 "He . . . fell at once *MSW,* 213.

159 "each thinking that now *ED,* 162; and see *CWNG,* 30.

159 "They were all young *MSW,* 214.

160 "looted clean C. Stanley Smith, letter to Mission Board, 1927, PHS.

161 "My roots *MSW,* 217–18.

161 "It was a godsend JLB interview, NSC. For the lost novel, see *MSW,* 209; PB letter to EW, November 12, 1954, NSC.

161 "I fret sometimes PB, letter to GY, January 1, 1941, NSC; ED, 219–20.

CHAPTER 6

162 "Almost every night JLB, letter to Bucks, April 15, 1927, NSC.

162 "But the longer time goes on This and the next quote are from PB, letter to B. Reisner, April 16, 1927, NSC.

163 "When I saw her *MSW,* 221.

163 "The little cottage *ED,* 164.

163 "I can't imagine why THi, 136. For this trip, see *MSW,* 223–24; *CWNG,* 35, JLB interview, NSC.

164 "I have the habit of forgetting *My Mother's House,* by PB, 1981, 11. The following amnesiac quotes are from *MSW,* 36, 81, 91, 221, 200.

165 "That Shanghai Christmas *MSW,* 231.

165 "embossed with a spare branch This and the following quote from "Christmas Away from Home," article, no provenance, NSC.

165 "We feel that helping the farmer This and the next quote are from "The Building of a Rural Church," *CR* 58, July 1927, 408.

166 "The farming implements "Indigenous Country Evangelism," by AS, *CR* 59, July 1928, 435–39. For PB's identical opinion, see *MSW,* 139.

166 "I do think she had a bad time This and the next two quotes are from Lilliath Bates interview NSC. On JLB's refusal to leave China, see PB, letter to EW, January 4, 1929, NSC.

166 "She entered very much GY interview NSC. JLB interview, NSC, confirms this.

166 "I'm not going to fail *TPH,* 125.

166 "I should like to tell you PB, letter to Bucks [summer 1917], NSC. The next quote is from PB, letter to Bucks, September 20, [1925], NSC.

167 "His house explained so much PB, letter to MCG, January 16, 1936, NSC.

167 "You'd have to understand Clifford Buck NS interview, January 5, 1976, NSC.

167 "It was Mr. Holm's hands *Other Gods,* by PB [1938], Toronto, 1940, 82, 200. For PB's confirmation that this book was based on her own first marriage, see THi, 258.

168 "a tall, thick-necked, oafish *TN,* 180. The next quote is from *TN,* 186.

168 "I clung to it *CWNG,* 30.

168 state institution THi, 172; and see *TN,* 330.

169 Interrogated by Pearl—For Lu Sadze's second marriage, see *MSW,* 232–34, and interviews with Lilliath Bates, James Thomson, and Nancy Thomson Waller, NSC.

169 "I have never seen the creative power *ED,* 165.

169 "They hugged them Lilliath Bates interview, NSC.

170 "Doubtless they felt *CWNG,* 26.

170 "Hours every day *ED,* 154.

170 "It's not a crime *CWNG,* 21.

170 "You can hear them almost Lilliath Bates interview, NSC.

171 "She was not really learning *CWNG,* 36. The next quote is from *CWNG,* 49.

171 "Missionaries in all Nationalist PB, letter to EW, April 4, 1928, NSC; JLB, letter to Mission Board, February 21, 1928, NSC.

172 "He was a soldier *MSW,* 247, 253.

172 "I feel as if I were living *MSW,* 230.

172 "like street dogs" This and the next three quotes are from *HD,* 67, 68, 331.

173 "that brilliant mind This and the next quote are from *MSW,* 179.

173 visit to Nanjing—Xu came from Peking to act as interpreter for Rabrindranath Tagore, who gave a single lecture in Nanjing on May 18 before leaving with Xu for the USSR. "Hsu Chi-Mo: Notes on a Biography," by Chang Chun-Ku, typescript 1970, NSC.

173 husband in "A Chinese Woman Speaks," THi, 125.

173 "sickening romanticism" MSW, 179. The next two quotes are from MSW, 178, 228–29.

174 Agnes Smedley See *Agnes Smedley,* by J. R. MacKinnon and S. R. MacKinnon, London, 1988, 43, 366, n.17.

174 "She was just the wife Christine Lewis interview, NSC.

174 "more like my old self PB, letter to EW, January 4, 1928, NSC; Emma White interview, NSC.

175 evidence for this affair—Nora Stirling claimed that the affair was confirmed by "Sara Burton" (pseudonym for Lilliath Bates), in PB's correspondence with Emma Edmunds White and by an anonymous secretary in the United States (NS, 86), but there is nothing to support this in NSC, which contains emphatic refutations in writing by Prof. Liang Shi-chiu (January 12, 1978), who knew both Xu and PB, and by Xu's friend and editor, Prof. Shau Wing Chan (April 14, 1979). All other interviewees denied the possibility, including Pearl's sister, Grace (who changed her mind twenty years later, in her eighties; see PC, 103, 397, n. 63). There is no evidence to support allegations that Xu was either the nameless friend in the United States who urged PB to publish "A Chinese Woman Speaks" (NS, 67) or the anonymous Chinese in Nanjing who advised her not to cut *GE* (NS, 102–3).

175 "She was stout Liang Shih-chiu letter to NS, January 12, 1978, NSC.

175 "she imagined herself THi, 125.

175 hero of *Letter from Peking* THi, 82, 102. See also p. 67 in this book.

175 "It is the privilege THi, 83.

176 All previous bids—For PB's publishing history, see FW, xx–xxii; *MSW,* 231; "Christmas Away from Home," n.d., NSC.

176 even the gardenia bushes *MSW,* 189.

177 "Locked in behind these high walls EWWW, p 228–29. "Repatriated" is in FW.

177 no intention of moving PB, letter to EW January 4, 1928, NSC.

177 he persuaded her—My account of the Bucks' return to Nanjing is based on PB, letter to EW, January 4, 1929; JLB, letter to Bucks, July 27, 1928, NSC; *MSW,*

235–39; reports to the Mission Board by A. R. Kepler in July 1927 and W. J. Drummond, October 29, 1927, both in PHS.

178 Jack Williams's grave *ED,* 166; PB, letter to EW, January 4, 1929, NSC.

178 "Twenty families of refugees *FA,* 260.

178 eighty-thousand farmers *The Stubborn Earth: American Agriculturalists on Chinese Soil, 1898–1937,* by Randall E. Stross, California, 1986, 175.

179 "The Communists in China This and the next quote are from *MSW,* 243, 244; see also "The New Road" in *FW.*

180 "these young men *HD,* 299.

180 "They were arrested This and the next quote are from *MSW,* 248, 247.

181 U. S. Department of Agriculture For JLB's professional career, see JLB and Ardron B. Lewis interviews, NSC; note to p. 191 below.

181 "I realize I must PB, letter to EW, January 4, 1929 NSC.

182 "the hardest thing Margaret Bear interview, NSC. PB's observations are in *CWNG,* 37–40.

182 "These too were human beings *CWNG* 40. The next three quotes are from *CWNG,* 43, 45.

182 "If I had known PC, 114, 399, n. 94.

183 "I continually marvel PB, letter to EW, January 4, 1929, NSC. For the Vineland School and parting from Carol, see *CWNG,* 42–48; THi, 141.

183 Grace Yaukey believed ED, 167; PB, letter to GY, September 3, 1931, Helen Snow interview, NSC.

183 "it would not be fair PB, letter to Mission Board, June 10, 1929, NSC.

184 "The house in Nanjing was empty *MSW,* 250.

184 "The rains of late winter *HD,* 330–32.

185 "That is, I think a Chinese intellectual PB, letter to EW, October 15, 1945, NSC.

185 "its energy was the anger *MSW,* 250.

185 "The Revolutionist," Published in *Asia,* vol. 28, no. 9, September 1928, and as "Wang Lung" in *FW.*

185 For "Lao Wang the Farmer," see *CR* 57, April 1926, 237–44. For "Lao Wang's Old Cow," see *CR* 63, February 1932, 102–7.

185 Shao Teh-hsing (Shao Dexin) 1894–1991 I am deeply indebted to Ye Gongping for piecing together Shao's career (he changed his name to Shao Chang-hsiang, or Zhongxiang).

186 "seemed to have been in her EDts.

186 "sounds biblical but is pictorial This and the next quote are from Christine Lewis interview, NSC.

186 "her speech presentation KL, 42.

186 "One can hardly believe "Pearl S. Buck's Reception in China Considered," by Liu Haiping in Lipscomb et al., *The Several Worlds of Pearl S. Buck,* 60, 66, n. 20.

186 "It was all on the tips of my fingers THii, 221.

187 "there was no one else." *MSW,* 255.

187 "many years planned NS, 103; Lilliath Bates and GY interviews, NSC.

187 *East Wind, West Wind* For its publishing history, see preface to *FW* and correspondence with Richard Walsh in NS, 103–5.

188 "admiration, even awe James Thomson, in Lipscomb et al., *The Several Worlds of Pearl S. Buck,* 11; James Thomson interview, NSC.

189 "It's difficult to distinguish JLB, letter to Mission Board, December 3, 1930, NSC.

189 two Chinese scholars I am grateful for this information to Prof. Liu Haiping, and Ye Gongping, whose source was Prof. David T. Roy of Chicago, a pupil of Zhao Yanan in 1949–50.

189 "She could hear them talk John C. Ferguson, *Quarterly Missive of Chinese Bibliography,* vol. 1, National Library of Peiping, China, March 1934, 20.

189 "In the Communists *MSW,* 251. The next quote is from *MSW,* 255.

190 "It's the papers and grades PB, letter to EW July 5, 1926; information from Prof. Liu Haiping.

190 "I miss eternally the person *CWNG,* 55.

190 "there was that great, greedy *Mo,* 125.

190 "It was very specific GY interview NSC; see *MSW,* 256.

190 "I simply cannot stand it PB, letter to EW September 17, 1933, NSC; see *TN,* 309.

191 standing over her own bed—PC, 102, 397, n. 60.

191 "open delight in the body PC, 117.

191 "She turned . . . and faced him. PB, *Other Gods,* 375.

191 "For editing I am greatly indebted Preface to JLB, *Chinese Farm Economy.*

191 "The project brought boom times Paul B. Trescott, *Jingji Xue: The History of the Introduction of Western Economic Ideas to China, 1850–1950,* Hong Kong, 2007, 171. My account of JLB's career is based primarily on Trescott's chapter 9, "John Lossing Buck and Agricultural Economics at Nanjing University"; on *Biology and Revolution in Twentieth Century China* by Laurence A. Schneider, Lanham, MD: Rowman & Littlefield, USA, 2003; and on papers given at the conference in honor of JLB, "Rural Reform and Development: Meeting New Challenges of the 21st Century," held at Nanjing University in November 2008.

192 "She was always thinking JLB interview, NSC.

192 "Do they know PC, 122.

192 "or knowing had forgotten it." *MSW,* 261.

192 "I think I would have been PB, letter to EW, March [1931], NSC.

192 "That first novel Andrea Lloyd interview, NSC.

193 "He could feel in his hands *The Long Love,* by PB, New York [1949], Cardinal Pocket Books, 1959, 146–47.

193 "it seemed to be about agriculture PC, 124, 41, n.9.

193 "Words were to her GE, 51.

193 "Nobody thought anything Helen Snow interview, NSC.

194 the Age of Contempt 1849–1937; KL, 47–64.

194 "He is politeness himself," "The Little Critic," by Lin Yutang, in *The China Critic,* Shanghai, June 11, 1931. Lin Yutang wrote this column from 1930 to 1935.

194 All night through the dark streets *GE,* 138–39. The next two quotes are from *GE,* 81, 82.

195 "a weird landscape This and the next quote from *Journey to the Beginning,* by Edgar Snow, New York, 1959, 9.

195 "To educate the masses KL, 39.

196 "It's a change in us Lilliath Bates interview, NSC.

196 "She was the first Helen Snow, interview with NS, July 9, 1976, NSC.

Chapter 7

197 "Her stories came from her THi, 141.

197 "come creeping and crawling *MSW,* 258.

197 "lapping at its base THi, 64.

197 a comprehensive survey—For JLB'a flood survey, see JLB, *Development of Agricultural Economics at the University of Nanjing,* 40; reports in *CR,* November and December, 1931.

198 Hu Zhongchi—Hu's 1933 preface to *GE,* reprinted in *Saizhenzhu Pinglunji,* ed. Guo Yingjian, Guangxi, China, 1999. I am grateful to Ye Gongping for pointing this out to me and supplying a translation.

198 "I miss him dreadfully!" PB, letter to GY, September 3, 1931, NSC. See *ED,* 171; PB, "In Memoriam," typescript NSC; PB, letter to EW November 13, 1931, "In Remembrance," in *CR,* 62, December 1931.

198 "During the past two years *MSW,* 257.

198 "We carve this tablet—The tablet can still be seen in Zhenjiang in the house commemorating the eleventh-century scientist and sage Shen Kuo. I am grateful to Zhou Weijing and Ye Gongping for this translation.

199 She had stopped going to church—JLB interview NSC; Rev. J. Graham, letter to Mission Board, February 4, 1933, PHS.

199 "several pages of blistering rebuke" *MSW,* 262. See also PC, 128–29, 402, n. 25.

199 "Of course . . . it *isn't* This and the next quote are from PB, letter to EW, May 29, 1931, NSC.

199 "sex is the devil PB, letter to Edgar Sydenstricker, May 26 [1931], PSBI.

199 "The study of peasant G. T. Yeh in *Chinese Social and Political Science Review,* vol. 15, no. 2, National Tsing-hua University, July 1931, 453.

200 "I was surprised This and the next quote from Helen Snow, interview with NS, August 15, 1977, NSC.

200 "Yuan could not bear it. *HD,* 154.

200 "The story is set—"John Lossing Buck the Person," by Shi Sanyou, in *Unofficial History of Nanjing,* Jiangsu People's Publishing House, Nanjing, 1985, kindly supplied and translated by Ye Gongping.

201 "It is very tense PB, letter to EW, September 24, 1931.

201 "We crawled up PB, letter to GY, March 14, 1932, NSC; information from Janice Walsh.

201 "a somber, wild, fierce landscape PB cited in *ED,* 173.

201 "It was in Peking *MSW,* 303. The next quote is from *MSW,* 311.

202 "like a common brown hen PC, 141.

202 "I shall avoid all publicity stuff PB, letter to EW, September 24, 1931, NSC.

203 "How can I know *ED,* 177–78. For PB's reception, see PC, 145, 406, n. 75.

203 Chinese students at Columbia *MSW,* 327.

204 "I did not know what to do THi, 308.

204 "It gave us cold chills C. B. McAfee, letter to Merlin A. Chappe, November 7, 1932, PHS.

204 "It is too much to expect This and the next two quotes from "The Conflict of Viewpoints," *CR* 54, September 1923, 539–44.

205 "More insidious in its pessimism This and the next quote are from "Is There a Place for the Foreign Missionary?" *CR* 58, February 1927, 100–107.

205 "I grew up among such *CR* 63, July 1932, 450–52.

206 I have seen the missionary PB, *Is There a Case for Foreign Missions?,* Methuen, UK, 1933, 8–9. The next two quotes are from 17, 20–21.

207 "ruthless, heartless, insane Rev. Marvin M. Walters, Grace Presbyterian Church, Green Bay, Wisconsin, letter to Dr. McAfee, November 1932, PHS; *"The Dirty Mud"* from Rev. F. W. Backemeyer, First Presbyterian Church, Gary, Indiana, letter to McAfee, April 12, 1933, PHS. My account of this affair is based on extensive PHS papers.

208 "wasted on a man *BP,* 109.

208 "Sympathy and understanding appreciation NS, 128.

209 "He was an impresario *BP,* 114, 152.

209 "Pearl dropped into my office *ED,* 179; clipping from *New York Sun,* March 8, 1932, NSC.

209 "He presented her Natalie Walsh Coltman interview, NSC.

210 Machen's challenge Correspondence, reports, and press clippings relating to this affair are in PHS.

211 "Everything she has uttered This and the next quote are from Rev. James Graham's report, February 4, 1933, PHS.

211 "I am only a humble—Mrs. Guthrie, letter to Dr. Machen and Foreign Mission Board, May, 1 1933, PHS.

211 "Some of the things *Chicago Defender,* May 6, 1933, PHS; *Madras Mail,* May 1933, PHS.

212 In July the Bucks set out—My account of the Bucks' return to China is based on Ardron B. Lewis and JLB interviews, NSC; *MSW,* 283–88; *ED,* 183.

213 "He was taken by surprise. THi, 154.

213 "I was busy, busy JLB interview, NSC.

213 "frankly if I am to live PB, letter to EW, September 17, 1933, NSC.

213 She gave interviews—For PB's Shanghai welcome, see Liu Haiping in Lipscomb et al., *The Several Worlds of Pearl S. Buck,* 67, n.27; *MSW,* 287–88.

213 "Dr. Buck's prestige This and the following quotes are from "J. Lossing Buck," a memoir by Ardron B. Lewis, typescript dated October 19, 1979, NSC. See also *The Breach in the Wall: A Memoir of The Old China,* by Lewis's secretary, Enid Saunders Candlin, London, 1974, 247.

214 "unquestionably the most detailed study Trescott, *Jingji Xue: The History of the Introduction of Western Economic Ideas to China, 1850–1950,* Hong Kong 178.

214 My account is based on the successive rehabilitation of JLB, after decades of vilification under Mao, carried out by Lewis in his memoir, and interview, NSC; by Laurence A. Schneider in *Biology and Revolution in Twentieth Century China,* 2003; by Trescott; and by papers given at the Nanjing conference 2008.

214 "It laid a solid foundation "John Lossing Buck," by Cui Zechun (the son of Buck's colleague R. H. Tsui), translation by Ye Gongping.

214 "The strain was practically impossible PB, letter to EW, September 17, 1933, NSC.

214 "Oh, so we've got a secretary James Thomson interview, NSC.

215 "the publisher Walsh" Cui Zechun, "John Lossing Buck"; JLB's comment from NS interview , NSC.

215 pulling off her wedding ring *Pearl S. Buck: The Final Chapter,* by Beverly Rizzon, Palm Springs, California, 1989, 179–80. For this journey, see MSW, 291–307.

215 "I wanted as little as possible MSW, 291.

216 Lin Yutang PB, letter to Richard Walsh, October 12, 1933, PSBI. For Snows and Timperley, see Helen Snow interview, NSC.

216 "It is always better for the Chinese For Lu Xun, see Liu Haiping in Lipscomb et al., *The Several Worlds of Pearl S. Buck,* 62–63; PC, 425, n.116; KL, 43; PB's review in *New York Herald Tribune,* June 3, 1941.

217 "It opened many doorways Edgar Snow, *Journey to the Beginning,* 132–33; see also PB's review of *Living China* by Edgar Snow, *Asia,* March 1937.

217 "Her beautiful gray-green eyes Helen Snow typescript, NSC; also see Helen Snow letters and interview, NSC.

218 "The chase had . . . been This and the next three quotes from *BP,* 112–13.

218 Adultery meant social ostracism Margaret Bear and Lilliath Bates interviews, NSC. See *MSW,* 307; THi, 166.

219 his publishing house faced bankruptcy See NS, 154–56.

220 "It is Carol all over again PB, letter to EW, April 29, 1934, NSC; GY interview, NSC.

220 Pearl took the opportunity MSW, 319–23; PB, letter to EW, April 15, 1935, NSC.

221 "not the dapper white trees THi, 162–63; see *MSW,* 312–13.

222 "She was proud Natalie Walsh Coltman interview, NSC.

222 "I guess we questioned it GY interview, NSC.

222 Pearl told Richard PB, letter to Richard Walsh, April 12, 1933, in NS, 127–28.

222 "It was a blow *MSW,* 275.

223 "I didn't write THi, 173.

224 "Of my work I must be PB, letter to EW, April 29, 1934, NSC.

224 "I accepted their decision *SS,* 191.

224 "I conceived the idea *MSW,* 287.

225 "fields big enough *HD* 143.

225 "Pearl sponsored it Helen Snow interview, NSC.

225 "I have seen him *BP,* 113.

226 "a screening mind William A. Smith, NS interview, NSC.

226 "He was the *only* one Edgar Walsh to author.

226 "His outlines remained ghostly *FA,* 9; see *ED,* 191.

226 "her steadfast eye *Sons,* 45.

226 Nor can I tolerate *FA,* 54.

227 a posthumous edition—For Sydenstricker's New Testament, see *A History of Nanjing Theological Seminary, 1911–61,* by F. W. Price, privately printed, New York, 1961, 24. The cotranslator was Sydenstricker's collaborator, Zhu Baohui.

227 "I am just *so* happy" GY, letter to PB, February 20, 1936, NSC.

227 "All the political propaganda KL, 129.

228 "Carie Sydenstricker was *The Presbyterian,* November 4, 1936. Mrs. Junkin's father was Hampden Coit du Bose, head of station in the Sydenstrickers' first posting at Suzhou. See also James Bear interview, NSC.

228 "Her mother was a very Lilliath Bates interview, NSC.

229 "bridge between the civilizations PC, p. 376.

229 "No other book Liu Haiping, in Lipscomb et al., *The Several Worlds of Pearl S. Buck,* 58, 66, n.9. On the obstruction of the film crew, see letter from PB in *The China Critic,* Shanghai, vol. 13, no. 3, April 16, 1939 PSBI; *MSW,* 392–95; PC, 159.

230 "They may form the majority *New York Times,* January 15, 1933. A shortened version with PB's reply is in *MSW,* 278–81. See also Liu Haiping, in Lipscomb et al., *The Several Worlds of Pearl S. Buck,* 61; KL, 21–22. Professor Jiang, 1883– 1954, was a classical scholar, an official in the Manchu Ministry of Justice, and founder of the Chinese Socialist Party. I am grateful to Ye Gongping for this information.

230 "The withdrawal heralded KL, 42; the next quote is from KL 64.

230 Sai Zhenzhu Lu Haiping, in Lipscomb et al., *The Several Worlds of Pearl S. Buck,* 58, 66, n. 8; conversation with Professor Lu.

230 "Nothing in Communist theory *MSW,* 255.

231 "as the inevitable future leader PB, "China and the West," 118.

231 "Yesterday in New York *MSW,* 255.

Postscript

233 a character who was a version THi, 269–70.

233 "where she could go THi, 137. The next quote is from THi, 142.

233 a deliberate self-portrait *ED*, 196–97; EDts; THi, 210.

234 "desire stirred in her *TPH*, 48. The next quote is from *TPH*, 49.

234 "when I speak the names THi, 96.

234 "Each day when she opened *TPH*, 118. The following quotes are from *TPH*, 125, 93, 295, 115.

235 "The book told of the difficulty THi, 211.

236 fame dehumanized her *SS*, 66; *MSW*, 275. The next quote is from *MSW*, 275.

236 "Madness was about her *Other Gods*, 65. The next quote is from *Other Gods*, 133–34.

237 "Then I never look Helen Snow, interview with NS, July 9, 1976. My account of PB's working method is based on interviews with Aline McMahon, Andrea Lloyd, and Robert Hill, John Day's managing editor, NSC.

237 "The kid is nuts." *CWNG*, 165.

237 "he said it was fun *BP*, 95.

238 "No one really got close Janice Walsh, interview with author; further information from Edgar Walsh.

238 *The Townsman* Natalie Walsh Coltman interview, NSC; NS, 213–14; THi, 296. *The Townsman* was published under the name "John Sedges."

239 "a basically single-handed crusade KL, 79; see also 81, 136.

239 "Pearl had a very good mind Helen Snow interview by Jane M. Rabb, RCA.

240 "The fact remains This and the next quote are from THi, 259.

240 her alter ego *The Long Love,* by PB, [1949], Pocket Cardinal, New York, 1959, 205.

240 "She did not think *The Hidden Flower,* by PB, [1952], Pocket Cardinal New York, 1954, 205.

241 "He would have been pained *FA* 54–55.

242 "trick of self-suspension" *VH*, 436. The following quotes are from *VH*, 409, 424, 434, 481.

243 "possibly the only one Helen Snow interview with NS, July 9, 1976, NSC.

243 "The worst thing any man Paul Roebling interview, NSC.

244 "When Walsh and Lloyd were gone Andrea Lloyd interview NSC. For McCarthy and the FBI, see PC, 299–301, 318, 321, 326–28.

245 a platonic romance—On Ernest Hocking, see THi, 352–58; Rizzon, *Pearl S. Buck: The Final Chapter,* 128, 134. Hocking was the model for Edwin Steadly in *The Goddess Abides,* 1972.

245 "She loses her grip See KL, 310.

246 "I have to make all I do *TPH*, 189.

246 "You could see Pearl Andrea Lloyd and Sarah Rowe interviews, NSC.

247 "Mr. Harris was presenting Pearl Natalie Walsh Coltman interview, NSC.

247 "the Arthur Murray crew," John Anderson interview, NSC. My account of Harris is based on his own books; interviews with his associates in NSC; NS, 280–86; PC, Chapter 9.

247 She also made a will NS, 334; PC, 362 and 376.

248 "She imagined herself a queen John Anderson interview, NSC.

248 "aspects of imperial grandeur." James Thomson interview, NSC.

248 "the true ruler *IW,* 162.

248 "that seemed . . . twice as long James Thomson interview, NSC.

248 "Magnificence became her *IW,* 103.

249 "The Dancing Master," See NS, 297–300, and "Crumbling Foundation," *Time* (July 25, 1969).

250 "Destiny compelled her *IW,* 91. The next quote is from *IW,* 170–71.

250 "I take my prestige NS, 282.

250 She told a journalist Ross Terrill, in PC, 372.

251 "By birth and ancestry *PB, Is There a Case for Foreign Missions?,* London, 1933, 58.

251 "taken an attitude of distortion For the full text, see PC, 373. I am grateful to Liu Haiping for information about Zhou Enlai.

251 "They were the communications THii, viii.

251 "I could pass her Mary Graves and Natalie Walsh Coltman interviews, NSC.

252 "what I called her Rizzon, *Pearl S. Buck: The Final Chapter,* 173.

252 "As I remember James Thomson interview, NSC.

252 "Her spirit dwelt in loneliness *IW,* 221.

252 "The scene was beautiful Rizzon, *Pearl S. Buck: The Final Chapter,* 418.

253 "We were told a lot Bertha Reisner interview, NSC.

NOTE ON TRANSLITERATION

Current names of places and people with their equivalents in Pearl Buck's time:

Anhui	Anhwei
Beijing	Peking
Guangzhou	Canton
Guling	Kuling
Hangzhou	Hangchow
Huaiyin or Huaiyuan	Tsingkiangpu
Hubei	Hupeh
Jiangsu	Kiangsu
Lao She	Lao Hsieh
Lu Xun	Lu Hsun
Nanjing	Nanking
Nanxuzhou [Suzhou]	Nanhsuchou
Sai Zhenzhu (Pearl Sydenstricker)	Sai Tseng-tsu
Shandong	Shantung
Siqian	Hsuchien
Xu Zhimo	Hsu Chih-Mo
Xuzhou	Hsuchowfu
Zhenjiang	Chinkiang

INDEX